LSAT®

PREMIUM PREP

30th Edition

The Staff of The Princeton Review

PrincetonReview.com

Penguin
Random
House

The Princeton Review
110 East 42nd Street, 7th Floor
New York, NY 10017

Published in the United States by Penguin Random House LLC, New York.

ISBN: 978-0-593-51862-5
ISSN: 2687-8747

Editor: Selena Coppock
Production Editors: Lea Osborne and Liz Dacey
Production Artist: Deborah Weber
Content Contributor: Chad Chasteen

Printed in the United States of America.

10 9 8 7 6 5 4 3 2 1

30th Edition

For customer service, please contact **editorialsupport@review.com**, and be sure to include:

- full title of the book
- ISBN
- page number

Acknowledgments

A successful LSAT program is a collaborative effort. We'd like to thank Spencer LeDoux, Karen Hoover, and Jennifer Wooddell for their expertise, and most especially Chad Chasteen, the National Content Director of LSAT Programs for The Princeton Review. A special thank you to Blaise Moritz for his persistence in making this improved version of *LSAT Premium Prep* a reality.

Special thanks to Adam Robinson, who conceived of and perfected the Joe Bloggs approach to standardized tests and many of the other successful techniques used by The Princeton Review.

Contents

Get Your Real **LSAT®** Content at **PrincetonReview.com/prep**

As easy as 1•2•3

1 Go to PrincetonReview.com/guidebooks or scan the **QR code** and enter the following ISBN to register your book: **9780593518625**

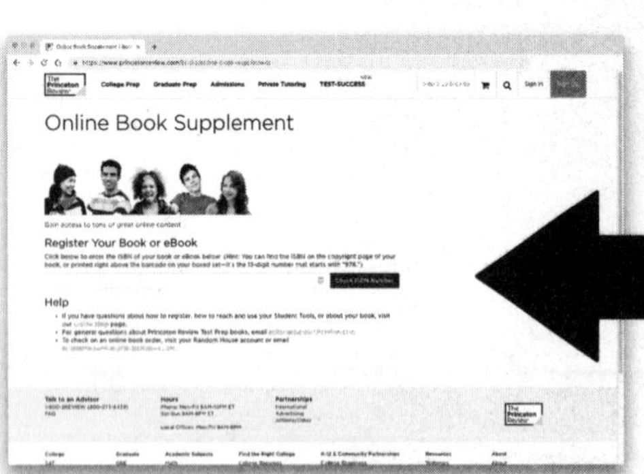

2 Answer a few simple questions to set up an exclusive Princeton Review account. *(If you already have one, you can just log in.)*

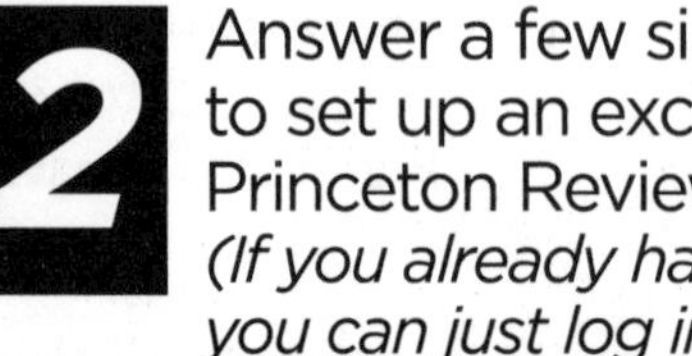

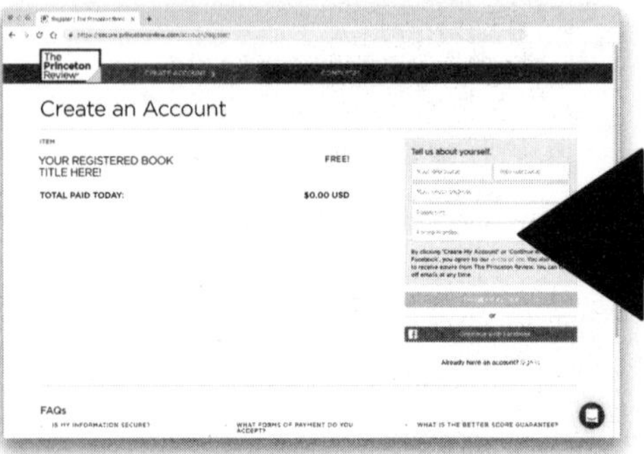

3 Enjoy access to your **FREE** content!

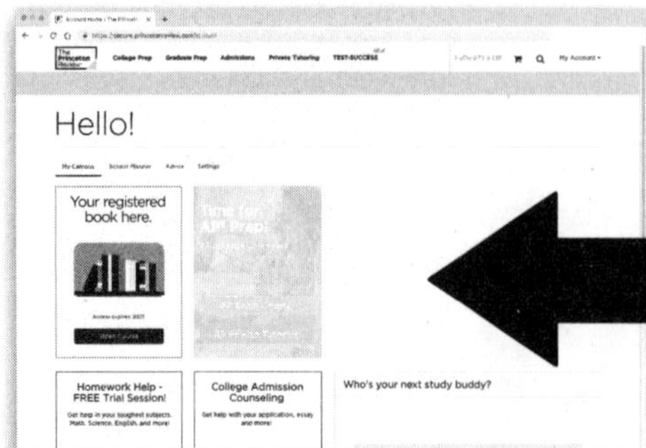

Once you've registered, you can...

- Access 2 Official LSAT PrepTests, plus detailed answers and explanations for every question and online score reports
- Plan your review sessions with study guides based on your schedule—4 weeks, 8 weeks, 12 weeks
- Read important opinions and advice about the LSAT and law school
- Access detailed profiles for hundreds of law schools to help you find the school that is right for you
- Find out more information about financial aid and scholarships to help you pay for law school
- Check out top 10 rankings including Best Professors, Most Competitive Students, Best Career Prospects, and tons more

Need to report a potential **content** issue?

Contact **EditorialSupport@review.com** and include:

- full title of the book
- ISBN
- page number

Need to report a **technical** issue?

Contact **TPRStudentTech@review.com** and provide:

- your full name
- email address used to register the book
- full book title and ISBN
- Operating system (Mac/PC) and browser (Chrome, Firefox, Safari, etc.)

Look For These Icons Throughout The Book

 ONLINE PRACTICE TESTS

 ONLINE ARTICLES

 PROVEN TECHNIQUES

 APPLIED STRATEGIES

Chapter 1
General Information and Strategies

In this chapter, we're going to give you an overall preparation plan for the LSAT. Before we hit you with some test-taking techniques, we want to make sure that you know all that we know about the LSAT itself. We'll start with a few pages' worth of information on the test. Make sure you read all this information carefully so you'll know exactly what you're up against.

To access LSAT PrepTests 129, 148, along with their answers and explanations, follow the instructions on pages vi–vii of this book.

APPROACHING THE LAW SCHOOL ADMISSION TEST

We hope you've bought this book at least a few months before the date of the LSAT you plan to take, so you'll have time to (a) work through the specific problems in Chapters 2, 3, and 4 (at least twice), and (b) actually follow the suggestions we make, including working on Official LSAT PrepTests released by the Law School Admission Council (LSAC)—two of which are available to you, with purchase of this book, in your online Student Tools.

If you've bought this book only a few weeks before the LSAT, read through this chapter and absorb the test-taking tips that we give you; then work through Chapters 2, 3, and 4. Finally, try to take at least one of the tests that you can find online in your Student Tools.

If you've bought (or are merely opening) this book for the first time only a few *days* before the LSAT, well, we admire your bravado. Take a complete test to see approximately what you would score on a real LSAT. If it's more than five or six points below where you want to be, consider skipping the test and taking it at a later date. The best way to improve your score dramatically is to work steadily on hundreds of problems throughout the course of a few months.

WHAT IS THE LSAT?

The LSAT is a tightly timed, multiple-choice test that almost always consists of 74 to 76 questions. By *tightly timed*, we mean that the test is designed so that the "average" test-taker (someone scoring around the 50th percentile) should not be able to comfortably complete all the questions in the time allotted. The LSAT also includes a 50-minute Writing Test. The LSAT is accepted by every American Bar Association (ABA)-certified law school in the United States—if you want to go to a U.S. law school, you not only have to take the LSAT, but you must do pretty well on it to boot. (The ABA recently added a small asterisk to this policy and will now accept other tests' scores for admission, but not every school will allow students to take another test, such as the GRE. So, the LSAT is still king.)

The LSAC Website

You should go to www.lsac.org as soon as you decide to take the test. Spend some time exploring the website. On the site, you can sign up for the LSAT and for the Credential Assembly Service (CAS), you can order previously released LSATs, and you can obtain information about law schools and the application process. Some testing sites fill up very quickly, so you should register for a location as soon as possible.

WHEN IS THE LSAT GIVEN?

The LSAT is administered multiple times per year, typically in January, February, April, June, August, September, October, and November. Visit https://www.lsac.org/lsat/lsat-dates-deadlines-score-release-dates for information about specific dates. Some law schools will continue accepting applications until July for fall admission that same year. See Chapter 6 on Law School Admissions for more information about when and how to apply to law school.

HOW IMPORTANT IS THE LSAT?

The LSAT is not only accepted by every single ABA-approved U.S. law school, but also weighted very heavily in the admissions process. For many schools, it is weighted just as heavily as (or even more heavily than) your undergraduate grade point average (GPA). That's the number that you worked very hard on in college, remember? The fact that a four-hour, multiple-choice test—one that is a questionable indicator of how well you'll do in law school—is considered as important as your undergraduate performance over the course of four *years* seems unjust. If you feel this way, you are not alone, but there isn't anything you can do about it. Instead, you need to focus on reaching your highest potential score.

HOW IS THE LSAT SCORED?

The LSAT is scored on a scale of 120 to 180, with the median score being approximately 152. You need to get about 44 questions right (out of 74–76) to get that median score of 152, which means you need to bat about 60 percent. Very few people get a perfect score, mainly because the test is designed so that very few people can answer all the questions correctly, let alone do so in the time allotted.

Along with your LSAT score, you will receive a percentile ranking. This ranking compares your performance with that of everyone else who has taken the LSAT for the previous three years. Because a 152 is the median LSAT score, it would give you a percentile ranking of approximately 50. A score of 156 moves you up to a ranking of about 70. A 164 pulls you up to a ranking of 90. And any score over 167 puts you above 95 percent of all the LSAT takers.

As you can see, small numerical jumps (five points or so) can lead to a huge difference in percentile points. That means you're jumping over 20 percent of all test-takers if, on your first practice test, you score a 150, but on the real test, you score a 155. Small gains can net big results.

The following table summarizes the number of questions you can skip or miss and still reach your LSAT goal. Notice that 93 percent of those taking the test make *more* than 15 errors. Take this into consideration as you develop your strategy of exactly how many questions you intend to answer or skip.

Approximate Number of Errors (Out of 76)	LSAT Score	Approximate Percentile Rank
1	180	99+
4	175	99+
8	170	98+
14	165	93+
22	160	82+
30	155	66+
37	150	46+
43	145	27+
48	140	14+
52	135	5+

What Is a Good Score?

A good score on the LSAT is one that gets you into the law school you want to attend. Many people feel that they have to score at least a 160 to get into a "good" law school. That's pure myth. Remember, any ABA-approved law school has to meet very strict standards in terms of its teaching staff, library, and facilities. Most schools use the Socratic method to teach students basic law. Therefore, a student's fundamental law school experience can be very similar no matter where they go to school—be it NYU or Quinnipiac Law School. Read through Chapter 6 for a much more comprehensive discussion of "good" scores and where to go to law school.

WHO'S RESPONSIBLE FOR THIS, ANYWAY?

The LSAT is brought to you by the wonderful folks at LSAC, based in Newtown, Pennsylvania. They work with the law schools and the ABA on many facets of the admissions process. You will register for the Credential Assembly Service (CAS), and that too is run by LSAC. See Chapter 6 for a full discussion of this alphabet soup.

WHAT EXACTLY IS ON THE LSAT?

The LSAT is made up of four 35-minute multiple-choice sections. Two multiple-choice sections will be Logical Reasoning (Arguments), and one will be Reading Comprehension. The remaining section will be an experimental section that will not count toward your score. During this section, you will do 35 minutes of unpaid work for LSAC, allowing them to test new types of questions on a representative audience. This experimental section can be Arguments or Reading Comprehension. The LSAT Writing Test is administered separately through the LSAC website and will not count toward your score, though the schools you apply to will receive a copy of it.

For instance, your LSAT could look as follows:

Section 1: Arguments (35 minutes)

Section 2: Experimental Reading Comprehension (35 minutes)

10-minute intermission

Section 3: Reading Comprehension (35 minutes)

Section 4: Arguments (35 minutes)

LSAT Writing Test—Administered online separately

As you can see, it's just over two hours of focused work. And because online administrators check your ID and confirm your computer system meets the requirements of the test before the test begins, you can add another hour's worth of administrative mumbo-jumbo to that number. That's why we say that you should prepare very well for this test—so you have to take it only once.

The Structure of an Arguments Section

There will be two scored Arguments sections, each lasting 35 minutes, on your LSAT. Each section has between 24 and 26 questions. Tests in the past frequently attached two questions to one argument, but LSAC has more or less phased out this style of question; you will almost certainly see one question per argument. Typically, the argument passages are no more than three or four sentences in length, but they can still be very dense. Since every word is potentially important, critical reading is the key skill on this section. The arguments are not arranged in strict order of difficulty, although the questions near the beginning of a section are generally easier than those at the end.

The Structure of a Reading Comprehension Section

In this 35-minute section, you will be given four reading comprehension passages, of about 60 to 80 lines each. Three of the passages will be written by one author; the fourth will be a combination of two shorter passages from two different sources discussing the same general subject. In each case, between five and eight questions will be attached to each passage. This is probably something you're familiar with from the SAT, the ACT, or any of the other myriad standardized tests you might have taken over the years. These passages are not arranged in any order of difficulty.

WHAT DOES ALL THIS TEST?

According to the LSAC, "The LSAT is designed to measure skills that are considered essential for success in law school: the reading and comprehension of complex texts with accuracy and insight; the organization and management of information and the ability to draw reasonable inferences from it; the ability to think critically; and the analysis and evaluation of the reasoning and arguments of others." This means that the LSAT tests a few different things in order to measure your ability to think like a lawyer. The most important is your ability to read a passage or argument very closely and figure out what the author is and is not saying. On some questions, you'll have to figure out what the author is *implying*, and on others, what the author is *assuming to be true*. You'll find that the ability to read efficiently and identify the salient parts of a passage will be very useful on the test.

Online Articles
Access your Student Tools for more opinions and advice on the LSAT.

The schools all have access to your complete undergraduate transcript, your academic and professional recommendations, and your essays. They could also ask for some of your undergraduate papers if they wanted to. However, all this reading would take too much time and cost admissions offices too much money—hence, they've got a neat little shortcut in the form of the LSAT. When they combine this with your undergraduate GPA, they generate your index, a number that allows them to quickly sort your application into one of a few preliminary piles to make the process of evaluating the increasing number of applications more efficient.

The overriding point is that whatever it's testing, your goal is to do as well as possible on the LSAT and take it only once. That's exactly what we're going to show you how to do.

GENERAL STRATEGIES

The following are several key things you should do when taking any multiple-choice test, especially the LSAT. Make sure you follow all of these mantras—they are the sum of more than 20 years' worth of our experience in researching and preparing hundreds of thousands of test-takers to take the LSAT.

Proven Techniques
Let's dive in!

Technique #1: Don't Rush

Most test-takers believe that the key to success on the LSAT is to go faster. Realize, though, that your *accuracy*—your likelihood of getting a question right when you work it—is also a key factor in how well you perform. Generally speaking, the faster you work, the lower your accuracy will be. What this means is that there's a pacing "sweet spot" somewhere between working as fast as you can and working as carefully as you can. Practice on real LSAT sections is important because you need to find the proper balance for yourself on each of the three section types.

Don't let the tight timing of the LSAT scare you into rushing. Most test-takers do their best when they don't try to answer every question on every section.

On most LSAT questions, you'll find that you can eliminate two or three answer choices relatively easily. Some test-takers simply pick the best-looking answer from the remaining ones and move on; this is poor strategy. It's only once you're down to two or three remaining choices that the real work on this test begins. Don't let the clock force you into bad decisions.

Your mantra: *I will fight the urge to rush and will work more deliberately, making choices about where to concentrate my energies so I can answer questions more accurately and end up with a higher score.*

Technique #2: Select an Answer for Every Question

Unlike some tests, the LSAT has no penalty for guessing, meaning that no points are subtracted for wrong answers. Therefore, even if you don't get to work on every question in a section, you want to make sure to answer every question before time is called. Even if you do only 75 percent of the test, you'll get an average of five more questions correct by picking a "letter of the day" and selecting it for the remaining 25 percent of the questions. Make sure you watch the time carefully. Just to be safe, assume you'll need the last minute to guess on any unanswered questions. If you still have time remaining, you can change your answers on any questions you have time to work through.

Unanswered questions will display white ovals so you can easily spot which questions still need an answer.

This is a key concept that you should remember when you're practicing on your PrepTests online and other, previously administered LSATs. Some people want to wait until test day to answer the questions they don't get to, thinking that they should see what their "real" score will be on practice tests. However, if you answer every question you didn't get to on your practice tests, you *are* finding out what your real score would be. And this will ensure that you won't forget to do it on test day—guessing could be the difference between a 159 and a 161, for instance.

Your mantra: *I will always remember to select an answer for every question, even the ones I don't get to, thereby getting a higher score.*

Technique #3: Use Process of Elimination

One solace (perhaps) on multiple-choice tests is the fact that all of the correct answers will be in front of you. Naturally, each will be camouflaged by four incorrect answers, some of which will look just as good as, and often better than, the credited response. But the fact remains that if you can clear away some of that distraction, you'll be left staring at the credited response. Don't expect that the correct answers will just leap off the page at you. They won't. In fact, those choices that leap off the page at you are often very attractive *wrong* answers. Remember that the test-writers have to be sure that they end up with a normal curve when they administer the test. Making a wrong answer look very appealing (with a small, camouflaged flaw) is a great way to make sure that not everyone gets all the questions right.

Process of Elimination (POE) may be a very different test-taking strategy from what you are used to. If you look first at the answer choices critically, with an eye toward trying to see what's wrong with them, you'll do better on almost any standardized test than by always trying to find the right answer. This is because, given enough time and creativity, you can justify the correctness of any answer choice that you find appealing. That skill may be useful in certain situations, but on the LSAT, creativity of that sort is dangerous.

Your mantra: *I will always try to eliminate answer choices using Process of Elimination, thereby increasing my chances on each question and getting a higher score.*

Technique #4: Be Prepared for Anything

You will be. Honest. You might not always feel that way, but you will be. True, you'll be nervous on test day, but a little nervousness is good because it can keep you focused. Just don't let this test psych you out. Remember that when you go into the test, you'll have worked through reams of LSAT problems and will be a lot more prepared than all the other people who didn't put in the same amount of work you did. You'll have absorbed all the techniques we've given you, and you'll be wise to all the tricks and traps that the LSAT can throw at you.

Therefore, don't let anything get to you. If the room is too cold for you, you've brought along a sweater. If the room gets too warm, you've layered your clothing and can get comfortable. If the people sitting next to you are scratching away loudly or coughing nervously, you've practiced working in an environment with similar distractions and know how to tune them out and stay focused on the task at hand. Relax and stay focused; you're prepared for anything.

No matter how prepared you are, it may happen that you lose focus temporarily. If you find yourself getting distracted or anxious, take a moment to focus and move on with confidence.

Your mantra: *I'm fully prepared to succeed. Nothing will distract me on test day. Nothing.*

Technique #5: Practice Consistently on Real LSATs

This book gives you access to two real LSATs and about 105 practice questions licensed from the Law School Admission Council. The best way to prepare for the LSAT is by practicing on actual LSAT questions, and that is exactly what you will be doing throughout this book. Unfortunately, that's just the tip of the iceberg. You should plan to take *at least* six additional recent, real tests from LSAC (www.lsac.org or 215-968-1001), if not more. LSAC offers free access to a few practice tests online through LawHub and a one-year subscription for access to a larger library of digital tests called LSAT PrepPlus. Here's a rough study plan for you over a two-month period.

Week 1: Create a LawHub account to access LSAT practice tests online. Take one of the LSATs timed. Stick to the time allotted and follow the LSAT guidelines so that your practice score is as legitimate as possible.

Week 2: Work through the Arguments chapter in this book; redo the Arguments questions from the test you took in week 1. Take the first of the two practice LSATs available through your online Student Tools.

Week 3: Work through the Reading Comprehension chapter; redo the Reading Comprehension passages from the test you took in week 1. Take the second of the two practice LSATs available through your online Student Tools.

Week 4: Read through Chapter 5 in this book for pacing tips. Review the practice LSAT you took in week 3. Review your mistakes on the work you did in week 3.

Practice Material

If possible, subscribe to LSAT PrepPlus so you have access to a full library of online practice tests. If you're beginning the preparation process more than two months in advance, plan to take more than six full-length practice tests online.

Week 5: Work untimed through one of the real LSATs you've ordered from LSAC; time yourself on another one.
Week 6: Review your mistakes on the work you did in week 5 and review the Arguments and Reading Comprehension chapters in this book. Work the specific problems again.
Week 7: Work untimed through another real LSAT you've ordered from LSAC; time yourself on another one (this should be the fourth real LSAT you've looked at).
Week 8: Review all the general techniques in this book, and review any specific problems you might be having in Arguments and Reading Comprehension. Read the Writing chapter in this book (Chapter 4). Take one more real LSAT timed and analyze your performance thoroughly.

If you follow this plan, you'll be well prepared for the LSAT when it comes around. Don't worry too much about your scores on any of these practice tests. Your performance on the real LSAT should be a bit higher than any of your practice tests if you've been working steadily. You should be taking the LSAT at the culmination of your studies, and if you follow the plan above, you will be. Never let more than one or two days pass without looking at LSAT problems once you've started this workout. You'll waste valuable study time relearning techniques that you would have remembered if you had been practicing steadily. The best athletes and musicians are the ones who practice daily—follow their example and you'll be totally prepared for the LSAT on test day.

Your mantra: *I will work steadily and consistently to master the techniques in this book by practicing them on real LSATs found online in my Student Tools and additional, real LSATs that I've ordered from LSAC.*

Technique #6: Choose Your Battles

Not all questions on the LSAT are created equal, yet each is worth the same one raw point. Also, most test-takers won't have enough time to finish all the questions and still maintain a high level of accuracy. Clearly, it is in your best interest to choose carefully which questions to work through and, even more important, which questions to skip if you don't have time for them all. By knowing the test and by knowing yourself, you will be able to make good *predictions* about which questions are your friends and which are your enemies before you start working on them; this approach will save you time, prevent frustration, and ultimately get you more points.

Your mantra: *I will fight my urge to work aimlessly through all of the questions in the order they are presented. Instead, I will make good decisions based on sound reasoning that will ultimately get me the most points.*

Technique #7: Keep Your Cursor and Pen Moving

During almost any standardized test, you can find people who have just completely lost their concentration. Losing concentration can take different forms, but we've all experienced it—staring at the same question for too long, reading and rereading without really having anything sink in. Needless to say, you don't want to join this group of test zombies.

Using your cursor and other online test tools is a surprisingly easy way to stay focused and on task, and it can help to ensure that you're sticking with the method and visualizing information.

You should constantly be eliminating incorrect answers, highlighting, underlining, and then on scratch paper, using a pen to jot down key pieces of information, take notes, draw diagrams, and so on. Don't let the test take *you*—take the test on your own terms; attack the test. Keeping your cursor and pen involved in the process prevents you from getting passive and losing touch. Stay engaged, stay aggressive, and stay confident.

Your mantra: *I will use my cursor and pen to stay engaged with the test and maximize my performance.*

Summary: General Strategies

Take the mantras from this chapter, learn them well, and—most important—use them. They are the distilled wisdom of much test-taking expertise. Here they are again.

- I will fight the urge to rush and will work more deliberately, making choices about where to concentrate my energies so I can answer questions more accurately and end up with a higher score.
- I will always remember to select an answer for every question, even the ones I don't get to, thereby getting a higher score.
- I will always try to eliminate answer choices using Process of Elimination, thereby increasing my chances on each question and getting a higher score.
- I'm fully prepared to succeed. Nothing will distract me on test day. Nothing.
- I will work steadily and consistently to master the techniques in this book by practicing them on real LSAT questions found in this book and full Official LSAT PrepTests found online.
- I will fight my urge to work aimlessly through all of the questions in the order they are presented. Instead, I will make good decisions based on sound reasoning that will ultimately get me the most points.
- I will use my cursor and pen to stay engaged with the test and maximize my performance.

Got 'em? Good. Now let's break the test down section by section.

Chapter 2
Arguments

For better or for worse, Arguments (logical reasoning, in LSAT-speak) questions make up half of the LSAT. For the past six years, there have been between 50 and 52 Arguments questions on the LSAT. The good news is that if you can substantially increase your Arguments performance, you will take a major step toward achieving the LSAT score you need. How do you go about improving your Arguments score? Well, let's get right to it.

WHAT DOES THIS SECTION TEST?

The Arguments section of the LSAT tests a very useful skill: the ability to read closely and critically. It also tests your ability to break down an argument into parts, to identify flaws and methods of reasoning, and to find assumptions. Many arguments contain flaws that you have to identify to be able to get the correct answer. It's a minefield.

WHY IS THIS SECTION ON THE LSAT?

Of all the sections on the test, this section relates the most to your future career as a lawyer. Evaluating an argument for its completeness, identifying assumptions, and making sound inferences are skills that will be useful to you in law school and beyond.

Memorize the Instructions

If you took the advice in Chapter 1, you've already completed a real LSAT (preferably one from the last year or two), and you're familiar with the directions that appear at the start of each Arguments section. Here they are again.

> Directions: Each question in this section is based on reasoning presented in a brief passage. In answering questions, you should not make assumptions that are by commonsense standards implausible, superfluous, or incompatible with the passage. For some questions, more than one of the choices could conceivably answer the question. However, you are to choose the **best** answer; that is, choose the response that most accurately and completely answers the question.

By the time you're ready to take the real LSAT, you'll no longer need to read these directions—in fact, doing so would be a waste of time—but you can learn something from them. First, they tell you that the tasks you will be asked to perform will revolve around the reasoning used in each argument. They also indirectly tell you how important it is to stick only to the information presented on the page and not to consider any outside information. As for the part about picking the best answer, we'll get to that a little later on—first you'll learn how to simply and efficiently understand the reasoning of an LSAT argument.

THE SECTION ITSELF

There are two scored Arguments sections on the LSAT that will have between 24 and 26 questions. Some Arguments passages may be followed by two questions, although most Arguments passages, especially on recent tests, are followed by a single question. The fact that you are presented with 25 or so arguments to do in a 35-minute period indicates that the Arguments section is just as time-intensive as the Reading Comprehension section.

ARGUMENTS: STRATEGIES

The next few pages cover the general strategies you need to use during the Arguments sections of the LSAT. These pages contain a few simple rules that you must take to heart. We've taught hundreds of thousands of students how to work through arguments, and these strategies reflect some of the wisdom we have gained in the process.

Always Read the Question First

Why should you read the question first? Because often, the question will tell you what you should be looking for when you read the argument—whether it be the conclusion of the argument, a weak spot in the argument, how to diagram the argument, or something else. If you don't read the question until after you've read the argument, you'll often find that you need to read the argument *again*—wasting valuable time—after you learn what your task is. The question is a tip-off, so use it.

Your mantra: *I will always read the question first.*

Pay Close Attention

Reading arguments too quickly is a recipe for disaster, even though they appear short and simple. Usually, the arguments are merely three sentences, and the answer choices are just a sentence each. But their brevity can be deceptive because very often, complex ideas are presented in these sentences. The answers often hinge on whether you've read each word correctly, especially words like *not*, *but*, or *some*. You should be reading as closely as if you were deconstructing Shakespeare, not as if you were reading the latest thriller on the beach. Most arguments also follow predictable patterns of reasoning that can help you deconstruct the argument. Slow down, and pay attention!

Your mantra: *I will slow down and read the arguments and answer choices carefully the first time.*

Choose Your Battles

What should you do if you read the first sentence of the argument and you don't understand what it's saying? Should you read sentence two? The answer is NO. Sentence two is not there to help you understand sentence one. Neither is sentence three. Nor are the answer choices—the answer choices exist to generate a bell curve, not to get you a 180. If you start reading an argument and you are confused, make sure you're focused and read the first sentence again more slowly. If this still doesn't help, skip that question. There are 24 to 26 arguments in the section—do another one! It doesn't matter which Arguments questions you work on, just that you do good work on those that you choose to do. Focus your time first on the questions you know you can get right. The LSAT rewards confidence, so it's important to maintain a confident mindset. Working through difficult questions when there are other, more manageable ones still available is not good form. Yes, you will feel as if you should finish the argument once you've invested the time to read part of it. But trust us; you'll benefit by leaving it. Remember, you can always come back to it later when there are no better opportunities to get points. Just mark the argument so you can find it if you have time later. Come back to it when it won't affect other questions that are more likely to yield points. After all, that's what you're after—points.

Strategy
Each question is worth the same number of points, so focus first on questions you can do without struggling.

Your mantra: *If I don't understand the first sentence of an argument and I don't see a common purpose or pattern of reasoning, I will skip to another argument that I do understand.*

Answer Each Question as You Go

Each question will appear on screen individually. When you're confident you've found the credited response, select your answer and move to the next screen. If you aren't sure of an answer, be sure to flag the question so you can return to answer it later. If you don't think you'll have time to return to the question, use Process of Elimination (POE) for as many choices as you can and select one from the remaining choices. Flag it so you can return if you have time and move on to the next screen.

Your mantra: *I will select answers to every question as I go and flag questions that I'm skipping for the time being.*

Here Are Your Arguments Mantras

I will always read the question first.

I will slow down and read the arguments and answer choices carefully the first time.

If I don't understand the first sentence of an argument and I don't see a common purpose or pattern of reasoning, I will skip to another argument that I do understand.

I will select answers to every question as I go and flag questions that I'm skipping for the time being.

I will take a 10-second break after every five or six arguments.

Breathe

Please remember to do this! You will, of course, feel some anxiety, but this energy can actually be helpful because it keeps your adrenaline pumping and can help keep you focused. So, don't get so stressed out that you lose the thread of reality. After finishing five or six questions, take 10 seconds, close your eyes, and inhale deeply three times. You'll invest only about a minute over the course of the entire section for these short breaks, but the payback will be enormous because they will help you to stay focused and to avoid careless errors. Trust us on this one.

Your mantra: *I will take a 10-second break after every five or six arguments.*

ARGUMENTS: HOW TO READ THEM

The first step in tackling LSAT Arguments is to make sure you're thinking critically when you read. Maybe you've had a lot of practice reading critically (philosophy and literature majors, please stand up) or maybe you haven't. Perhaps you haven't been in an academic environment for a while and you're out of practice. The next few pages show you on what level you need to be reading arguments to be able to answer questions correctly.

Argument Basics

So, what is an argument? When people hear the term *argument,* they often think of a debate between two people, with each party trying to advance their own view. People often are emotionally invested in an argument, and thus arguments can become heated quickly. On the LSAT, it's crucial that you don't develop such an emotional response to the information.

Here's a definition of arguments that applies to the LSAT: "An argument is the *reasoned presentation* of *an idea* that is *supported by evidence* that is *assumed to be true.*" Notice that we've italicized certain words for emphasis. We explain these phrases in detail below.

Reasoned presentation: The author of an LSAT argument has organized the information presented according to a predictable, logical structure, however flawed the end result may be.

An idea: The conclusion of the author's argument is really nothing more than an idea. Just because it's on the LSAT doesn't mean it's valid. In fact, the only way to evaluate the validity of an author's conclusion is to examine the evidence in support of it and decide whether the author makes any leaps of logic between the evidence and their conclusion.

Supported by evidence: All of the arguments on the test in which an author is advancing a conclusion—there are a few exceptions to this, which we'll refer to as "passages" rather than "arguments"—have some kind of evidence presented in support of the author's conclusion.

Arguments and Flaws

Keep in mind that it is generally difficult to make an airtight case for a point of view if you have only three or four sentences in which to get that point across. Yet that's exactly the format of an argument on the LSAT. What can you take from that? The vast majority of the arguments you run across on this test are flawed in some way. That's a valuable thing to know because it reminds you to maintain a critical stance when evaluating these arguments. As you read an argument, always pay attention to *what* the author is trying to persuade you of, *what evidence* the author is using to make the case, and *where* the author has lapsed in making a solid connection. Developing an eye for the common purpose and reasoning patterns will also help you evaluate arguments more quickly and efficiently.

Assumed to be true: On the LSAT, you are not allowed to question the validity of the *evidence* presented in support of a claim. In other words, you have to assume that whatever information the author presents as evidence is, in fact, true, even when the evidence includes arguable statements. You can question the validity of the *argument* by evaluating whether the evidence alone is able to support the conclusion without making a large leap.

Your Goal: Conclusions and Premises

Remember that arguments are constructed to persuade you of the author's idea. Thus, you should always get a firm grasp on the argument's conclusion (whether or not you think it's valid) and how the arguer structured the evidence to reach that conclusion. If you understand the conclusion and the reasoning behind it, you've won half the battle because most of the questions in Arguments revolve around the hows and whys of the arguer's reasoning.

Sample Argument #1

Let's start with something fairly simple. Although this argument is simple, its structure is similar to that of many real LSAT Arguments that you will see. Here it is.

> Serena has to move to Kentucky. She lost the lease on her New York apartment, and her company is moving to Kentucky.

Okay, now what? You've got to make sure you understand the following things about this argument:

- the point that the author is trying to make (we'll call this the author's conclusion)
- the evidence or reasons the author presents in support of their argument (we'll refer to these as the author's premises)

If you are able to identify the conclusion and premises, you are well on your way to being able to tackle an LSAT question about the argument. After reading the argument again, try to identify the following elements:

- author's conclusion
- author's premises

Careful!
Though a great starting point, signal words can sometimes be a trap. Not all signal words introduce a conclusion.

What's the author's conclusion? When looking for the author's conclusion, try to figure out what the author is attempting to persuade us of. Ultimately, the author is trying to persuade you that Serena has to move to Kentucky. The rest of the information (about the lease and her company's move) is given in support of that conclusion. Often, the author's conclusion is signaled by words such as *thus*, *therefore*, or *so*, or is a recommendation, a prediction, or an explanation of the evidence presented.

What if I didn't properly identify the author's conclusion? Getting the author's conclusion and understanding the reasoning behind it is crucial to tackling an argument effectively and performing whatever task the question demands of you. But let's face it, not every argument will be as simplistic as this one. It would be a good idea to have a technique to use when you aren't sure of an argument's conclusion. This technique is called the Why Test.

The Why Test

The Why Test should be applied to verify that you have found the author's conclusion. Let's take the previous example to see how the Why Test works. If you had said that the author's conclusion was that she had lost her lease, the next step is to ask *Why did Serena lose her lease?* There is absolutely no evidence in the argument to answer that question. Therefore, that statement can't be the author's actual conclusion.

Now, let's say that you had chosen the fact that Serena's company was moving to Kentucky as the proper conclusion. You would ask *Why is Serena's company moving to Kentucky?* Once again, the argument does not answer that question. But notice what happens when you use the Why Test on the author's actual conclusion: that she has to move to Kentucky. *Why does she have to move to Kentucky?* Now you have some answers: because she lost the lease on her New York apartment, and because her company is moving to Kentucky. In this case, the Why Test works perfectly. You have identified the author's conclusion.

What are the author's premises? So, why does the author think that Serena has to move to Kentucky? (1) She lost the lease on her apartment in New York, and (2) her company is relocating to Kentucky. Each of these is a premise in support of the conclusion. Now you know the author's conclusion and the premises behind it. This should be the first step you take in analyzing almost every argument on the LSAT. After taking a look at this argument, however, you might be thinking that Serena may not have thought this whole thing through. After all, couldn't she get another apartment in New York? And does she really have to stick with this company even though it's moving halfway across the country? If you're asking these kinds of questions, good! Hold on to those thoughts for another few minutes—we'll come back to these questions soon.

Use the Why Test to determine whether you've properly identified the conclusion of the argument.

Sample Argument #2

Now let's take a look at another argument that deals with a slightly more complicated subject, one that's closer to what you'll see on the LSAT.

> The mayor of the town of Shasta sent a letter to the townspeople instructing them to burn less wood. A few weeks after the letter was delivered, there was a noticeable decrease in the amount of wood the townspeople of Shasta were burning on a daily basis. Therefore, it is obvious that the letter was successful in helping the mayor achieve his goal.

Later we'll see that this is an argument with a "causal" flaw.

Now, let's identify the conclusion and premises in this argument.

What's the author's conclusion? The author is trying to persuade you that the letter was, in fact, the only cause of the townspeople's burning less wood. Notice the phrase "it is obvious that," which indicates that a point is being made and that the point is debatable. Is there enough information preceding this statement to completely back it up? Can two short sentences persuade us that there is an "obvious" conclusion that you should come to when evaluating this information? Not if you're thinking about the issue critically and thinking about some of the other possible causes for this effect.

What are the author's premises? Use the Why Test here. If you've identified the right conclusion, asking "why" will provide the author's premises. *Why did the author conclude that the letter was successful in getting the townspeople of Shasta to burn less wood?* The author's premises are that the mayor sent a letter, and that the townspeople started burning less wood a few weeks later.

What's missing? Remember when we said that you need to be critical and ask questions? Well, here's your chance. Arguments on the LSAT are full of holes, so be skeptical and poke holes in this author's reasoning.

What do you think about the author's conclusion that the letter was responsible for helping the mayor achieve their goal? In evaluating the author's argument, you should start with their premises—they're the only facts that you have to go on. The purpose of this argument is to simply interpret the one piece of evidence given. The mayor sends a letter to the townspeople, urging them to burn less wood, and a few weeks later, the townspeople start to burn less wood. (Remember that you have to accept these facts at face value. You have to accept that, for instance, there was in fact a noticeable decrease in the amount of wood being burned in Shasta.) Now, do you know *for certain* that the mayor's letter is what caused the decline in burning? Couldn't it have been something else? This author evidently doesn't think so—they think that there couldn't be any other factors involved and this is the only way to interpret the evidence. You could probably come up with a hundred possible reasons that might explain why the residents of Shasta started to burn less wood, other than the mayor's letter. (For example, the price of firewood could have doubled right before the decline in burning.) But by asking these questions, you know the important thing—that this author *assumes* that there wasn't any other cause.

What is an assumption? An assumption, both in life and on the LSAT, is a leap of logic that we make to get from one piece of information to another. For instance, if you see a friend of yours wearing a yellow shirt and you conclude that your friend likes yellow, you would be making the following assumptions:

- Your friend isn't wearing the yellow shirt only as their work uniform.
- Your friend was not threatened by a madman who said that, unless they wore a yellow shirt for one month straight, their house would be burned to the ground.
- Your friend was not down to their last clean shirt, the one that they wear only when everything else needs to be washed.
- Your friend...

You get the point. You make these assumptions because you've seen a particular effect (in this case, your friend wearing a yellow shirt), and you think you've identified the proper cause (in this case, that your friend likes yellow and not that they are wearing a uniform or need to do some laundry). Then, whether or not it's true, you *assume a connection* between the cause and the effect. You've made a leap of logic.

Assumptions on the LSAT

The assumptions made in the arguments on the LSAT are also leaps of logic. Sometimes, the logic is so simple that it looks as if the author has actually stated it but really hasn't. The author's assumption is never explicitly stated in the passage. By definition, it is always unstated.

> In LSAT terms, an assumption is an unstated premise that is required in order to make an argument's conclusion valid.

Go back to the wood-burning argument. Here, you have an observed effect: the townspeople of Shasta burning less wood. You have a possible cause: the mayor's letter. On the LSAT, the arguer will often try to make a direct connection between these two pieces of information—in this case, that the letter *caused* the wood-burning decrease.

However, as you've seen from the above example, you're also assuming the following:

- that the decrease in the burning of wood was not because of an increase in the price of wood
- that the town didn't experience unexpectedly warm temperatures, lessening the demand for wood as a heat source
- that the townspeople actually received and read the letter the mayor sent out
- that...

Once again, you get the point. The author actually made many assumptions when she made the leap of logic from the letter being sent and people burning less wood on one hand and the conclusion that the letter was successful on the other hand. They all revolve around two basic assumptions: that the letter could have caused the decline in firewood use and that no other factor was the cause of the decline.

This Is All Really Exciting, But...

You want to get to the answer choices, don't you? Well, we will—soon. But what has been the point of the last several pages? To show you how to read the argument itself in a critical way. This will help you immensely in evaluating the answer choices because you will already understand the author's conclusion and the premises on which it is based, and you'll also have spotted any potential problems with the argument. This means that many times you'll have the answer to the question in mind before you read any answer choices, and you can simply eliminate any that don't match.

The reason we want you to stop and think before going to the answer choices is that the answer choices are not there to help you get a good score on the LSAT. Four of the answer choices are going to be wrong, and their purpose is to distract you from the "best" answer choice. True, many times this "best" choice will merely be the least sketchy of five sketchy answer choices. Nonetheless, the more work you put into analyzing the argument before reading the choices, the better your chance of eliminating the four distractors and choosing the "credited response."

Why do we hammer this into you, anyway? Because you may or may not have had a lot of practice reading critically. You're not simply reading for pleasure, or reading the newspaper or a menu at a restaurant—here, you've got to focus your attention on these short paragraphs. Read LSAT Arguments critically, as if you're reading a contract you're about to sign. Don't just casually glance over them so you can quickly get to the answer choices. You'll end up spending more time with the answer choices trying to determine the credited response if you don't have a solid understanding of the author's conclusion and how she got there. The single most important thing to read extremely carefully is the author's conclusion, whenever it is explicitly stated. Take the time to think critically about the argument, to break it down, and to be sure that you can paraphrase what the author is saying and articulate any flaws in their reasoning. Doing this will actually save you time by enabling you to evaluate the answer choices more quickly and efficiently.

WORKING ARGUMENTS: A STEP-BY-STEP PROCESS

We have developed a four-step process for working LSAT Arguments. It is a very simple process that will keep you on task and increase your odds of success if you follow it for every argument that you do. Here are the steps.

Step 1: Assess the question
Step 2: Analyze the argument
Step 3: Act
Step 4: Answer using Process of Elimination

Now let's look at these steps in more detail.

Step 1: Assess the question Sound familiar? This is one of your mantras. Reading the question first will tip you off about what you need to look for in the argument. Don't waste time reading the argument before you know how you will need to evaluate it for that particular question. If you don't know what your task is, you are unlikely to perform it effectively.

Analyze
Some question types don't require you to find the conclusion, premises, and flaws. We'll cover these types later in the chapter.

Step 2: Analyze the argument This is what we've been practicing for the last few pages. You've got to read the argument *critically*, looking for the author's conclusion and the evidence used to support it. When the author's conclusion is explicitly stated, use the underline tool to make a note of it. If necessary, jot down short, simple paraphrases of the premises and any flaws you found in the argument on your scratch paper.

To find flaws, you should keep your eyes open for any shifts in the author's language or gaps in the argument. Look for common purpose and reasoning patterns. Remember that the author's conclusion is reached using *only* the information on the page in front of you, so any gaps in the language or in the evidence indicate problems with the argument. You'll always want to be sure that you're reading critically and articulating the parts of the argument (both stated and unstated) in your own words. This will take a few extra seconds, but the investment will more than pay off by saving you loads of time in dealing with the answer choices.

Step 3: Act The particular strategy you'll use to answer a given question will be determined by the type of question being asked (one more reason to start by focusing on the question task). Each question task will have different criteria for what constitutes an acceptable answer. You'll want to think about that before going to the choices.

The test-writers rely on the fact that the people who are taking the LSAT feel pressured to get through all the questions quickly. Many answer choices will seem appealing if you don't have a clear idea of what you're looking for before you start reading through them. The best way to keep yourself from falling into this trap is to predict what the right answer will say or do before you even look at the choices, and write that prediction down on your scratch paper!

Step 4: Answer using Process of Elimination
We first mentioned Process of Elimination (POE) in Chapter 1. It's a key to success on every section of the LSAT, especially Arguments and Reading Comprehension.

Process of Elimination
Most people look for the best answer and, in the process, end up falling for answer choices that are designed to look appealing but actually contain artfully concealed flaws. The part that looks good looks *really* good, and the little bit that's wrong blends right into the background if you're not reading carefully and critically. The "best" answer on a tricky question won't necessarily sound very good at all. That's why the question is difficult. But if you're keenly attuned to getting rid of those choices with identifiable flaws, you'll be left with one that wasn't appealing, but *didn't have anything wrong with it.* And that's the winner because it's the "best" one of a group of flawed answers. If you can find a reason to eliminate a choice, you've just improved your chances of getting the question right. So be aggressive about finding the flaws in answer choices that will allow you to eliminate them. At the same time, don't eliminate choices that you don't understand or that don't have a distinct problem.

THE ELEVEN TYPES OF ARGUMENTS QUESTIONS

Almost every question in the Arguments section of the exam will fit into one of the following eleven categories: Main Point, Necessary Assumption, Sufficient Assumption, Weaken, Strengthen, Resolve/Explain, Inference, Reasoning, Flaw, Principle, and Parallel-the-Reasoning. Each of these types of questions has its own unique characteristics, which we'll cover in the following pages. At the end of each question type, you'll find a chart summarizing the most important things to remember. The chart will be repeated in full at the end of the chapter for all eleven categories.

So, Are You Ready?

We're finally going to give you an entire LSAT argument. First, we'll give you the whole argument, and you can approach it by using the process we just outlined. Then, you can compare your results against ours. Finally, after each Arguments "lesson," we'll explain some extra techniques that you'll want to absorb. That way, by the end of Lesson 11, you'll know everything you need to answer any Arguments question the LSAT might throw at you. This first lesson is about Main Point questions. Good luck!

LESSON 1: MAIN POINT QUESTIONS

These questions are relatively rare, but because finding the main point is essential to answering most other Arguments questions correctly, it's a good place to start.

The Argument

1. Mayor McKinney's policies have often been criticized on the grounds that they benefit only wealthy city residents, but that is not a fair evaluation. Some of McKinney's policies have clearly benefited the city's less affluent residents. McKinney actively supported last year's proposal to lower the city's high property taxes. Because of this tax decrease, more development is taking place in the city, helping to end the housing shortage and stabilize the rents in the city.

   Which one of the following most accurately expresses the main conclusion of the argument?

(A) It is impossible to tell whether McKinney is more committed to the interests of the wealthy than to those of the poor.

(B) McKinney's policies have often been criticized for benefiting only wealthy city residents.

(C) The decrease in property taxes that McKinney supported caused more development to take place in the city.

(D) The criticism that McKinney's policies benefit only the wealthy is unjustified.

(E) McKinney's efforts helped end the housing shortage and stabilize the rents in the city.

PrepTest 118, Section 4, Question 1

Here's How to Crack It

Step 1: Assess the question Did you remember to read the question before you started reading the argument? Here it is again.

> Which one of the following most accurately expresses the main conclusion of the argument?

This question asks for the main conclusion of the argument, so analyze the argument with the goal of identifying the author's conclusion.

Assess
Always read the question first.

Step 2: Analyze the argument Read the argument. Read it slowly enough that you maintain a critical stance and identify the author's conclusion and premises. Here it is again.

Hint:
Always underline the conclusion of an argument so that you can quickly refer back to it.

> Mayor McKinney's policies have often been criticized on the grounds that they benefit only wealthy city residents, but that is not a fair evaluation. Some of McKinney's policies have clearly benefited the city's less affluent residents. McKinney actively supported last year's proposal to lower the city's high property taxes. Because of this tax decrease, more development is taking place in the city, helping to end the housing shortage and stabilize the rents in the city.

Keep in mind that you need to find only the conclusion and premises when you're working on a Main Point question. Finding assumptions won't help you, so don't waste precious time trying to figure them out. Here's what we found for the author's conclusion and premises.

- Author's conclusion: *Mayor McKinney's policies have often been criticized on the grounds that they benefit only wealthy city residents, but that is not a fair evaluation.*
- Author's premises: *The mayor's policies have lowered property taxes, which have in turn increased development and decreased the housing shortage, which have stabilized rents.*

If you had trouble identifying the conclusion, try thinking about why the author wrote this argument. The purpose of the argument is to disagree with someone else's conclusion—those criticizing the mayor's policies as benefiting only the wealthy. Therefore, the conclusion is the opposite of the criticism. The purpose of an argument—whether it is intended to interpret facts, solve a problem, or disagree with a position—is intimately connected to the main point.

Remember to use the Why Test to check the author's conclusion if you're not sure. Let's go to Step 3.

Step 3: Act Now that you've broken down the argument and have all the pieces clear in your mind, it's time to make sure that you approach the answer choices knowing what it is that you've been asked to find. If you're not sure about exactly what you're supposed to be looking for, you will be much more likely to fall for one of the appealing trap answer choices designed to distract you from the credited response. Just to be sure you're ready for the next step, we said that the author's conclusion was that it's not fair to evaluate the mayor's policies on the grounds that they benefit the wealthy.

The credited response to a Main Point question will articulate the author's conclusion.

Step 4: Answer using Process of Elimination Okay, now let's look at each of the answer choices. Your goal is to eliminate four of the choices by removing anything that doesn't match the paraphrase of the author's main point. If any part of it doesn't fit, the whole thing is wrong and you need to get rid of it.

 It is impossible to tell whether McKinney is more committed to the interests of the wealthy than to those of the poor. 

Does this sound like the author's conclusion? No, the conclusion is that the criticism is not fair, not that it's impossible to tell whose interests the mayor is more committed to. Eliminate it.

 McKinney's policies have often been criticized for benefiting only wealthy city residents. 

Is this the author's conclusion? No, this is a paraphrase of the position that the author is disagreeing with. Eliminate it.

 The decrease in property taxes that McKinney supported caused more development to take place in the city. 

This may look pretty good if you expect the conclusion to be the last sentence of the argument—a common trap answer. This is actually evidence for why the criticism is unfair. Eliminate it.

(D) **The criticism that McKinney's policies benefit only the wealthy is unjustified.** 

Does this sound like the author's conclusion? Yes. Keep it.

 McKinney's efforts helped end the housing shortage and stabilize the rents in the city. 

This choice has the same problem as (C). This answer is another paraphrase of a premise in the argument, not the conclusion. Eliminate it. Well, it looks like you've got (D), the right answer here. Nice job!

Arguments Technique: Use Process of Elimination

Let's go into a bit more depth with Process of Elimination. Choices (A), (B), (C), and (E) above all presented you with specific reasons for eliminating them. Following are ways in which you can analyze answer choices to see if you can eliminate them.

Make Sure the Answer Is Relevant

LSAT Arguments have very specific limits; the author of an argument stays within the argument's scope in reaching his conclusion. Anything else is not relevant. When you read an argument, you must pretend that you know only what is written on the page in front of you. Never assume anything else. Thus, any answer choice that is outside the scope of the argument can be eliminated. You did this for (A) in the last example. Many times, answer choices will be so general that they are no longer relevant. Arguments are usually about specific things—such as Mayor McKinney's policies benefiting the wealthy—as opposed to "being more committed." The ultimate deciding factor about what is or is not within the scope of the argument is the *exact wording* of the conclusion.

Watch Out for Extreme Language

Pay attention to the wording of the answer choices. For some question types (most notably Main Point and Inference), extreme, absolute language (*never, must, exactly, cannot, always, only*) tends to be wrong, and choices with extreme language can often be eliminated. Keep in mind, however, that an argument that uses strong language can support an *equally* strong answer choice. You should always note extreme language anywhere—in the passage, the question, or the answer choices—as it will frequently play an important role.

Careful!
Think of extreme language as a red flag. You should always check it against what was specified in the passage before using it to eliminate an answer choice.

Beware of Premises

Make sure that you have clearly identified the conclusion using the Why Test so you don't mistakenly choose an answer choice that is a paraphrase of a premise. You saw this in (B), (C), and (E) in the last example.

Arguments Technique:
Watch Out for the Word *Conclusion*

You'll notice that we've labeled these first questions "Main Point" questions. Your task on these questions is to determine the author's conclusion. You might be wondering why we don't just call them *conclusion* questions. Well, there is a method to our madness. You'll find that words such as "conclusion" or "concluded" may appear in other types of questions as well. You'll see this when we get to Lesson 7 on Inference questions.

Summary: Main Point Questions

Check out the chart below for some quick tips on Main Point questions. The left column of the chart shows some of the ways in which the LSAT folks will ask you to find the conclusion. The right column is a brief summary of the techniques you should use when approaching Main Point questions.

Sample Question Phrasings	Act
What is the author's main point? *The main conclusion drawn in the author's argument is that...* *The argument is structured to lead to which one of the following conclusions?*	• Identify the conclusion and premises. • Use the Why Test, and then match your conclusion against the five answer choices. • Be careful not to fall for a premise in the answer choices. • When down to two choices, look for extreme wording and relevance to eliminate one choice and be left with the credited response.

LESSON 2: NECESSARY ASSUMPTION QUESTIONS

Assumption questions ask you to pick the choice that fills a gap in the author's reasoning. A *necessary* assumption is something that the argument relies on but doesn't state—something that *needs* to be true in order for the argument to work.

The Argument

2. In addition to the labor and materials used to make wine, the reputation of the vineyard where the grapes originate plays a role in determining the price of the finished wine. Therefore, an expensive wine is not always a good wine.

   Which one of the following is an assumption on which the argument depends?

(A) The price of a bottle of wine should be a reflection of the wine's quality.

(B) Price is never an accurate indication of the quality of a bottle of wine.

(C) The reputation of a vineyard does not always indicate the quality of its wines.

(D) The reputation of a vineyard generally plays a greater role than the quality of its grapes in determining its wines' prices.

(E) Wines produced by lesser-known vineyards generally are priced to reflect accurately the wines' quality.

PrepTest 117, Section 2, Question 9

Here's How to Crack It

Step 1: Assess the question Here's the question again.

> Which one of the following is an assumption on which the argument depends?

It includes not only the word *assumption*, but also the word *depend*. This sort of language—*relies on*, *depends on*, *requires*—is a sure sign of a Necessary Assumption question.

If Assumed
Sometimes a question will ask you, "Which of the following, if assumed, allows the conclusion to be properly drawn?" This is a Sufficient Assumption question, not a Necessary Assumption question. We'll discuss Sufficient Assumption questions in the next lesson.

Step 2: Analyze the argument On a Necessary Assumption question, you analyze the argument by finding its conclusion and premises, as before. But there's something else you need to do. If possible, you need to find what's wrong with the argument before you go to the answer choices. Do this by maintaining a skeptical attitude and looking for differences in wording in the conclusion and premises.

Here's the argument again.

> In addition to the labor and materials used to make wine, the reputation of the vineyard where the grapes originate plays a role in determining the price of the finished wine. Therefore, an expensive wine is not always a good wine.

One thing to look for in any argument like this is a new idea or a judgment call in the conclusion. On the LSAT, you're always looking for a gap in the reasoning between the premises and the conclusion. If an important idea is missing from the premises, or a new idea is introduced in the conclusion, then that's a serious problem with the argument. Here's what we came up with.

Answer Choice Wording

We've written assumptions in language that matches the tone of the LSAT for the purposes of this book, but you don't have to come up with anything that fancy while you're working under timed conditions. Just locate the potential problems with an argument and leave writing the answer choices to the LSAC.

- Author's conclusion: *Therefore, an expensive wine is not always a good wine.*
- Author's premises: *In addition to the labor and materials used to make wine, the reputation of the vineyard where the grapes originate also plays a role in the price of the finished wine.*
- Author's assumption: *Labor, materials, and reputation of a vineyard do not guarantee the quality of the wine.*

Where did we get our assumptions? By noticing that the premise discusses the factors that determine the price of a bottle of wine, but the conclusion introduces the idea of a "good" wine.

You may be looking at the assumption we found and asking, "Didn't the argument basically say that?" In the premises, we're told that several things determine the price of a finished wine. That may explain why a wine might be expensive, but does it explain why the expensive wine might not always be a good wine?

Not really. In fact, when you look at it closely, it is a pretty big jump. The connection between price and quality is never explained.

When you're looking for the problems in an argument, it's important not to give the argument the benefit of the doubt because it seems to make sense or seems reasonable. Be skeptical and examine the language of the conclusion very closely.

Step 3: Act Once you've found one or more problems with the argument, you're almost ready to go. Realize that an assumption will not only *help* the argument, usually by fixing one of the problems you've identified, but it will also be essential to the argument. Here, you want something that supplies the idea that the factors that determine the price of a wine do not guarantee its quality.

> The credited response to a Necessary Assumption question will be a statement that is essential for the argument's conclusion to be valid.

Step 4: Answer using Process of Elimination Let's take the choices one at a time.

 The price of a bottle of wine should be a reflection of the wine's quality. 

Look carefully at the wording of this answer: it is actually the opposite of the assumption you are looking for. The author's position is that price is NOT a reflection of quality. Eliminate it.

 Price is never an accurate indication of the quality of a bottle of wine. 

This one seems to go along with the argument more or less, but notice how demanding this choice is. It says that price is *never* an accurate indication of quality. That language is too strong. An assumption is something the argument *needs*, but we don't want to pick a choice that's *more* than what the argument needs. This falls into that category; eliminate it.

 The reputation of a vineyard does not always indicate the quality of its wines. 

Notice how careful the language here is. This choice uses the phrase "does not always" rather than "never." It also connects a part of the premise—reputation of the vineyard—with the conclusion—quality of the wine. Keep this one for now.

 The reputation of a vineyard generally plays a greater role than the quality of its grapes in determining its wines' prices. 

Initially this one may look tempting, since the reputation of the vineyard may very well play a greater role than the quality of its grapes in determining its wines' prices. After all, isn't it reasonable to think that could be why an expensive bottle of wine might not be as good as a cheap one? If the argument's primary concern were to point out the factor that plays a greater role in determining the price of a wine, then this answer choice would be relevant. But the relevance of the choice is determined by what the argument is trying to do—its *scope*.

To determine the exact scope of the argument, look at the conclusion. Is the argument primarily concerned with identifying which factor plays a greater role in price? No. You can now be certain that this choice isn't relevant and eliminate it.

 Wines produced by lesser-known vineyards generally are priced to reflect accurately the wines' quality. 

Even if it is true that the price of wines from vineyards reflects their quality, this fact is not relevant to either the premise or the conclusion. Eliminate it.

To check out the "Toughest Law Schools to Get Into," visit PrincetonReview.com

You're left with (C), which is the credited response. Notice that (C) isn't exactly what we came up with when we analyzed the argument; this is quite common on the LSAT. But we recognized that it related to a part of the conclusion that was problematic (introducing the new idea of "good"), that it connected this idea back to the factors of pricing discussed in the premises, and that it had the proper strength for this argument. Noting that an important idea is missing from the premises, or a new idea is introduced in the conclusion, and recognizing that it's a serious problem with the argument will help you recognize assumptions, even when they don't exactly match the assumptions you expected to find.

Arguments Technique: How to Spot an Assumption

Finding an assumption can be one of the most difficult things to do on the LSAT. But as we said before, sometimes looking for a language shift between the conclusion and the premises will help you spot it. Let's look at an example of how this works. Consider the following argument.

> Ronald Reagan ate too many jelly beans. Therefore, he was a bad president.

All right. You probably already think you know the assumption here; it's pretty obvious. After all, how do you get from "too many jelly beans" to "bad president"? This argument just doesn't make any sense, and the reason it doesn't make sense is that there's no connection between eating a lot of jelly beans and being a bad president.

But now consider this argument.

> Ronald Reagan was responsible for creating a huge national debt. Therefore, he was a bad president.

Suppose you were a staunch Reagan supporter, and someone came up to you and made this argument. How would you respond? You'd probably say that the debt wasn't his fault, that it was caused by Congress, Jimmy Carter, or the policies of a previous administration. You would attack the premise of the argument rather than its assumption. But why? Well, because the assumption here might seem reasonable to you. Consider the following parts of the argument:

- Conclusion: *Ronald Reagan was a bad president.*
- Premise: *Ronald Reagan was responsible for creating a huge debt.*

As far as the LSAT is concerned, the assumption of this argument works in basically the same way as the assumption of the first version. Initially, we saw that the link from "ate too many jelly beans" to "bad president" was what the argument was missing. Here, what's missing is the link from "huge national debt" to "bad president." In the first case, the assumption stands out more because it seems ridiculous. It's important to understand, though, that your real-world beliefs about whether or not an assumption is plausible play no role in analyzing arguments on the LSAT. Even if you consider it reasonable to associate huge national debt with being a bad president, this is still the connection the argument needs to establish in order for its conclusion to be properly drawn. Of course, assumptions that you consider reasonable are more difficult to spot, because unless you pay very close attention, you may not even realize they're there.

It's also important to understand, as you analyze arguments, that there is a *big difference* between an assumption of the argument and its conclusion. The conclusions of the two arguments above are the same: "[Ronald Reagan] was a bad president." The conclusion of an argument is the single, well-defined thing that the author wants us to believe. Once you start thinking about *why* we should believe it, you're moving past the conclusion into the reasoning of the argument. Also consider the purpose of these arguments. In both cases, you are given a fact (premise) and then a conclusion. The purpose for both of these is the same—to interpret the evidence. Once you recognize the purpose structure of the argument, it becomes easier to find the assumptions even if you didn't see them initially.

Finally, don't make your life too difficult when you're analyzing an argument to find its assumptions. You don't need to write LSAT answer choices in order to have a good sense of what's wrong with an argument. In the national debt argument above, for example, it's enough to know what the argument does wrong: that it's missing the connection from "huge debt" to "bad president." Knowing that this is the link your answer will need to supply is plenty to get you ready to evaluate the answer choices.

Arguments Technique: The Negation Test

We said before that a necessary assumption is something the argument *needs* in order for its conclusion to follow from the premises. We've described a number of ways to find necessary assumptions for yourself, but when you're doing Process of Elimination on Necessary Assumption questions, there is something you can do that will tell you for certain whether a particular fact is essential to an argument.

We call it the Negation Test.

Careful!
The Negation Test works only for Necessary Assumption questions. Sufficient Assumption questions, which we'll look at next, must be cracked differently.

> Negate the answer choice to see whether the conclusion remains intact. If the conclusion falls apart, then the choice is a valid assumption and thus the credited response.

Think of an argument as a canyon that you need to get across. On one side of the gap is the premise, and on the other side is the conclusion. You need a bridge—the assumption—to get from one side to the other. What happens if you take out the bridge? You can no longer get from the premises to the conclusion. Because a necessary assumption is required by the argument, all you have to do is suppose the choice you're looking at is *untrue*. If the choice is essential to the argument, then the conclusion and premises should no longer be connected without it. It takes a bit of practice, but it's the strongest elimination technique there is for Necessary Assumption questions.

Try it with two choices from the first example in this lesson—the one about the price of wine on page 29. If you need to, flip back to review the conclusion and premises of the argument. Then take a look at your answer.

The reputation of a vineyard does not always indicate the quality of its wines.

Hint:
If it's hard to tell where to throw in a NOT, simply say, "It's not true that…" followed by the answer choice.

To negate a choice, often all you have to do is negate the main verb. In this case, here's how it looks.

The reputation of the vineyard DOES always indicate the quality of its wines.

What does this mean? That the reputation of the vineyard guarantees the quality of the wine. Supposing that this is true, how much sense does the argument make? Not much. After all, the whole point was that the factors that determine price, including the reputation of the vineyard, do not determine the quality of a wine.

Notice that the same method can be used to eliminate answers as well as confirm them. Take this other choice from the same question.

The price of a bottle of wine should be a reflection of the wine's quality.

Negated, it looks like this.

The price of a bottle of wine should NOT be a reflection of the wine's quality.

If this is true, it doesn't destroy the bridge (assumption) that the author is using to connect the premises with the conclusion. Remember the author's assumption—*Labor, materials, and reputation of a vineyard do not guarantee the quality of the wine.* Negated, this answer choice *agrees* with the assumption! This is the opposite of what you need it to do.

Certainly, the Negation Test can be confusing to do in some cases, especially if the answer is long and convoluted to start with. For this reason, the Negation Test shouldn't be a first-line elimination method for you. The best time to use negation is when you're down to two choices, or to confirm your final choice. If you make the effort to practice using the Negation Test on Necessary Assumption questions, you'll find it gets easier to do.

Now let's try another Necessary Assumption question.

The Argument

3. Bram Stoker's 1897 novel *Dracula* portrayed vampires—the "undead" who roam at night to suck the blood of living people—as able to turn into bats. As a result of the pervasive influence of this novel, many people now assume that a vampire's being able to turn into a bat is an essential part of vampire myths. However, this assumption is false, for vampire myths existed in Europe long before Stoker's book.

   Which one of the following is an assumption on which the argument depends?

(A) At least one of the European vampire myths that predated Stoker's book did not portray vampires as strictly nocturnal.

(B) Vampire myths in Central and South America, where real vampire bats are found, portray vampires as able to turn into bats.

(C) Vampire myths did not exist outside Europe before the publication of Stoker's *Dracula*.

(D) At least one of the European vampire myths that predated Stoker's book did not portray vampires as able to turn into bats.

(E) At the time he wrote *Dracula*, Stoker was familiar with earlier European vampire myths.

PrepTest 117, Section 2, Question 18

Here's How to Crack It

Step 1: Assess the question As always, read the question first. Here it is again.

> Which one of the following is an assumption on which the argument depends?

The words *assumption* and *depends* tell you that this is a Necessary Assumption question. You know that you'll need to identify the conclusion and the premises and that you'll need to think about the gap in the author's logic.

Step 2: Analyze the argument Read the argument. Identify the important parts. Here it is again.

> Bram Stoker's 1897 novel *Dracula* portrayed vampires—the "undead" who roam at night to suck the blood of living people—as able to turn into bats. As a result of the pervasive influence of this novel, many people now assume that a vampire's being able to turn into a bat is an essential part of vampire myths. However, this assumption is false, for vampire myths existed in Europe long before Stoker's book.

Don't Forget!
Always mark the conclusion on all Necessary Assumption questions.

One common purpose structure you will see on the LSAT occurs when the author disagrees with something. The conclusion will be phrased as the opposite of someone else's opinion. (You saw this on the Mayor McKinney question in the previous section.) You're told that many people now assume that a vampire's being able to turn into a bat is an essential part of vampire myths. Notice the word *however* at the beginning of the last sentence. This tells you that the author is about to disagree with the previous statement, and you can quickly identify the conclusion as the last line of the argument: "this assumption is false...."

What information is given to support this? That vampire myths existed in Europe long before Stoker's book. If you notice that this premise never mentions whether vampires were able to turn into bats, you're on your way to finding the assumption.

- Author's conclusion: *...this assumption (a vampire being able to turn into a bat is essential to vampire myths) is false...*
- Author's premises: *...for vampire myths existed in Europe long before Stoker's book.*
- Author's assumption: *When the purpose of the argument is to disagree, the author makes an assumption that both points of view cannot be valid at the same time. In this case, since we know the author disagrees with the portrayal of vampires turning into bats, then he assumes that the earlier myths did not portray vampires as able to turn into bats.*

Step 3: Act Remember that the right answer will have to link the conclusion and the premise together somehow. Use that as your first Process of Elimination (POE) criterion and move to the answer choices.

Step 4: Answer using Process of Elimination Here we go.

 At least one of the European vampire myths that predated Stoker's book did not portray vampires as strictly nocturnal. 

Does this suggest a link between the pre-existing myths and Stoker's portrayal that vampires could turn into bats? No, so eliminate it.

(B) Vampire myths in Central and South America, where real vampire bats are found, portray vampires as able to turn into bats. 

Does this suggest a link between the pre-existing myths and Stoker's portrayal that vampires could turn into bats? Well, it does mention myths and bats, so it's okay to hold onto this for your first pass.

(C) Vampire myths did not exist outside Europe before the publication of Stoker's *Dracula*.

Does this suggest a link between the pre-existing myths and Stoker's portrayal that vampires could turn into bats? It does mention both the book and the myths, so hold on to it.

(D) At least one of the European vampire myths that predated Stoker's book did not portray vampires as able to turn into bats. 

Does this suggest a link between the pre-existing myths and Stoker's portrayal that vampires could turn into bats? It mentions both the premise and the conclusion. Hold on to it.

 At the time he wrote *Dracula*, Stoker was familiar with earlier European vampire myths. 

Does this suggest a link between the pre-existing myths and Stoker's portrayal that vampires could turn into bats? No. It is not necessary that Stoker knew anything about the earlier myths, and there is no mention of bats, so eliminate it.

You're Down to Three This Time—Now What?

This will happen from time to time. You'll have to do some more thinking. Before you compare the answer choices, always reread the conclusion and the question. Here they are again.

> Author's conclusion: ...*this assumption (a vampire being able to turn into a bat is essential to vampire myths) is false...*
> Question: *Which one of the following is an assumption on which the argument depends?*

Let's start with (B). If you negate (B), it will read, "Vampire myths in Central and South America, where real vampire bats are found, DO NOT portray vampires as able to turn into bats." Remember that when you negate the correct answer, you should no longer be able to connect the premises and the conclusion. Negated, this answer choice does nothing to stop a connection between European myths and whether vampires can turn into bats. It becomes clear that myths in other countries aren't relevant. Eliminate it.

So, if myths in other countries aren't relevant to this argument, then what about (C)? Negated, it will read, "Vampire myths DID exist outside Europe before the publication of Stoker's *Dracula*." Again, this doesn't prevent a connection between the European myths and whether vampires could turn into bats. Get rid of it.

That leaves you with (D).

 At least one of the European vampire myths that predated Stoker's book did not portray vampires as able to turn into bats. 

Try negation. What if at least one of the European vampire myths that predated Stoker's book did not portray vampires as able to turn into bats? That would mean that NONE of the myths did not portray vampires as able to turn into bats, and if none of them did not, that means they ALL DID portray vampires as able to turn

Tip:
The negation of "at least one" is "none."

into bats. Wait—if they all said vampires could turn into bats, then the conclusion doesn't follow. The negated version of (D) destroys the argument and is therefore the credited response to the argument.

Negating (D) was trickier because it had the quantity "at least one" in it. When an answer has a quantity, negate that rather than the verb. If you get confused, remember to fall back on saying, "It's not true that..." followed by the answer choice.

Summary: Necessary Assumption Questions

We've just covered a ton of information regarding Necessary Assumption questions. Remember that a necessary assumption is something that the argument *needs* in order for its conclusion to be correctly reached. For that reason, any answer you pick on a Necessary Assumption question should, at a bare minimum, help the author's argument. If you negate the right answer on a Necessary Assumption question, what you'll find is that the argument either disintegrates entirely, or the connection between the premises and the conclusion is severed. Finally, watch out for choices that are too strongly worded or overly specific; these types of choices may seem right to you at first, but they frequently go too far or insist upon too much.

Below is a chart that summarizes Necessary Assumption questions.

Sample Question Phrasings	Act
Which of the following is an assumption on which the argument relies? *The argument above assumes which of the following?* *The writer's argument depends on assuming which of the following?*	• Identify the conclusion, premises, and assumptions of the author. • If you are having trouble finding an assumption, look for a gap between two different ideas in the argument. • The assumption will always at least mildly strengthen the author's conclusion and is NECESSARY for the conclusion to follow from the information provided. • When down to two choices, negate each statement to see if the argument falls apart. If it does, that's your answer.

LESSON 3: SUFFICIENT ASSUMPTION QUESTIONS

Sufficient Assumption questions have a lot in common with the Necessary Assumption questions you just looked at it. Both ask you to identify the missing gap in the author's reasoning.

Sufficient Assumption questions, however, differ in that they aren't asking you for an assumption that is *required* by the argument; rather, they are simply asking you for an assumption, that, if true, would allow for the conclusion to follow. In other words, they are asking you for information that would *prove* the conclusion is true.

Because of this, Sufficient Assumption questions will often have credited answers that are stronger, broader, or more far-reaching than credited responses on Necessary Assumption questions. Let's revisit Ronald Reagan to see why.

> Ronald Reagan ate too many jelly beans. Therefore, he was a bad president.

Now, when we originally analyzed this argument, we identified the huge assumption that the argument makes: namely, that eating a certain quantity of jelly beans reflects in some way upon one's skill at being leader of the free world.

This is a necessary assumption; if eating jelly beans didn't reflect at least *somewhat* upon Reagan's ability to be president, then this argument has no hope of proving its conclusion.

But what if the LSAT was willing to grant to you a premise that said that the number of jelly beans one eats is the *only* indicator of one's ability to preside? Would that do it for the argument? We don't *need* jelly beans to be the only factor, but if they were, would the conclusion follow logically? You bet it would.

Try the Negation Test though. If eating jelly beans wasn't the only indicator of Ronald Reagan's presidential prowess, would the argument fall to pieces? Not necessarily—you needed to know only that jelly beans have something to do with his abilities as a president.

This is what separates Sufficient Assumption questions from Necessary Assumption questions. The credited responses can be more extreme, and the Negation Test can't help us.

Let's look at an example from a real, past LSAT.

The Argument

4. The only preexisting recordings that are transferred onto compact disc are those that record companies believe will sell well enough on compact disc to be profitable. So, most classic jazz recordings will not be transferred onto compact disc, because few classic jazz recordings are played on the radio.

   The conclusion above follows logically if which one of the following is assumed?

(A) Few of the preexisting recordings that record companies believe can be profitably transferred to compact disc are classic jazz recordings.

(B) Few compact discs featuring classic jazz recordings are played on the radio.

(C) The only recordings that are played on the radio are ones that record companies believe can be profitably sold as compact discs.

(D) Most record companies are less interested in preserving classic jazz recordings than in making a profit.

(E) No recording that is not played on the radio is one that record companies believe would be profitable if transferred to compact disc.

PrepTest 118, Section 4, Question 22

Here's How to Crack It

Step 1: Assess the question What makes this a Sufficient Assumption question? Here it is.

> The conclusion above follows logically if which one of the following is assumed?

The word *assumed* can reliably tell you that you're looking at an assumption question of some sort. Notice, however, that the test-writers aren't asking you for an assumption on which the argument relies or depends, as they did with Necessary Assumption questions. Rather, they're giving you a hypothetical: if you plug this answer choice into the argument as a missing premise, would it be enough to prove the conclusion is true?

Step 2: Analyze the argument Just as you did with Necessary Assumption questions, you'll start off by looking for the argument's conclusion and premises. Here's the argument one more time.

> The only preexisting recordings that are transferred onto compact disc are those that record companies believe will sell well enough on compact disc to be profitable. So, most classic jazz recordings will not be transferred onto compact disc, because few classic jazz recordings are played on the radio.

And here's what our analysis reveals.

- Author's conclusion: *So, most classic jazz recordings will not be transferred onto compact disc.*
- Author's premises: *The only preexisting recordings that are transferred are those that record companies believe will sell well enough to be profitable. And...because few classical jazz recordings are played on the radio.*
- Author's assumption: *The purpose of this argument is to interpret evidence. Notice that the premises are facts—not problems or another opinion—and the conclusion is not disagreeing or offering a solution. So, the assumption is that there are no other factors that determine why record companies might transfer a recording to a CD.*

Step 3: Act The good thing about Sufficient Assumption questions is that the correct responses don't introduce new information. Instead, they make the connection between the premises and the conclusion as strong as possible. Go ahead; make a wish for the answer choice that would do the best job of sealing the deal on the conclusion, and you're likely to find something similar in the answer choices.

In this case, there is a language shift between sales of CDs being profitable and recordings played on the radio and which recordings record companies will transfer to CD. You'd love to see an answer choice telling you that the only recordings that would be profitable are ones that are played on the radio. Keep your wish in mind as you go to the answer choices.

> The credited response to a Sufficient Assumption question will make an explicit connection between the premises and the conclusion—strong enough to prove the conclusion.

Step 4: Answer using Process of Elimination Now go to the answer choices, keeping in mind that your correct answer choice must prove the conclusion and will not bring in new information. Let's take a look.

 Few of the preexisting recordings that record companies believe can be profitably transferred to compact disc are classic jazz recordings. 

This may seem helpful at first, but how does this link to the recordings being played on the radio? If anything, it's more a rehash of the conclusion. This doesn't create a link between the premises and the conclusion that *proves* the conclusion is true. Get rid of it.

 Few compact discs featuring classic jazz recordings are played on the radio. 

Here's our missing radio link, but now where is the link to profitability? This answer looks like an existing premise, which certainly helps the conclusion but doesn't prove the conclusion is true. Eliminate it.

 The only recordings that are played on the radio are ones that record companies believe can be profitably sold as compact discs. 

Be careful here! You may decide to keep this on the first pass since it links radio play with profitability. Read this choice again and notice the direction of this answer—that profitability proves radio play. We need to prove that radio play guarantees profitability. So close, but it has to go!

 Most record companies are less interested in preserving classic jazz recordings than in making a profit. 

This choice is bringing in new information that doesn't tie the idea of profitability with radio play. It is out of scope, so eliminate it.

 **No recording that is not played on the radio is one that record companies believe would be profitable if transferred to compact disc.** 

Wait, what did that say? The double negative makes the answer difficult to decipher, but you should keep it on the first pass through the answers because it includes both radio play and profitability. On the second pass, get rid of the double negative—"No recording that is not" becomes "A recording that is." So now the answer reads, "A recording that is played on the radio is one that record companies believe will be profitable if transferred to compact disc." Aha! This is exactly what you wanted in an answer choice! If you add this to the premises, the conclusion clearly follows directly from the premises. It is the missing link, shoring up the gap between the language of the premises and the language of the conclusion.

Summary: Sufficient Assumption Questions

Sufficient Assumption questions always bring up ideas in the conclusion that are not discussed in the premises. The credited response will make an explicit connection between the two, positively sealing the deal on the conclusion. On more difficult Sufficient Assumption questions, you may see conditional statements or answer choices that seem very similar. Focus on proving the conclusion and making sure the answer choice goes in the right direction, eliminating answer choices that bring in new information that doesn't get you any closer to the conclusion. Look for the strongest answer.

Sample Question Phrasings	Act
Which one of the following, if assumed, would enable the conclusion to be properly drawn? *The conclusion follows logically if which one of the following is assumed?*	• Identify the conclusion, premises, and assumptions of the author. • Look for language in the conclusion that is not accounted for in the premise. • Paraphrase an answer that would strongly connect the premises to the conclusion and shore up the language gap. • Eliminate answer choices that bring in new information.

LESSON 4: WEAKEN QUESTIONS

Weaken questions ask you to identify a fact that would work against the argument. Sometimes the answer you pick will directly contradict the conclusion; at other times, it will merely sever the connection between the premises and the conclusion, destroying the argument's reasoning. Either way, the right answer will exploit a gap in the argument.

The Argument

5. The top 50 centimeters of soil on Tiliga Island contain bones from the native birds eaten by the islanders since the first human immigration to the island 3,000 years ago. A comparison of this top layer with the underlying 150 centimeters of soil—accumulated over 80,000 years—reveals that before humans arrived on Tiliga, a much larger and more diverse population of birds lived there. Thus, the arrival of humans dramatically decreased the population and diversity of birds on Tiliga.

   Which one of the following statements, if true, most seriously weakens the argument?

(A) The bird species known to have been eaten by the islanders had few natural predators on Tiliga.

(B) Many of the bird species that disappeared from Tiliga did not disappear from other, similar, uninhabited islands until much later.

(C) The arrival of a species of microbe, carried by some birds but deadly to many others, immediately preceded the first human immigration to Tiliga.

(D) Bones from bird species known to have been eaten by the islanders were found in the underlying 150 centimeters of soil.

(E) The birds that lived on Tiliga prior to the first human immigration generally did not fly well.

PrepTest 117, Section 2, Question 4

Here's How to Crack It

Step 1: Assess the question Always go to the question first. Here it is.

Which one of the following, if true, most seriously weakens the argument?

The word *weakens* or one of its synonyms—*undermines, calls into questions, casts doubt upon*—is a clear indication of the kind of question you're facing here. You want to find a way to hurt the argument's conclusion.

Step 2: Analyze the argument As usual, start by finding and marking the conclusion and the premises. And because the right answer on a Weaken question will often attack a conspicuous problem with the argument's reasoning, you also need to look for the purpose and common patterns of reasoning before you proceed. Here's the argument again.

> The top 50 centimeters of soil on Tiliga Island contain bones from the native birds eaten by the islanders since the first human immigration to the island 3,000 years ago. A comparison of this top layer with the underlying 150 centimeters of soil—accumulated over 80,000 years—reveals that before humans arrived on Tiliga, a much larger and more diverse population of birds lived there. Thus, the arrival of humans dramatically decreased the population and diversity of birds on Tiliga.

And here's what we came up with from our analysis.

- Author's conclusion: *The arrival of humans dramatically decreased the number and diversity of birds on Tiliga.*
- Author's premises: *The archaeological record shows the bones of birds eaten by the islanders after humans arrived on Tiliga, and that the bird population was larger and more diverse before the arrival of humans.*
- Author's assumption: *Humans, and no other factors, are responsible for the birds' decline.*

This assumption falls under one of the common patterns of reasoning. The author sees that two events occurred at roughly the same time and assumes that one must have caused the other, and that nothing else could have been a factor—that there is no other cause.

Step 3: Act On a Weaken question, you don't have to predict the exact content of the right answer. You know what's wrong with the argument, and the chances are that the right answer will exploit that flaw somehow. In this case, you anticipate that the answer choice you want will describe something else that could have caused the drop in bird population and diversity.

> Remember that the premises must be accepted as true. The credited response to a Weaken question will give a reason why the author's conclusion might not be true, despite the true premises offered in support of the conclusion.

Step 4: Answer using Process of Elimination Keep your eyes on the prize; remember that what you want is something that hurts the conclusion that humans are responsible for the birds' decline.

 The bird species known to have been eaten by the islanders had few natural predators on Tiliga. 

Does this hurt the conclusion? If the birds had few natural predators other than humans, then this choice doesn't hurt the conclusion. If anything, it could strengthen the conclusion by showing humans were the biggest predators of the birds. This choice goes in the wrong direction, so eliminate it.

 Many of the bird species that disappeared from Tiliga did not disappear from other, similar, uninhabited islands until much later. 

Does this hurt the conclusion? If the same birds that disappeared from Tiliga after the humans arrived did not disappear from other islands, then it is more likely that humans caused the decline on Tiliga. This choice also goes in the wrong direction, so eliminate it.

 **The arrival of a species of microbe, carried by some birds but deadly to many others, immediately preceded the first human immigration to Tiliga.** 

Does this hurt the conclusion? You might initially be turned off by the mention of a microbe, but remember that you are looking for another reason for the birds' decline. If a microbe that kills many birds was introduced to the island just before the humans arrived, then the microbe could be responsible for the decline. If so, that would hurt the conclusion, so keep it.

POE Hint:
Answer choices for question types that contain the words "if true" in the question stem sometimes bring in new information. If the new information is relevant, the fact that it's "new" is not a reason to eliminate it.

 Bones from bird species known to have been eaten by the islanders were found in the underlying 150 centimeters of soil. 

Does this hurt the conclusion? Not really. So the same birds eaten by the islanders were there before the humans were. Nice to know, but this isn't a potential reason for the decline of the other birds. Eliminate it.

 **The birds that lived on Tiliga prior to the first human immigration generally did not fly well.** 

Does this hurt the conclusion? Well, it depends how not flying well impacted the birds' ability to survive. You may want to keep this on the first pass.

You have two choices left, a circumstance you'll frequently encounter on the LSAT. How do you make up your mind?

Arguments Technique: Look for Direct Impact

On Weaken questions, your task is to find the strongest attack on the conclusion. There might be more than one answer that seems to be working against the overall reasoning, so you need to go back, make sure you understand the conclusion fully, and then look for the one that has the most direct impact on it.

Things that can be important here are quantity words and the overall strength of language involved. Generally speaking, because you want a clear attack, you'll often see strong wording in the right answer. More important, you want to make sure that the answer you pick hits the conclusion squarely. Try comparing the impact of your two remaining choices in the previous example.

As a reminder, here's the argument's conclusion.

> The arrival of humans dramatically decreased the number and diversity of birds on Tiliga.

And here's (C).

> The arrival of a species of microbe, carried by some birds but deadly to many others, immediately preceded the first human immigration to Tiliga.

Does this really hurt the conclusion? Since the reasoning of this argument assumes a causal link between the arrival of the humans and the decline of the birds, then by offering another possible cause—say, a microbe—this answer makes a direct attack on the conclusion. Keep it.

By contrast, here's (E).

> The birds that lived on Tiliga prior to the first human immigration generally did not fly well.

Does this really hurt the conclusion? While this choice may seem to have potential, it lacks the detail needed to tell definitively if this was a problem that could have caused the birds to decline. You don't know if the birds never flew well—like penguins or ostriches—even when they were thriving, or if this was a new development that made them easier prey for predators. Remember that if you have to justify an answer, or you find yourself saying, "It could be true if…", then the answer is wrong. This is not as strong as (C), so eliminate it.

When more than one answer choice seems to do the job, make sure you go back to the conclusion and look for the choice that attacks it most directly.

Arguments Technique: Common Patterns of Reasoning

There are a few classic flawed patterns of reasoning that show up repeatedly on the LSAT. It's helpful to become familiar with these so that you can more easily recognize the assumptions that are built into them.

Causal Arguments

"Causal" is shorthand for cause and effect. A causal argument links an observed effect with a possible cause for that effect. A causal argument also assumes that there was no other cause for the observed effect. The argument on page 45 is an example of a causal argument.

Take a look at this simple causal argument.

> Every time I walk my dog, it rains. Therefore, walking my dog must be the cause of the rain.

Absurd, right? However, this is classic causality. You see the observed effect (it's raining), you see a concurrent event (walking the dog), and then the author connects the two by saying that walking his dog caused the rain, thereby implying that nothing else caused it. So why are causal assumptions so popular on the LSAT? Because people often confuse *correlation* with *causality*. Let's call the possible cause (A) and the effect (B); then let's map out what the common assumptions are when working with a causal argument.

1. Something caused B—that is, B didn't occur by chance.
2. Nothing other than A could have caused B.
3. B did not cause A.

Of course, causal arguments on the LSAT won't be that absurd, but they'll have the same basic structure. The great thing about being able to identify causal arguments is that once you know where their potential weaknesses are, it becomes much easier to identify the credited response for Assumption, Weaken, and Strengthen questions.

- On Necessary and Sufficient Assumption questions, the credited response will be a paraphrase of the causal assumption you've identified.
- For Weaken questions, the credited response will suggest an alternate cause for the observed effect.
- For Strengthen questions, the credited response will eliminate a possible alternate cause or give more evidence linking the stated possible cause with the stated effect.

Sampling Arguments

Another popular type of Argument on the LSAT is the *sampling* or *statistical* argument. These arguments have a conclusion that is based on a survey of a selected group or a statistic from a study. This assumes that a given statistic or sample is sufficient to justify a given conclusion or that an individual or small group is representative of a large group.

Sampling Assumptions

- A given statistic or sample is representative of the whole.
- The sampling was conducted correctly.

Whenever you see something about a group used as evidence to conclude something about a larger population, remember that the argument's potential weakness is that the sample is skewed because the small sample is unrepresentative.

Arguments by Analogy

A third type of common flawed reasoning on the LSAT is argument *by analogy*. These arguments use a comparison to draw a conclusion about a certain group. In this case, the author assumes that a given group, idea, or action is logically similar to another group, idea, or action without providing evidence that the items are similar.

Analogy Assumption

One group, idea, or action is the same as another, with respect to the terms of the argument.

To strengthen arguments that have faulty analogies, provide evidence that the groups, ideas, or actions are comparable. To weaken such an argument, you would need to find a relevant way in which the two things being compared are dissimilar.

The Argument

6. Barr: The National Tea Association cites tea's recent visibility in advertising and magazine articles as evidence of tea's increasing popularity. However, a neutral polling company, the Survey Group, has tracked tea sales at numerous stores for the last 20 years and has found no change in the amount of tea sold. We can thus conclude that tea is no more popular now than it ever was.

Which one of the following, if true, most seriously weakens Barr's argument?

(A) The National Tea Association has announced that it plans to carry out its own retail survey in the next year.

(B) A survey by an unrelated polling organization shows that the public is generally receptive to the idea of trying new types of tea.

(C) The Survey Group is funded by a consortium of consumer advocacy groups.

(D) The stores from which the Survey Group collected information about tea sales are all located in the same small region of the country.

(E) Tea has been the subject of an expensive and efficient advertising campaign funded, in part, by the National Tea Association.

PrepTest 117, Section 4, Question 5

To check out law schools with the "Most Liberal Students," visit PrincetonReview.com/law-school-rankings

Here's How to Crack It

Step 1: Assess the question This question might be familiar. Here it is again.

Which of the following, if true, most seriously weakens Barr's argument?

Clearly, you're out to weaken the argument.

Step 2: Analyze the argument Read the argument carefully. Identify the conclusion, the premises the author offers as evidence, and any assumptions he makes. Here's the body of the argument.

> Barr: The National Tea Association cites tea's recent visibility in advertising and magazine articles as evidence of tea's increasing popularity. However, a neutral polling company, the Survey Group, has tracked tea sales at numerous stores for the last 20 years and has found no change in the amount of tea sold. We can thus conclude that tea is no more popular now than it ever was.

Did you recognize this as a sampling argument? The conclusion suggests that tea has not gained in popularity over the last 20 years. What is the author's evidence? A survey/study. Whenever the argument uses a survey or poll or study as its premises, be on the lookout for flawed sampling reasoning.

What are the automatic assumptions that an author makes in a sampling argument? That the sample represents the larger group and that the sampling was conducted correctly. Here, the disagree purpose structure helps you as well. The author is disagreeing with the National Tea Association's position and using the study as evidence. He assumes that the data from the tracked stores applies to all tea sales everywhere.

Let's summarize:

- Author's conclusion: *Tea is no more popular now than it ever was.*
- Author's premises: *The Survey Group has found no change in the amount of tea sold at numerous stores over the last 20 years.*
- Author's assumption: *That the Survey Group data is representative of the tea market everywhere.*

Step 3: Act You're looking for evidence that the sample in the Survey Group's data is not representative, or that there is some problem with the way the Survey Group collected its information.

Step 4: Answer using Process of Elimination Be careful here. Because you're looking for a potential problem with the data, the right answer might seem out of scope because it introduces new information that doesn't necessarily refer to something in the body of the argument. Let's look at them one by one.

The National Tea Association has announced that it plans to carry out its own retail survey in the next year.

Does this show a potential problem with the data collected by the Survey Group? Even if the National Tea Association does plan to do its own survey, that doesn't invalidate the Survey Group's information. Eliminate it.

(B) A survey by an unrelated polling organization shows that the public is generally receptive to the idea of trying new types of tea.

Does this show a potential problem with the data collected by the Survey Group? Well, different results from a different source could potentially weaken the initial data. Keep this one for now.

(C) The Survey Group is funded by a consortium of consumer advocacy groups. 

You can also find law schools with the "Most Conservative Students," at PrincetonReview.com/law-school-rankings

Does this show a potential problem with the data collected by the Survey Group? There is not enough information here to connect how the group is funded with the findings of the group. This is out of scope of the argument. Get rid of it.

(D) The stores from which the Survey Group collected information about tea sales are all located in the same small region of the country.

Does this show a potential problem with the data collected by the Survey Group? This is what you need to be careful of. The choice may seem irrelevant at first glance, but if all the stores were in the same region, it is possible that tea sales have increased in other regions. Weakening an argument doesn't require destroying it; casting doubt by pointing out how the data might not be representative of the larger group is all that's required of the credited response. This effectively weakens the argument.

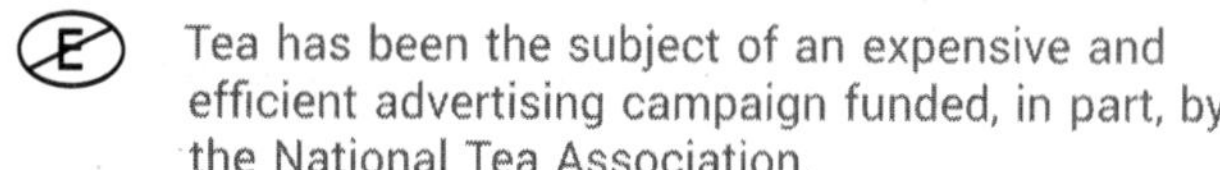

(E) Tea has been the subject of an expensive and efficient advertising campaign funded, in part, by the National Tea Association. 

Does this show a potential problem with the data collected by the Survey Group? Even if tea has been the subject of an advertising campaign, you don't know if the campaign worked or that tea has become more popular. Eliminate it.

You did keep (B) at first, but compared with (D), it's not as good. Just because people are more receptive to the idea of trying new types of tea does not prove that tea is more popular. Choice (D) does not require additional justification to make it weaken the argument, so it is the better choice.

Summary: Weaken Questions

Remember these two key ideas when answering Weaken questions: the correct answer will probably attack one of the author's assumptions, and you should treat each answer choice as hypothetically true, looking for its direct negative impact on the conclusion. On more difficult Weaken questions, there will often be an appealing answer that, with just a little interpretation, looks right. The key is to avoid making any new assumptions when you try to determine the impact of an answer. Look to eliminate, not justify.

Sample Question Phrasings	Act
Which one of the following, if true, would most undermine the author's conclusion? *Which of the following statements, if true, would most call into question the results achieved by the scientists?*	• Identify the conclusion, premises, and assumptions of the author. • Read critically, looking for instances in which the author made large leaps in logic. • Then, when you go to the answer choices, look for a choice that has the most negative impact on that leap in logic. • Assume all choices to be hypothetically true.

LESSON 5: STRENGTHEN QUESTIONS

Strengthen questions are the flipside of Weaken questions. Now what you're asked to do is pick a new fact that confirms the conclusion, or at the very least, helps the conclusion seem more likely. If there are problems with the argument, the answer here will most often address them.

The Argument

7. Increases in the occurrence of hearing loss among teenagers are due in part to their listening to loud music through stereo headphones. So a group of concerned parents is recommending that headphone manufacturers include in their product lines stereo headphones that automatically turn off when a dangerous level of loudness is reached. It is clear that adoption of this recommendation would not significantly reduce the occurrence of hearing loss in teenagers, however, since almost all stereo headphones that teenagers use are bought by the teenagers themselves.

Which one of the following, if true, provides the most support for the argument?

(A) Loud music is most dangerous to hearing when it is played through stereo headphones.

(B) No other cause of hearing loss in teenagers is as damaging as their listening to loud music through stereo headphones.

(C) Parents of teenagers generally do not themselves listen to loud music through stereo headphones.

(D) Teenagers who now listen to music at dangerously loud levels choose to do so despite their awareness of the risks involved.

(E) A few headphone manufacturers already plan to market stereo headphones that automatically turn off when a dangerous level of loudness is reached.

To check out law schools with the "Most Diverse Faculty," take a look at your online Student Tools. If you haven't registered yet, go to PrincetonReview.com/prep

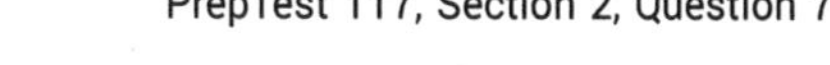

PrepTest 117, Section 2, Question 7

Here's How to Crack It

Step 1: Assess the question As always, begin with the task at hand. Here it is.

> Which of the following, if true, provides the most support for the argument?

Note the use of the word *support* here. This word and the word *strengthen* are the two most frequently seen clues that you're looking at in a Strengthen question. As you'll see later, however, it's important to make sure what's supporting what on a question like this. You're asked to pick the *answer* that supports the *argument*. This is the pattern you see in Strengthen questions.

Step 2: Analyze the argument Once you've identified the question, you know how much analysis you need to do. As with Weaken and Assumption questions, start by finding the conclusion and the premises. Then look for the purpose or any patterns of reasoning. Here's the argument for this question.

> Increases in the occurrence of hearing loss among teenagers are due in part to their listening to loud music through stereo headphones. So a group of concerned parents is recommending that headphone manufacturers include in their product lines stereo headphones that automatically turn off when a dangerous level of loudness is reached. It is clear that adoption of this recommendation would not significantly reduce the occurrence of hearing loss in teenagers, however, since almost all stereo headphones that teenagers use are bought by the teenagers themselves.

And here's a quick analysis.

- Author's conclusion: *It is clear that adoption of this recommendation would not significantly reduce the occurrence of hearing loss in teenagers.*
- Author's premises: *Teenagers buy their own headphones.*
- Author's assumption: *Since the purpose of this argument is to reject a proposed solution, it is assuming that teenagers will not buy the headphones that shut off when dangerous levels of loudness are reached.*

Step 3: Act Since the author does not come right out and say that teens won't buy the headphones, chances are that you'll find an answer that makes this connection. Failing that, you'll need to keep in mind that you're broadly looking for choices that agree with the author's conclusion. In this case, that the parents' headphone solution will not work.

> The credited response to a Strengthen question will provide information in support of the conclusion, or it will weaken an alternate interpretation of the premises.

Step 4: Answer using Process of Elimination Remember that you want something that helps the conclusion here.

 Loud music is most dangerous to hearing when it is played through stereo headphones. 

Does this show that the parents' solution won't work? This is not relevant because it doesn't matter whether listening through headphones is the most dangerous. The argument does not compare different methods of listening to music. Eliminate this one.

 No other cause of hearing loss in teenagers is as damaging as their listening to loud music through stereo headphones. 

Does this show that the parents' solution won't work? This choice would strengthen a causal argument (no other cause), but since that reasoning isn't in play in this argument, this choice doesn't work. Eliminate it.

 Parents of teenagers generally do not themselves listen to loud music through stereo headphones. 

Does this show that the parents' solution won't work? Be careful not to fall into the trap of thinking that if the parents don't listen to their own advice then neither will their teenagers. This isn't about common sense; it's about what you can prove from the information in the argument. This does not work without a lot of justification, so get rid of it.

 **Teenagers who now listen to music at dangerously loud levels choose to do so despite their awareness of the risks involved.** 

Does this show that the parents' solution won't work? If the teenagers are aware of the risk and want to listen to dangerously loud music anyway, then this shows that they are unlikely to buy the new headphones. This rules out the possibility that perhaps the teens were unaware of the danger. Keep this choice for now.

Careful!
Watch out for Weaken answers on Strengthen questions, and vice versa.

 A few headphone manufacturers already plan to market stereo headphones that automatically turn off when a dangerous level of loudness is reached. 

Does this show that the parents' solution won't work? The author thinks that teenagers won't buy the headphones. If the manufacturers already plan to sell the safe headphones, then they think people will buy them. If anything, this strengthens the parents' position and weakens the author's position. The problem is that there still isn't any direct link between making the headphones and getting teens to use them, or showing that the teens won't use them.

Principle Strengthen

Another type of Strengthen question asks you to find a "principle" to "justify" the argument. This time, instead of a specific fact or piece of evidence, the correct answer will be a general rule that will strengthen the argument as a whole. These tend to prove the conclusion is true, very much like sufficient assumption questions. The answer may help the conclusion in an unexpected or rather extreme way, so don't shy away from answers that are strongly worded.

The Argument

8. In order to expand its mailing lists for e-mail advertising, the Outdoor Sports Company has been offering its customers financial incentives if they provide the e-mail addresses of their friends. However, offering such incentives is an unethical business practice, because it encourages people to exploit their personal relationships for profit, which risks damaging the integrity of those relationships.

Which one of the following principles, if valid, most helps to justify the reasoning in the argument?

(A) It is unethical for people to exploit their personal relationships for profit if in doing so they risk damaging the integrity of those relationships.

(B) If it would be unethical to use information that was gathered in a particular way, then it is unethical to gather that information in the first place.

(C) It is an unethical business practice for a company to deliberately damage the integrity of its customers' personal relationships in any way.

(D) It is unethical to encourage people to engage in behavior that could damage the integrity of their personal relationships.

(E) Providing a friend's personal information to a company in exchange for a financial reward will almost certainly damage the integrity of one's personal relationship with that friend.

PrepTest 127, Section 2, Question 16

Assess
There are two kinds of Principle questions. Some ask you to "justify" or strengthen the conclusion. Some ask for a principle that "conforms" or matches information (see Lesson 10). When the question asks you to justify a conclusion, be sure to find the conclusion and premises.

Here's How to Crack It

Step 1: Assess the question As always, look at the question first.

> Which one of the following principles, if valid, most helps to justify the reasoning in the argument?

Now you're looking to "justify"—basically, to strengthen—the argument about Outdoor Sports Company. Notice how the question also includes the proviso "if valid," just as a Strengthen question would include "if true." Remember that your choices are going to be generally worded rules rather than specific facts.

Step 2: Analyze the argument Just as you would on a Strengthen question, analyze the argument by finding the conclusion (the judgment you're looking to justify) and the premises (the circumstances involved). You'll also want to see if you can find a conspicuous gap in the reasoning. Take a look at the argument.

> In order to expand its mailing lists for e-mail advertising, the Outdoor Sports Company has been offering its customers financial incentives if they provide the e-mail addresses of their friends. However, offering such incentives is an unethical business practice, because it encourages people to exploit their personal relationships for profit, which risks damaging the integrity of those relationships.

Here's how to break it down:

- Author's conclusion: *...offering such incentives is an unethical business practice.*
- Author's premises: *[financial incentives to provide a friend's email address] encourages people to exploit their personal relationships for profit...*
- Author's assumption: *The argument never explicitly links the premise that exploiting a personal relationship for profit and risking damage to a relationship with the conclusion about a business practice being unethical. The argument assumes that causing a customer to risk the integrity of a friendship for profit is unethical.*

To check out the "Schools with the Best Quality of Life," take a look at your online Student Tools. If you haven't registered yet, go to PrincetonReview.com/prep

Step 3: Act You're looking for an answer that supports the position that it is unethical to cause a customer to risk the integrity of a relationship. The credited response will probably do this by somehow connecting the *threat* of doing harm to the *act* of doing harm.

Step 4: Answer using Process of Elimination Make sure you take each answer choice back to the argument and see whether it supports the conclusion. Since you're looking for an answer that justifies, or proves, the conclusion, the stronger the answer choice, the better.

 It is unethical for people to exploit their personal relationships for profit if in doing so they risk damaging the integrity of those relationships. 

Does this prove that a financial incentive for customers to exploit a personal relationship is unethical? This choice focuses on the ethics of the customer instead of the business. Eliminate this answer.

 If it would be unethical to use information that was gathered in a particular way, then it is unethical to gather that information in the first place. 

Does this prove that a financial incentive for customers to exploit a personal relationship is unethical? This choice makes the unethical business practice predicated on the use of the data after the fact, but the argument does not address whether using the data is unethical or not. Eliminate this answer choice.

 It is an unethical business practice for a company to deliberately damage the integrity of its customers' personal relationships in any way. 

Does this prove that a financial incentive for customers to exploit a personal relationship is unethical? Maybe—take a close look at this one. The choice certainly connects the business practice to a customer damaging the integrity of a personal relationship. But check the argument again to make sure it is the same. The argument says it is unethical because a person *risks* damaging the integrity of a personal relationship and it never mentions whether the company is doing so *deliberately*. This is one way that Principle Strengthen questions can be tricky. Eliminate this answer.

 **It is unethical to encourage people to engage in behavior that could damage the integrity of their personal relationships.** 

Does this prove that a financial incentive for customers to exploit a personal relationship is unethical? Since the author claims the business practice would cause a customer to exploit a personal relationship and risk damaging the integrity of that relationship, it seems the answer is yes. Keep this answer.

 Providing a friend's personal information to a company in exchange for a financial reward will almost certainly damage the integrity of one's personal relationship with that friend. 

Does this prove that a financial incentive for customers to exploit a personal relationship is unethical? Not quite. This proves the risk of a customer damaging a relationship is almost certain, but it does not address whether that makes the business practice mentioned in the argument *unethical.* Eliminate this choice.

This means the credited response to this Principle Strengthen question is (D).

Understanding Principle Strengthen Questions

In Principle Strengthen questions, a principle that "justifies" the conclusion may legitimately help the conclusion using a method that's a little different from the one in the original argument. Make sure you know what kind of Principle question you are dealing with: Principle Strengthen or Principle Match, which requires a somewhat different method.

What If I Can't Find an Assumption?

We've been talking quite a bit about what an important role the assumptions play in weakening or strengthening arguments on the LSAT. You may be asking yourself, "What am I supposed to do if I can't find an assumption?" Well, there's still hope. Finding assumptions is one of the trickier skills for many students to develop. In addition to identifying the purpose structure and looking for the common flawed patterns of reasoning, here are two ideas to keep in mind.

First, look for any shifts in the author's language. Anytime the author makes a conclusion, evaluate that conclusion *only* on the basis of the evidence you're given in support of that conclusion. If there are any changes in language between the premises and the conclusion, these changes clue you into assumptions. This shift can be blatant, as when something that was never mentioned before suddenly shows up in the conclusion. Or it can be more subtle, such as if the author makes a statement that is more strongly qualified than the evidence. For instance, if you had evidence about what "almost always" is the case and concluded something that "will" happen, that would require a leap in logic.

Remember also that arguments can have multiple assumptions. Even if you identify an assumption correctly, it might not be the "right" one (meaning it might not be the one the credited response hinges on).

What if you can't articulate an assumption, or you find the "wrong" one? Don't worry; there's *still* hope. As we've been saying, you should approach the answer choices with an assumption or at least an understanding of the gap between the conclusion and premises. This is because it's not necessary for you to be able to *generate* the assumption to find the best answer. You can also be prepared to *recognize* an assumption (or an answer that will impact it, in the case of Weaken and Strengthen questions). Sure, you might find that you can get through POE more quickly if you have a neatly paraphrased assumption jotted down, but if you've at least identified any gaps in the argument, you'll be able to evaluate the answer choices and recognize the ones that don't have the proper impact.

Arguments Technique: What to Do When You're Down to Two

As you do more LSAT Arguments, you may find yourself falling into a predictable pattern in which you find it easy to eliminate three of the answer choices but then have no clear idea of which one of the two remaining choices is correct. There's the first problem. You should know that it isn't your job to determine which is the *correct* answer. The trickiest incorrect answers on LSAT Arguments are usually mostly right—they contain just a word or two that makes them wrong.

Very often these wrong answers will even sound better than the "credited response." The writers of the LSAT are experts at writing answers that are *almost* all correct, so if you spot anything that makes the choice wrong, even one word, eliminate it.

Now, what do you do when you get down to two choices? Well, you focus on finding something that makes one of them incorrect. There must be something appealing about each of them, or you would have eliminated one of them by now.

Here are a few steps to follow when you are down to two choices.

1. Identify how the answer choices are different.
2. Go back to the argument and reread, keeping the difference in mind. Use the difference that you've spotted to help you read the argument from a new, critical perspective. Try to find something in the language of the argument that points out a problem with one of the remaining two choices. Focus on the statement of the conclusion; this is very often what makes the final decision, especially if you didn't read it closely enough the first time.
3. Eliminate the choice with the flaw. Now that you've found the problem, eliminate that choice and move on.

This process will work on any type of Argument question—and, for that matter, on Reading Comprehension. Be critical and methodical, and you'll get results.

Summary: Strengthen Questions

With Strengthen questions, you once again looked for what impact each of the answer choices had on the argument—only this time, a favorable impact. Focus on finding the flaws that allow you to eliminate the attractive wrong answers and leave you with the only choice that has a direct impact on the argument. Look at the chart below.

Sample Question Phrasings	Act
Which one of the following statements, if true, would most support the author's conclusion? *Which one of the following statements, if true, would strengthen the author's argument?* *Which one of the following principles, if established, justifies the actions taken by Mia in the argument above?*	• Identify the conclusion, premises, and assumptions of the author. • Read critically, looking for where the author made large leaps in logic. • Then, when you go to the answer choices, look for a choice that has the most positive impact on that gap. • Assume all choices to be hypothetically true.

Careful!
Not all questions that use the word *support* are Strengthen questions. Strengthen questions ask you to support the argument's conclusion, but Inference questions ask you to use the passage to support an answer choice.

LESSON 6: RESOLVE/EXPLAIN QUESTIONS

So far, you've been working with arguments in which the author has presented evidence to support a conclusion. And with the exception of Main Point questions, you've been paying attention to any gaps in the argument that might help you to pinpoint the assumptions the author has made. The process for analyzing the argument (Step 2) has been almost identical for Main Point, Assumption, Weaken, and Strengthen question types.

Step 2 is a bit different in answering Resolve/Explain questions. That's because the "argument" attached to these questions is more like a passage. With these types of questions, the author will present a couple of pieces of information that don't seem to fit together. Your task will be to find the answer choice that will do the best job of *resolving* the apparent discrepancy between these two pieces of information and that will *explain* how both pieces of information could be true at once. The other steps remain the same; you just don't have the same pieces to break down what you've seen so far.

Look at a typical passage that would be used in asking a Resolve/Explain question.

> The ancient Dirdirs used water power for various purposes in the outlying cities and towns in their empire. However, they did not use this technology in their capital city of Avallone.

Your goal will be to spot an answer choice that resolves or explains the discrepancy or paradox.

Notice that there's no evidence provided to support a particular claim, just two pieces of information that don't really seem to fit with each other. Here you've got this ancient culture that has this certain type of technology but doesn't use it in the capital city. That's the discrepancy or paradox, right? Good. Your goal then will be to spot an answer choice that in some way resolves or explains that discrepancy or paradox. You might be able to think up a few reasons the Dirdirs had this technology and didn't use it, such as the following:

- There were no rivers or other bodies of water in or near Avallone.
- It was cheaper or more efficient to use another source of power in the capital, such as abundant labor.
- There was not enough space for the equipment in Avallone.

That's good for a start. You could actually come up with a multitude of theoretical reasons they didn't use this technology (the actual historical reason has something to do with the fact that it would have caused social unrest because this technology would have put too many people out of work), but the nice thing is that you don't have to come up with reasons! All you have to do is identify the discrepancy and be able to recognize the answer choice that allows both parts of the discrepancy to be true. That'll save you a lot of work and keep you from generating ideas that are far away from what the test-writers were thinking when they wrote the question. Now you will put this idea to work on a full question.

The Argument

9. In the past, combining children of different ages in one classroom was usually a failure; it resulted in confused younger children, who were given inadequate attention and instruction, and bored older ones, who had to sit through previously learned lessons. Recently, however, the practice has been revived with excellent results. Mixed-age classrooms today are stimulating to older children and enable younger children to learn much more efficiently than in standard classrooms.

   Which one of the following, if true, most helps to resolve the apparent discrepancy in the passage?

   (A) On average, mixed-age classrooms today are somewhat larger in enrollment than were the ones of the past.

   (B) Mixed-age classrooms of the past were better equipped than are those of today.

   (C) Today's mixed-age classrooms, unlike those of the past, emphasize group projects that are engaging to students of different ages.

   (D) Today's mixed-age classrooms have students of a greater range of ages than did those of the past.

   (E) Few of the teachers who are reviving mixed-age classrooms today were students in mixed-age classrooms when they were young.

PrepTest 117, Section 2, Question 3

Here's How to Crack It

Step 1: Assess the question Here it is again.

> Which one of the following, if true, most helps to resolve the apparent discrepancy in the passage?

This question is tipping your hand—it's telling you that there is something you need to *resolve* in the *passage*. When the question stem doesn't use the word "argument," you are not looking for any gaps in the reasoning. The information in the passage contains a *discrepancy* or *paradox*, and you're going to have to find an answer choice that resolves these seemingly opposing facts.

Step 2: Analyze the argument Read through the argument, looking for any situations or facts that seem contrary to one another. Here it is again.

Analyze
There's no need to find the conclusion and premises on Resolve/Explain questions.

> In the past, combining children of different ages in one classroom was usually a failure; it resulted in confused younger children, who were given inadequate attention and instruction, and bored older ones, who had to sit through previously learned lessons. Recently, however, the practice has been revived with excellent results. Mixed-age classrooms today are stimulating to older children and enable younger children to learn much more efficiently than in standard classrooms.

What is the apparent discrepancy? In the past, mixed-age classrooms were not successful, but now they are.

Step 3: Act Remember that there are probably a number of specific theories we could come up with to explain this discrepancy, and if one possible explanation jumps into your head, that's fine—it may turn out to be an answer choice. But fundamentally, you just need to be aware of the *discrepancy* and see what impact, if any, each of the answer choices will have on it.

> The credited response to a Resolve/Explain question will be a hypothetically true statement that explains how all aspects of the paradox or discrepancy can be true.

Step 4: Answer using Process of Elimination Just as with Weaken and Strengthen answer choices, you first have to accept each of the answer choices here as facts, and then apply them to the argument. One of these facts, when added to the argument, will resolve the apparent paradox, or explain the supposed discrepancy.

Let's see which one of the following choices does this.

 On average, mixed-age classrooms today are somewhat larger in enrollment than were the ones of the past. 

Does this explain why mixed-age classrooms were not successful but now are? No. A larger class size does not resolve the discrepancy in success. Eliminate it.

 Mixed-age classrooms of the past were better equipped than are those of today. 

Does this explain why mixed-age classrooms were not successful but now are? If mixed-age classrooms of the past were better equipped, then why would the new mixed-age classrooms be more successful? This makes the discrepancy worse. Get rid of it.

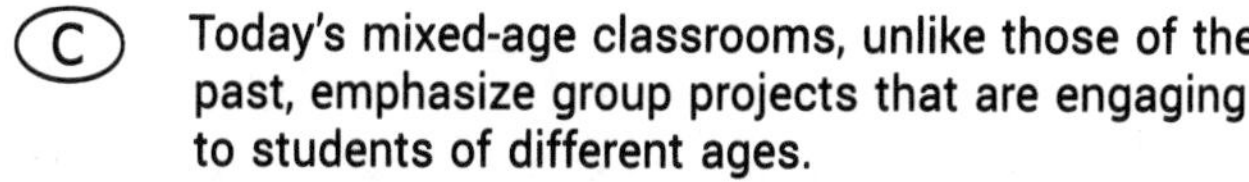
(C) **Today's mixed-age classrooms, unlike those of the past, emphasize group projects that are engaging to students of different ages.**

Does this explain why mixed-age classrooms were not successful but now are? Notice how this answer sets up a contrast between the student activities in today's mixed-age classrooms and those of the past. If the projects are engaging to students of different ages, then this could explain why today's classrooms are more successful. Keep this one.

 Today's mixed-age classrooms have students of a greater range of ages than did those of the past. 

Does this explain why mixed-age classrooms were not successful but now are? A wider age range does not clear up the difference in the success of the new classrooms versus the old ones. Eliminate it.

 Few of the teachers who are reviving mixed-age classrooms today were students in mixed-age classrooms when they were young. 

Does this explain why mixed-age classrooms were not successful but now are? Whether the teachers attended mixed-age classes is not relevant to the change in success. Eliminate it.

Some people find this type of question challenging because they can see how more than one of the answers could work. If this sounds like something you do, remember to follow the process and be crystal clear what you need the credited response to do. Asking yourself the same question as you do POE—in this case, "Does this explain why mixed-age classrooms were not successful but now are?"—will help you stay focused on the task at hand. If you find yourself wanting to justify any of the answers by supplying additional information to make them work, they are wrong and you need to eliminate them.

Arguments Technique: Using Process of Elimination with Resolve/Explain Questions

In using Process of Elimination (POE) with Resolve/Explain questions, you should remember that the correct answer will be some explanation that will allow *both* of the facts from the passage to be true. In the Dirdir question, the two facts were (1) they had water power, and (2) they did not use this technology in their capital city. In the mixed-age classrooms passage, the facts were (1) mixed-age classrooms in the past were usually a failure, and (2) mixed-age classrooms today are successful. The correct answer in each case allowed each of these facts to be true independently of the other and allowed both to make sense together.

Additionally, note that the phrasing of most Resolve/Explain questions contains the clause "if true." Your methodology should be exactly the same here as it is with Weaken and Strengthen questions—you assume each of the five answer choices to be hypothetically true and look for the impact of each one on the discrepancy. In the case of Resolve/Explain questions, the impact will relate to whether or not or how well the choice resolves an apparent discrepancy.

Summary: Resolve/Explain Questions

With Resolve/Explain questions, the only thing you must find before going to the answer choices is the apparent discrepancy or paradox. Remember that you have to work under the belief that the answers are true, regardless of how unreasonable they may seem. Evaluate what impact the answer choice would have on the discrepancy *if it were true.* Finally, look to see which one of the answer choices allows both of the facts or sides in the passage to be true at the same time. Only one of them will do this.

Sample Question Phrasings	Act
Which one of the following provides the best resolution to the apparent paradox described by the committee member? *Which of the following statements, if true, would explain the discrepancy found by the scientists?*	• Identify the apparent discrepancy or paradox. • Go to the answer choices and look for a piece of information that, when added to the information given, allows both facts from the passage to be true. • Assume all choices to be hypothetically true.

LESSON 7: INFERENCE QUESTIONS

Like the arguments attached to Resolve/Explain questions, most Inference arguments are not written in the familiar *conclusion supported by premises* format. Instead, they will be passages that may or may not seem to be headed somewhere. And the test-writers will ask you to find a piece of information that either must be true, based on the information provided in the argument, or will be best supported by the argument. That something can come from anywhere in the passage and doesn't have to come from anything important.

Here are a few tips right off the bat. You can't use any information that is not included in the passage, you don't have to find the main conclusion, and you have to pay very close attention to any qualifying language (*most, always, each, few, might*) that is used. Ready to put this information to work? Then let's get to it.

The Argument

10. Artists have different ways of producing contours and hatching, and analysis of these stylistic features can help to distinguish works by a famous artist both from forgeries and from works genuinely by other artists. Indeed, this analysis has shown that many of the drawings formerly attributed to Michelangelo are actually by the artist Giulio Clovio, Michelangelo's contemporary.

    If the statements above are true, then which one of the following must also be true?

(A) Contours and hatching are the main features that distinguish the drawing styles of different artists.

(B) Many of the drawings formerly attributed to Michelangelo are actually forgeries.

(C) No forgery can perfectly duplicate the contour and hatching styles of a famous artist.

(D) The contour and hatching styles used to identify the drawings of Clovio cited can be shown to be features of all Clovio's works.

(E) There is an analyzable difference between Clovio's contour and hatching styles and those of Michelangelo.

PrepTest 117, Section 4, Question 15

Here's How to Crack It

Step 1: Assess the question Inference questions can be worded in several ways. Here's a common one.

> If the statements above are true, then which one of the following must also be true?

You're looking for something that's an absolutely 100 percent airtight logical consequence of the material presented in the argument, which as you can see in this case is more like a short descriptive passage.

Step 2: Analyze the argument Sometimes on Inference questions there isn't a lot of analysis you can do. In those cases, just read the passage and do a quick paraphrase of the information given. Most often, these passages are not arguments, though when they are you still have to treat all the parts as true and not look for gaps in the reasoning. Sometimes there are a series of statements that appear to be begging to be put together. Look at the passage again.

> Artists have different ways of producing contours and hatching, and analysis of these stylistic features can help to distinguish works by a famous artist both from forgeries and from works genuinely by other artists. Indeed, this analysis has shown that many of the drawings formerly attributed to Michelangelo are actually by the artist Giulio Clovio, Michelangelo's contemporary.

Analyze
Do not look for the conclusion and premises on Inference questions.

Focus on the facts in this passage, and paraphrase them so you can more readily recognize any connections.

- Fact 1: *Analysis of certain stylistic features can help distinguish who the artist is.*
- Fact 2: *This analysis helped to show that some art is Clovio's instead of Michelangelo's.*

An inference is something you can prove from the information given. It is not to be confused with an assumption, which doesn't need proof. Once you have paraphrased the facts, look to see what you know to be true on the basis of them. If you notice a logical progression leading to a particular conclusion, it always pays to go ahead and combine the facts for yourself before you do POE. So, what do you know for sure from the facts above?

- *Artists stylistic features are different enough that they can be used to help identify who made the art.*
- *Since the analysis was used to differentiate between Clovio's work and Michelangelo's, there must be some differences between Clovio's style and Michelangelo's style.*

Step 3: Act These conclusions are very likely to figure into the right answer somehow, which is why you should bother to paraphrase the passage and look for them in the first place.

The credited response to an Inference question is the statement best supported by the passage.

Step 4: Answer using Process of Elimination When using POE on Inference question answers, look at the choices with an open mind. It is sometimes hard to predict exactly what inference will be in the answers. Combining facts is one way to make inferences on the LSAT, or sometimes the test-writers will make an inference by just taking a small logical step away from something said in the passage. Take each choice on its own merits and always go back to the passage for *proof!*

 Contours and hatching are the main features that distinguish the drawing styles of different artists. 

The passage mentions contours and hatching as examples of stylistic features, but it does not claim that these are the *main* features that distinguish artists' works. This choice is more specific and more demanding than our original, so eliminate the choice.

 Many of the drawings formerly attributed to Michelangelo are actually forgeries. 

A forgery is a fake meant to be passed off as an original work of art. Many Michelangelo works have now been attributed to Clovio, but there is no proof in the passage that those works were forgeries. You should eliminate this choice.

 No forgery can perfectly duplicate the contour and hatching styles of a famous artist. 

The passage states that stylistic differences "help to distinguish" works, which is not the same as claiming that no forgery can perfectly duplicate an artist's style. This goes too far, so eliminate it.

 The contour and hatching styles used to identify the drawings of Clovio cited can be shown to be features of all Clovio's works. 

There is no evidence in the passage that all of Clovio's works had the same style features. Be careful not to make an assumption here! All you know for sure is that the stylistic features are unique and that the styles of Clovio and Michelangelo are different. If you can't prove it, you can't choose it! Since you don't have enough information to prove this, eliminate it.

(E) There is an analyzable difference between Clovio's contour and hatching styles and those of Michelangelo. 

Here, at last, is the inference we came up with in the first place. Because some of Michelangelo's works have been reattributed to Clovio using analysis of contour and hatching styles, there must be a discernible difference. This is the choice you want.

Arguments Technique: Look for Extreme Language

Do you remember the Process of Elimination techniques used to get rid of wrong answer choices in Main Point questions in Lesson 1? They included relevance, opposites, and extreme language. Relevance is still certainly an issue with Inference questions because if there is something in an answer choice that wasn't mentioned in the argument, there's no way you could have inferred it from the information presented. However, when it comes to Inference questions, extreme wording (as you saw in some of the answers in the previous examples) plays a key role. It is much easier to say that something is *usually* true than to say that something is *always* true. It is much more difficult to back up the second phrase. Take a look at another example.

1. Most literature professors are skilled readers.
2. All literature professors are skilled readers.

There's only one difference between these two sentences: one has the word *most;* the other has the word *all.* Yet there is a vast difference between these two statements. Certainly, anyone who has reached such a high position has done more than her fair share of reading. Very rigorous standards must be met and outstanding academic performance must be demonstrated. This requires a ton of reading. It's reasonable to think that if someone's doing that much reading, they are probably a skilled reader. But if you were asked which of those statements *must be true,* you would have to eliminate the second statement. It would be incredibly difficult to prove that *all* literature professors are skilled readers. It would take only *one* person who never really liked to read, but was driven to this level of success for other reasons, to disprove the second statement. It would be much easier to prove the first statement because it leaves a lot more room for a few exceptions to the general rule. Both statements involve strong wording, but the second is *too* strong.

It's much easier to prove that something is usually true than it is to prove that something is always true.

Take a look at the following chart.

Safely Vague		Dangerously Extreme	
might could may can some	possible usually sometimes at least once frequently	always never at no time must will all	not positively absolutely unequivocally every

The sample Inference question you just worked through asked you to find the answer choice that could be "properly inferred," in other words, the one that *must be true* based on the information in the argument. Other Inference questions will require a slightly different task. Rather than finding the answer that must be true, you will be asked to find the one that would be best supported by the information in the argument. This may seem like a subtle difference, but it is important to pay attention to nuances in language such as this on the LSAT. Let's take a look at how these work.

The Argument

11. Coffee and tea contain methylxanthines, which cause temporary increases in the natural production of vasopressin, a hormone produced by the pituitary gland. Vasopressin causes clumping of blood cells, and the clumping is more pronounced in women than in men. This is probably the explanation of the fact that women face as much as a tenfold higher risk than men do of complications following angioplasty, a technique used to clear clogged arteries.

    Which one of the following statements is most strongly supported by the information above?

(A) Men, but not women, should be given methylxanthines prior to undergoing angioplasty.

(B) In spite of the risks, angioplasty is the only effective treatment for clogged arteries.

(C) Women probably drink more coffee and tea, on average, than do men.

(D) Prior to undergoing angioplasty, women should avoid coffee and tea.

(E) Angioplasty should not be used to treat clogged arteries.

PrepTest 117, Section 4, Question 12

Here's How to Crack It

Step 1: Assess the question Make sure that you're clear about your task. Notice that the question stem makes no mention of an argument—that's a classic sign that this is an Inference question. This question asks us to find the answer that is "most strongly supported" by the information in the passage. You don't have to be able to show that the answer *must be true* according to the information we have from the author. You still need evidence from the author's language, but it doesn't *have to be* true.

Step 2: Analyze the argument You still need to read the passage carefully. This step will be the same as it was with your first Inference question. Pay close attention to qualifying language, underlining key words and jotting down any notes you need to keep things straight. Here's the passage again.

> Coffee and tea contain methylxanthines, which cause temporary increases in the natural production of vasopressin, a hormone produced by the pituitary gland. Vasopressin causes clumping of blood cells, and the clumping is more pronounced in women than in men. This is probably the explanation of the fact that women face as much as a tenfold higher risk than men do of complications following angioplasty, a technique used to clear clogged arteries.

To summarize, a substance in coffee and tea increases vasopressin, which, in turn, causes clumping of blood cells. This clumping is more pronounced in women than in men, and may explain why women face a higher risk of complications after angioplasty.

Step 3: Act Remember that on Inference questions, you can't predict with any assurance what the test-writers will look for. Head right to the answer choices and start Step 4. Just be sure to go back to the passage for proof.

Step 4: Answer using Process of Elimination Check out each answer choice in turn and see which ones you can eliminate. Be on the lookout for answers that fall outside of the scope of the information that you've been given or are inconsistent with what you were told: answers that include extreme language and answers that make unwarranted comparisons. If any part of an answer choice isn't supported, get rid of it. Here we go.

Men, but not women, should be given methylxanthines prior to undergoing angioplasty.

What do you know from the passage? Methylxanthines increase vasopressin, which causes blood cell clumping. Clumping can lead to complications, so it would be bad to give men methylxanthines. Eliminate this choice.

 In spite of the risks, angioplasty is the only effective treatment for clogged arteries. 

The passage doesn't provide enough information to say that angioplasty is the only effective treatment for clogged arteries. "Only" makes this choice extreme and unsupported. Eliminate it.

 Women probably drink more coffee and tea, on average, than do men. 

You may be tempted by this at first, since women are at a greater risk for complications than men, but there is no support in the passage that the reason is that women drink more coffee and tea. All you know for sure is that the clumping is more pronounced for women than for men, but not why. Get rid of this one.

 **Prior to undergoing angioplasty, women should avoid coffee and tea.** 

What do you know from the passage? Because consuming methylxanthines increases the risk of blood cell clumping, which in turn increases the risk of complications after angioplasty, women would be well advised to avoid coffee and tea before undergoing angioplasty. Keep this one for now.

 Angioplasty should not be used to treat clogged arteries. 

This goes too far. Though the passage mentions complications of angioplasty, that's not enough to claim that the treatment should not be used. This one should be eliminated too.

There you have it. You found (D), which is the credited response. Notice that you can't say *for sure* that women should avoid coffee and tea before angioplasty, but this is a reasonable inference from the given facts.

In summary, when you have this kind of weaker inference, you have a little bit more latitude. You still need evidence from the passage to support the choice, but you don't have to be able to show that an answer *must be true.*

Arguments Technique: Watch Out for the Word *Support*

The word *support* shows up in two different types of Arguments questions, and you'll need to be able to keep them straight if you hope to approach the questions effectively. Take a look at a couple of sample questions.

> Which one of the following, if true, provides the most support for the argument?

> The passage provides the most support for which one of the following?

If you're not careful, you might mistakenly think that these two questions ask you to perform the same task. After all, they both talk about support, right? Actually, you have two different tasks here, and if you get them mixed up, you're going to have a difficult time with POE. Examine the first question more closely. Here it is again.

> Which one of the following, if true, provides the most support for the argument?

This should look familiar. Care to guess what your task is here? If you identified this as a Strengthen question, bravo! There are two indicators that will help you to properly identify it. First, notice the phrase "if true," referring to "the following," and recall that it is the answers on Strengthen questions that are hypothetically true. Second, notice that you are being asked to find the answer choice that *provides the most support for* the argument. In other words, you're being asked to evaluate the impact that each answer choice has on the author's conclusion. Sound familiar? We hope so.

Read Carefully!
"The statements above, if true, provide the most support for which one of the following?" Notice that "if true" refers to "the statements above." Because these statements are being used to support one of the answer choices, this is an *Inference* question, not a *Strengthen* question.

Here's the second question again.

> The passage provides the most support for which one of the following?

Notice the difference here. Aside from the obvious lack of the words *if true,* this question also asks for the support to happen, but *in the other direction.* Here you are asked to find the answer choice that *is best supported by* the passage. That's what you were just doing in the question you worked on a minute ago, so this is an Inference question.

Here, eliminate answers that aren't relevant because the passage doesn't offer enough evidence to support them, a pretty different mode of elimination from that used with Strengthen questions. The words *if true,* when referring to the choices, indicate hypotheticals in the answers, so it won't be an Inference question.

Two things to look for: If the *answer choices* are being used to support the *argument*, you have a Strengthen question. If the *passage* is being used to support one of the *answer choices*, you have an Inference question.

Arguments Technique: Look for Conditional Statements and Find the Contrapositive

Do you know what an "if...then" statement is? If you've taken any classes in logic, you might know it as a "conditional statement." Actually, it's very simple. Read this sentence.

If you hit a glass with a hammer, the glass will break.

When you run across a statement such as this, you can diagram it. A common way to diagram conditional statements is to use a symbol for each element in the statement—here we'll use "H" for hitting the glass with a hammer and "B" for breaking—and use an arrow to connect them, showing that the action leads directly to the effect. So H → B would represent the original statement.

This statement would seem reasonable to most people because it's what you would expect to happen in the real world. On the LSAT, you have to take this statement as true if it were part of an argument because, as we stated earlier, you have to accept all of the evidence presented in arguments at face value. This is true even when they aren't things that necessarily make reasonable sense.

With Inference questions, you are often asked to identify another statement—in the form of an answer choice—that also *must be true* if the statements in the argument are accepted as true.

Conditional Statements: Sufficient and Necessary

Once you diagram a conditional statement, use the terms *sufficient* and *necessary* to describe the function of each side of the diagram.

The left side is the sufficient side because it is enough, on its own, to know something else (the right side).

The right side is the necessary side because it is a requirement of something else (the left side).

You can use these terms to take apart and diagram difficult sentences containing conditional language by asking yourself, "Which factor is enough to know something else?" or "Which factor seems to be a requirement of something else?"

Here's the original statement.

> If you hit a glass with a hammer, the glass will break.

You can come up with a few other statements that you think would also have to be true.

For example, you could say

> If the glass is broken, it was hit with a hammer.

You would symbolize this as B → H. That seems like a reasonable outcome, but can you say that it *must be true* given our original statement?

Not *necessarily*. The glass could have been thrown out the window, stepped on by a giraffe, shot up with a Red Rider BB gun, and so on. If this were an answer choice on an Inference question in which the argument contained our original statement, what would you do? Hopefully, you would eliminate it because it doesn't have to be true. You could also suppose that

> If you don't hit a glass with a hammer, the glass won't break.

In this case, your symbolization would become ~H → ~B. Once again this seems reasonable in many cases, but does it *have to be true*? Again, not necessarily. It could have been thrown out the window, run over by a car, shattered by an opera singer's high C note, and so on. If this were an answer choice on an Inference question in which the argument contained our original statement, what would you do? Hopefully, you would eliminate it too because just like the last one, it doesn't have to be true.

How about this statement.

> If the glass isn't broken, it wasn't hit with a hammer.

This would be symbolized as ~B → ~H. This *must* be true. It makes sense if you think about it because you know for sure that if you hit the glass with a hammer, you're definitely going to break the glass. So if you come across an unbroken glass, there's no way it could have been hit with a hammer, at least not if you accept the truth of the original statement the way we have to on the LSAT. The only way that you could argue the truth of the above statement is by arguing the truth of the original. And while you can do that in real life, you can't do it on the LSAT.

This statement, which must always be true given that the original statement is true, is known as the *contrapositive*.

To create the contrapositive of a statement, take the original statement (or its symbolization, which is easier to work with) and perform the following two steps: Flip the order of the statements and then negate each of them.

Here's how it works with our original.

H → B

Flip the order of the statements and negate each of them to get the contrapositive.

~B → ~H

Now, what do you do if you have to negate something that's already negative? Let's take a look at an example.

If Pablo attends the dance, Christina won't attend the dance.

You can symbolize this as follows:

P → ~C

How do you negate ~C? Well, two negatives make a positive. When you negate a statement like "Christina won't attend the dance," it becomes "Christina will attend the dance." The contrapositive of your original statement is

C → ~P

With these examples, which are tied to real life and make reasonable sense, it might seem as if it's more work to learn how to apply this process than it would be to just reason out what the only other true statement would be. And it would be pretty reasonable to do that if you understand the way conditionals and contrapositives work and if the original statement makes sense. If only the LSAT were always that straightforward.

Instead, what will often happen is the original statement will be some abstract and complicated notion that's hard to get a handle on. For instance, you might see a conditional statement such as "Copper will not be added to the alloy only if aluminum is also not added to the alloy." Not nearly as intuitive, is it? Add to that the pressure of taking a timed, standardized exam and you'll wish you had memorized the simple symbols above.

These steps always work, so it's worth having them at your disposal. We're telling you all this because sometimes arguments contain "if…then" statements like the ones above. Usually the LSAT writers then ask an Inference question that requires you to find the answer that *must be true.* A couple of the answer choices will seem like reasonable things to believe. Another one or two may be variations on the original conditional statement, but won't be valid contrapositives.

It's possible that the credited response may just actually be the contrapositive—that depends on how complicated the argument is and how many pieces of information the passage contains—but regardless, knowing how to derive the contrapositive will help you eliminate wrong choices. Having both the original and contrapositive statements makes it easier to see the difference between what is *definitely* true and what merely *could* be true.

If…Then and Its Relatives

We showed you how to diagram basic "if…then" statements. The "if" always occurs on the left side of the arrow, while the "then" statement is always to the right of the arrow. However, these are not the only ways the LSAT will structure conditional statements. There are two other major conditional phrases that you need to be on the lookout for.

The first of these is the word "only" (or "only when" or "only if"). The word "only" establishes a requirement. Thus, whatever condition follows the word "only" should be placed to the right side of the arrow.

X will be In only if Y is Out.

The diagram for this is as follows:

X → ~Y

If your head is spinning with all this logic, fret not, intrepid tester! There is a fast way to ensure that you diagram the conditional correctly every time. Simply find the word "only" and draw the conditional arrow directly on top of it.

X will be In only if Y is out.

As you can see, the statement practically diagrams itself. One final note: just as with "if…then" statements, the order of the sentence does not affect the diagram. The same statement could have been written as follows:

Only if Y is Out will X be in.

Use the same method by drawing the arrow over the "only if" phrase. Since the arrow points to ~Y, that must be placed on the right side of the diagram.

Only if Y is Out will X be in.

Here's your rule of thumb: draw an arrow pointing to the right through the word "only." The thing on the point of the arrow should also be on the point of the arrow in your diagram. Be careful with these; it's easy to reverse them by mistake.

The next major word that the LSAT uses to create conditional statements is the word "unless." This one is a little harder for most people to wrap their heads around. However, consider the two sides to every conditional statement. The left side is sufficient—it provides enough information to know that something else has occurred or will occur. The right side is necessary—it provides some sort of requirement or rule that must be met. Now, try to apply that logic to the following statement.

X will not be In unless Y is Out.

It can be a little confusing, but thinking in terms of requirements, Y Out is the requirement for X In. Therefore, this can be diagrammed as follows:

X → ~Y

If this is confusing, don't worry. Just like the word "only," there is a fast way to figure out the diagram for these statements. Take the word "unless," and replace it with "if not."

if not
X will not be In ~~unless~~ Y is Out.

Now, diagram the statement mechanically.

~ (~Y) → ~X

Remember that two "not" become yes, so simplified we have

Y → ~X

Now take the contrapositive.

X → ~Y

We ultimately end up with the same result. The rule of thumb here is to cross out "unless" and write "if not," and then symbolize the clue as you would any "if… then" statement. The word "unless" is the most frequently misinterpreted clue; be extremely careful with these.

Tip!
While understanding the logic of conditionals is vital to mastering the LSAT, begin mechanically. Use the rules of thumb described here. Focus on understanding the logic during your self-analysis stage.

Conditionals with "And" or "Or"

On the LSAT, the word "and" means just what you think it does. "Or," on the other hand, means one or the other, or both. In other words, "A or B is chosen" could mean A, or B, or AB are chosen. Take a look at the following clue:

> If F is chosen, then G or H must also be chosen.

What does this mean? Well, whenever F is In, we know that at least one of G or H is In, and possibly both of them are. The only possibility this clue excludes is having both G and H Out.

How do we symbolize this? Since "and" and "or" appear so often on the test, we simply incorporate these words into our symbols.

F → G or H

Since the symbol implies both G and H as a possibility, we don't need to include anything else.

As always, we need to draw a symbol for the contrapositive of the clue. In order to elucidate the logic behind "and/or" statements, let's take a trip back to primary school. If you remember, the colors red and blue are both required to make purple. If you see that I have made purple, you know that I have mixed red and blue. This can be symbolized by writing

Purple → Red and Blue

Now imagine that I tell you that I cannot make purple today. What must be true? It is possible that I lack both red and blue, but that's a bit extreme. Only missing one of the required colors would prevent me from being able to make purple. Therefore, when I write the contrapositive, I need to falsify only one-half of the requirement to falsify the sufficient factor.

~Red or ~ Blue → ~Purple

Remember the rationale behind the contrapositive: we look for a case when the thing on the left-hand side must also be untrue. Apply this logic to the original example. What does it mean for "G or H" to be untrue? Well, the only way we can be sure that neither G nor H is In would be to have both of them Out. Put it another way, the contrary of the statement G is In or H is In (or both) is "G is Out and H is Out." Negating our "or" statement turns it into an "and" statement. Thus, the contrapositive here is as follows:

~G and ~H → ~F

This is how we negate the "or" statement. Not surprisingly, negating an "and" statement changes it into—you guessed it—an "or." After all, if we flip and negate the symbol we've drawn above, we should be back to our original symbol. In order to do that, we would turn the statement "not G and not H" into the statement "G or H."

Remember that when you're working with a statement involving "and" or "or," you have to negate every part of the statement. When you negate "and," it becomes "or"; when you negate "or," it becomes "and."

One last note of caution: be careful with the phrase "neither...nor." Many students mistakenly think that "nor" is the same as "or" since they sound alike. In reality, "neither A nor B" means "not A and not B." Consider the following phrase.

> If neither Harry nor Sally is at the party, then John will not be at the party.

This phrase literally means if not Harry *and* not Sally, then not John. Therefore, it should be symbolized as

~H and ~S → ~J
J → H or S

Do not make the mistake of thinking that because "or" and "nor" look alike, they must mean the same thing.

DIAGRAMMING CONDITIONALS DRILL

In order to practice diagramming conditionals, we've created a little quiz for you to practice these crucial skills and concepts. Make sure you translate each one carefully and generate the contrapositives before you move on.

1. If Jack attends, Mark must attend.

2. Ann will work only if Kate works.

3. Bob cannot work unless Gary is working.

4. Sid will attend the party only if Nancy attends.

5. If Will goes to the party, Cam won't go.

6. If Harry is invited, both Charles and Linda must be invited.

7. John will not speak unless neither Bill nor Harry speaks.

8. Doug will drive unless either May or Sue drives.

Cracking the Diagramming Conditionals Drill

We have placed each of these in table form, so that you have a quick reference guide for your notes as you study.

Clue	Symbol	Contrapositive
If Jack attends, Mark must attend.	J → M	~M → ~J
Ann will work only if Kate works.	A → K	~K → ~A
Bob cannot work ~~unless~~ (if not) Gary is working.	~G → ~B	B → G
Sid will attend the party only if Nancy attends.	S → N	~N → ~S
If Will goes to the party, Cam won't go.	W → ~C	C → ~W
If Harry is invited, both Charles and Linda must be invited.	H → C and L	~C or ~L → ~H
John will not speak ~~unless~~ (if not) neither Bill nor Harry speaks.	B or H → ~J	J → ~B and ~H*
Doug will drive ~~unless~~ (if not) either May or Sue drives.	~M and ~S → D	~D → M or S*

The two marked with an * deserve additional explanation. "Unless" statements with "and" or "or" can be incredibly challenging to diagram. Remember that when you negate, you have to negate the entire side. A more expanded diagram of John, Bill, and Harry is below.

~(~B and ~H) → ~J

The double negatives become positives and the "and" becomes an "or." Thus, the final diagram of

B or H → ~J

The last one is even trickier, but follows the same process by expanding out the diagram even more.

~ (M or S) → D

The negative applies to both M and S and the "or" becomes an "and." Thus, the final diagram of

~M and ~S → D

Arguments Technique: Look for Little Things That Mean a Lot

Another key to cracking Inference questions is to pay close attention to detail. Inferences are often made around seemingly innocuous words or phrases. For instance, anytime you see a term of quantity, comparison, or frequency, odds are it contains an inference.

Statement: *Most people like Picasso.*
Inference: *Some people may not like Picasso.*

Statement: *Unlike her jacket, mine is real leather.*
Inference: *Her jacket is not real leather.*

Statement: *Russ almost never shows up on time.*
Inference: *Russ rarely (or occasionally) does show up on time.*

Keep an eye out for details, and you'll stand a better chance of getting Inference questions right.

Summary: Inference Questions

With Inference questions, read the argument carefully and pay close attention to details such as qualifying language. Once you're at the answer choices, your goal is to eliminate the four answer choices that *don't have to be true* or are not *wholly supported* by evidence provided in the argument. You're also going to look out for relevance and, especially, issues of extreme language.

The way that Inference questions are phrased can be very tricky. See the "Sample Question Phrasings" column in the chart below for some examples.

Sample Question Phrasings	Act
Which one of the following statements can be validly inferred from the information above? *If the statements above are true, then which of the following must also be true?* *Which one of the following conclusions can be validly drawn from the passage above?** *Which one of the following conclusions is best supported by the passage above?**	• Read carefully, paying close attention to qualifying language, and then go to the answer choices. • Once there, eliminate any answer choices that are not *directly* supported by evidence in the passage. • Look for relevance and extreme language to eliminate answer choices. • Use the contrapositive if there are "if...then" statements contained in the passage and in the answer choices.

*Even though the stems in these questions contain the term "conclusions," they are not Main Point questions. Main Point questions ask you to find the conclusion, whereas Inference questions ask you for a conclusion, one of many that could possibly be derived from the passage. They are *Inference* questions, not *Main Point* questions. For contrast, review the sample Main Point question phrasings on page 28.

LESSON 8: REASONING QUESTIONS

So far, the questions you've seen in the Arguments section have been concerned with the literal contents: what's the conclusion, how do you attack or support it, or what does it assume? What piece of information will resolve two seemingly inconsistent pieces of information, or what else do you know to be true if the statements in the argument are true? Now you're going to look at some questions that deal with the arguments on a more abstract or descriptive level.

The first of these is the Reasoning question task, which asks you to determine not what the argument is about, but how the argument is made. This sounds quite straightforward, doesn't it? Well, sometimes it will be, but sometimes it will be rather difficult because of very attractive incorrect answers and deliberately impenetrable vocabulary. The answers to Reasoning questions will fall into one of two categories: general answers that don't actually mention the subject matter of the argument, and specific answers that do address the subject matter of the argument. Occasionally, the answer choices will be a mix of both.

So how do you approach questions such as these? Well, first you have to be able to identify the task. Then your goal is to describe what's happening in the argument—in other words, how the author arrived at their conclusion. Give one a try.

The Argument

12. An artificial hormone has recently been developed that increases milk production in cows. Its development has prompted some lawmakers to propose that milk labels should be required to provide information to consumers about what artificial substances were used in milk production. This proposal should not be implemented: just imagine trying to list every synthetic fertilizer used to grow the grass and grain the cows ate, or every fungicide used to keep the grain from spoiling!

The argument proceeds by

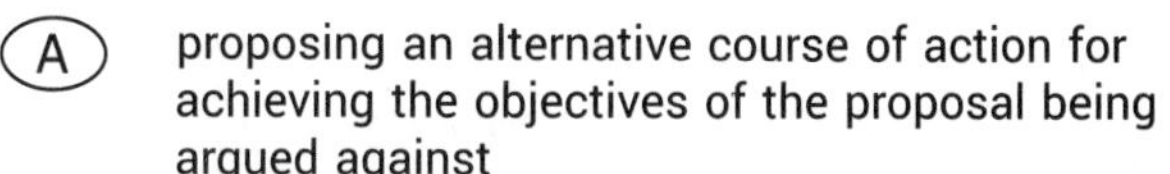
(A) proposing an alternative course of action for achieving the objectives of the proposal being argued against

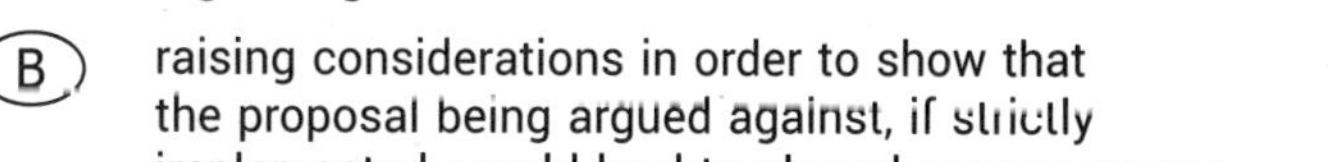
(B) raising considerations in order to show that the proposal being argued against, if strictly implemented, would lead to absurd consequences

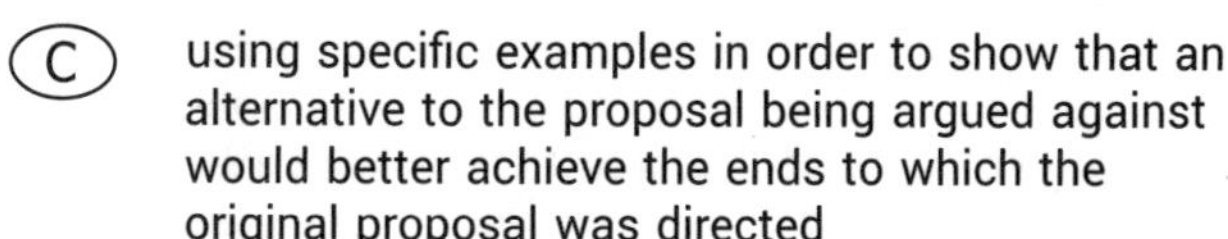
(C) using specific examples in order to show that an alternative to the proposal being argued against would better achieve the ends to which the original proposal was directed

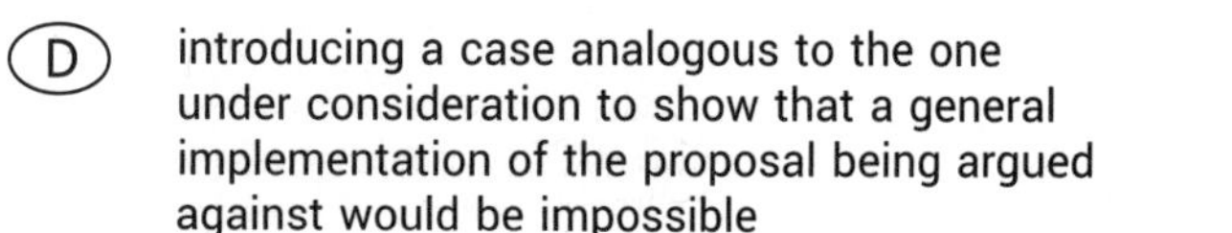
(D) introducing a case analogous to the one under consideration to show that a general implementation of the proposal being argued against would be impossible

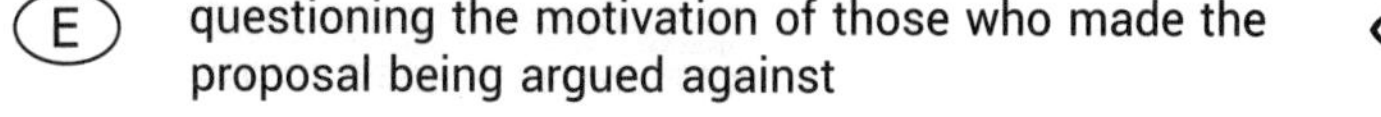
(E) questioning the motivation of those who made the proposal being argued against

PrepTest 118, Section 1, Question 7

Here's How to Crack It

Step 1: Assess the question You've read the question, but here it is again.

> The argument proceeds by

This asks you to describe the author's method of reasoning. Read the argument and look at the purpose structure of the argument to see how they get from the evidence to the main point.

Step 2: Analyze the argument Read the argument closely, paying attention to the author's reasoning. To do this, you'll have to identify the conclusion and the premises because this will allow you to understand the structure of the argument—in other words, how the author used the evidence to support their conclusion. You don't need to identify any gaps in the reasoning. Here it is again.

Analyze
Find the conclusion and premises on Reasoning questions.

> An artificial hormone has recently been developed that increases milk production in cows. Its development has prompted some lawmakers to propose that milk labels should be required to provide information to consumers about what artificial substances were used in milk production. This proposal should not be implemented: just imagine trying to list every synthetic fertilizer used to grow the grass and grain the cows ate, or every fungicide used to keep the grain from spoiling!

What is the purpose of this argument? To disagree—you can tell because the argument presents a proposal and then the author does not want the proposal implemented.

- Author's conclusion: *This proposal (that milk labels should be required to list artificial substances used in milk production) should not be implemented.*
- Author's premises: *Such labels would have to list so many synthetic products as to be impossible to implement.*

Step 3: Act Your goal here is simply to describe how the author made his argument. In this case, the author disagrees with implementing a proposal by presenting reasons that make the proposal too difficult to implement.

> The credited response to a Reasoning question will describe how the author constructed the argument.

Step 4: Answer using Process of Elimination Now you're going to approach the answer choices. The credited response will be a paraphrase of the author's reasoning: the proposal shouldn't be implemented because it will be unreasonable to do so. Check them out.

 proposing an alternative course of action for achieving the objectives of the proposal being argued against 

The author doesn't propose an alternative course of action, so eliminate it.

(B) 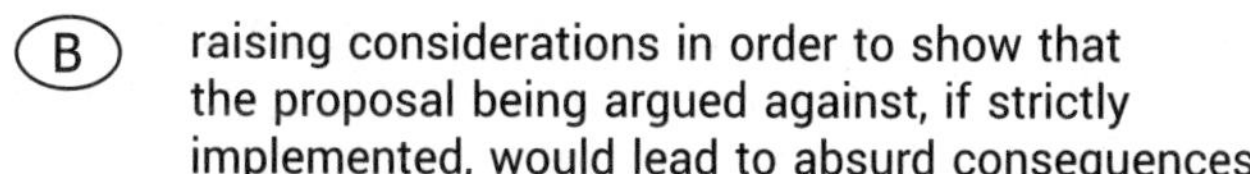
raising considerations in order to show that the proposal being argued against, if strictly implemented, would lead to absurd consequences

While the wording is different, it does line up with the disagree purpose structure and the author's position since he points out that there are too many ingredients to reasonably list. Keep it.

 using specific examples in order to show that an alternative to the proposal being argued against would better achieve the ends to which the original proposal was directed 

What alternative proposal? The author isn't trying to solve the problem, just point out that the current proposal shouldn't be implemented.

(D) introducing a case analogous to the one under consideration to show that a general implementation of the proposal being argued against would be impossible 

Although the author implies that the proposal would be impossible, he does not offer an analogous case to the one described in the argument. Eliminate it.

 questioning the motivation of those who made the proposal being argued against 

There is no mention of the motivation of those making the label proposal. Get rid of it.

That one was pretty straightforward. You were able to recognize the credited response pretty easily because you understood the author's reasoning and purpose structure before you approached the answer choices. Note how abstract the answers were. They didn't mention any of the specific details from the argument but took a much broader view.

Arguments Technique: Using Process of Elimination with Reasoning Questions

You may have noticed that when we discussed some of the answer choices, we took each word or phrase from the answer choice and asked, "Does this correspond to anything that actually occurred in the argument?" Most of the time, the answer to this question was no. The answer choices might sound abstract and technical, but unless you can go back to the argument and say, "Ah, yes, this is where the author gives the example and this is where they give the counterexample," then an answer choice that mentions "examples" and "counterexamples" will be wrong. This technique is the key to dealing with Reasoning questions; it should allow you to eliminate two or three answer choices every time. One other nice advantage of this technique is that it works even if you can't articulate the author's reasoning in your own words.

Hint:
On Reasoning questions, try to match each piece of the answer choice to a piece of the argument.

Look through the answers on Reasoning questions slowly and make sure to match each piece of the answer choice to a piece of the argument. When you come across something in an answer choice that doesn't correspond to anything in the argument, get rid of that choice. If it's even a little wrong, it's all wrong.

Summary: Reasoning Questions

In Reasoning questions, you should come up with your own description of how the argument unfolds. If you're able to come up with a terse, exact description of the argument, you can usually match it with one of the answer choices. Even if you can't come up with a good description, you can eliminate any answers that have elements that don't correspond with what actually happens in the author's argument. The vocabulary in the answer choices will probably be more esoteric than that which you used, but as long as the meaning is the same, you're fine.

Sample Question Phrasings	Act
The argument proceeds by... *Leah responds to Kevin by doing which of the following?* *The method the activist uses to object to the developer's argument is to...* *Dr. Jacobs does which of the following?* *Which one of the following most accurately describes the role played in the argument by the claim that...*	• Read the argument carefully and then describe what is happening in your own words, focusing on the purpose structure and the author's conclusion and premises. • Take this description and rigorously apply it to all the answer choices. • Once you're at the answer choices, use the technique of comparing the actions described in the answer choices against those that actually occur in the argument. • Eliminate anything that doesn't appear in the argument.

LESSON 9: FLAW QUESTIONS

Flaw questions are similar to Reasoning questions, but they're dissimilar enough that they call for a slightly different approach. On recent LSATs, Flaw questions have been far more common than have Reasoning questions. So what's the difference? Well, while a Reasoning question asks you to identify what the argument does or how it's argued, a Flaw question asks you what the argument does *wrong*. And as we mentioned before, if you find a problematic assumption in an argument, you've probably found its flaw. The approach to Flaw and Reasoning questions is the same, but with one important distinction: during Step 2, you should break down the argument into its parts and locate the assumption. After you've spotted the assumption, you just need to state what's wrong with the argument. Look at the following argument.

The Argument

13. According to some astronomers, Earth is struck by a meteorite large enough to cause an ice age on an average of once every 100 million years. The last such incident occurred nearly 100 million years ago, so we can expect that Earth will be struck by such a meteorite in the near future. This clearly warrants funding to determine whether there is a means to protect our planet from such meteorite strikes.

The reasoning in the argument is most subject to criticism on the grounds that the argument

(A) makes a bold prescription on the basis of evidence that establishes only a high probability for a disastrous event

(B) presumes, without providing justification, that the probability of a chance event's occurring is not affected by whether the event has occurred during a period in which it would be expected to occur

(C) moves from evidence about the average frequency of an event to a specific prediction about when the next such event will occur

(D) fails to specify the likelihood that, if such a meteorite should strike Earth, the meteorite would indeed cause an ice age

(E) presumes, without providing justification, that some feasible means can be found to deter large meteorite strikes

PrepTest 118, Section 4, Question 19

Here's How to Crack It

Step 1: Assess the question You've already read the question, but here it is again.

> The reasoning in the argument is most subject to criticism on the grounds that the argument

Now, you're expected to describe why the above argument is bad. Remember that this is different from "weakening" an argument, in which you'd hypothesize that the five answer choices were true. All you're looking for here is to describe the way in which the argument is bad, not add something that would make it worse.

Step 2: Analyze the argument Okay, so start by breaking it down into its parts.

- Author's conclusion: *This (likelihood of a large meteorite strike) clearly warrants funding to determine whether there is a means to protect our planet from such meteorite strikes.*
- Author's premises: *Earth is struck by a meteorite large enough to cause an ice age on an average of once every 100 million years. The last such incident occurred nearly 100 million years ago, so we can expect that Earth will be struck by such a meteorite in the near future.*
- Author's assumption: *How did the author get from an average time between meteor strikes to needing to prepare for an imminent meteor strike? He is interpreting the statistic incorrectly to assume that an average amount of time is an actual, predictable amount of time.*

Step 3: Act The correct answer to a Flaw question often draws attention to an assumption. If the assumption is that an average amount of time can be used to reliably predict the next meteorite strike, then the flaw is that the author fails to consider that the statistic might not be an accurate predictor. The credited response should draw attention to this weak link between the average and the prediction.

> The credited response to a Flaw question will describe how the premises don't necessarily lead to the conclusion, often drawing attention to a key assumption.

Step 4: Answer using Process of Elimination Now you're going to attack the answer choices. Let's see if you can find an answer choice that has something to do with the author making an analogy.

 makes a bold prescription on the basis of evidence that establishes only a high probability for a disastrous event 

This answer describes the progression of the argument, but this isn't what makes the argument's logic problematic. This describes the argument's conclusion and premises, but not the assumption, and the assumption is where the argument is flawed. Eliminate it.

 presumes, without providing justification, that the probability of a chance event's occurring is not affected by whether the event has occurred during a period in which it would be expected to occur 

Does this match the assumption that average time can be a reliable predictor? Let's match this to the specific details in the argument. The probability of a chance event (meteorite strike) is not affected by whether the event (meteorite strike) has occurred during a period of time (100 million years) it was expected to. This is the opposite of what we are looking for. Get rid of it.

 moves from evidence about the average frequency of an event to a specific prediction about when the next such event will occur 

Does this match the assumption that average time can be a reliable predictor? Well, it addresses the shift from average frequency (average time) to a specific prediction (the next meteorite strike), which lines up with the assumption. Keep this one for now.

 fails to specify the likelihood that, if such a meteorite should strike Earth, the meteorite would indeed cause an ice age 

This answer doesn't match the assumption because the argument is centered on the asteroid strike itself, not the results of such a strike. Eliminate it.

 presumes, without providing justification, that some feasible means can be found to deter large meteorite strikes 

Be careful here! You may think that the author believes this based on his conclusion that the possible meteorite strike warrants funding, but if you look carefully at this conclusion, the author wants funding to determine if there *is* a way to protect the planet, which may or may not involve deterring the meteor. This choice is not nearly as strong as (C), so get rid of it.

You know that Flaw questions deal with gaps or assumptions in an argument. You also know that they're pretty similar to Reasoning questions and that they can exhibit similar "traps" (such as overly wordy or confusing answers). Finally, you can use similar POE techniques on Flaw questions, such as trying to match each word or phrase in the answer choices with something in the argument.

Arguments Technique: Using Process of Elimination with Flaw Questions

One thing you might have noticed that we did when discussing some of the answer choices was again to take each word or phrase from the answer choice and ask, "Does this correspond to anything that actually occurred in the argument?" Most of the time, the answer is no. The answer choices might sound impressive ("the author assumes what he sets out to prove," "the author appeals to authority," and so on), but unless you can go back to the argument and say, "Ah, yes, *this* is where the author gives evidence" or "*this* is where the author makes a prediction," then an answer choice that mentions "examples" or "predictions" will be wrong. This technique is HUGE. It will eliminate two or three answer choices every time.

Therefore, take answer choices on Flaw questions very slowly, and make sure to match each piece of the answer choice to a piece of the argument. Once you come across something in an answer choice that doesn't correspond to anything in the argument, you can get rid of that answer choice. Once it's a little wrong, it's all wrong.

This process will allow you to eliminate two or three answer choices in most cases, but what about the ones that remain? You'll find that some of the answer choices on Flaw questions will be consistent with the argument but won't represent a flaw in the author's reasoning. Once you've eliminated any answer choices on Flaw questions that are not consistent with what actually happened in the argument, then go back to check the rest to see if they represent a logical flaw in the structure of the author's argument.

The Argument

14. Advertisement: Each of the Economic Merit Prize winners from the past 25 years is covered by the Acme retirement plan. Since the winners of the nation's most prestigious award for economists have thus clearly recognized that the Acme plan offers them a financially secure future, it is probably a good plan for anyone with retirement needs similar to theirs.

The advertisement's argumentation is most vulnerable to criticism on which one of the following grounds?

(A) It ignores the possibility that the majority of Economic Merit Prize winners from previous years used a retirement plan other than the Acme plan.

(B) It fails to address adequately the possibility that any of several retirement plans would be good enough for, and offer a financially secure future to, Economic Merit Prize winners.

(C) It appeals to the fact that supposed experts have endorsed the argument's main conclusion, rather than appealing to direct evidence for that conclusion.

(D) It takes for granted that some winners of the Economic Merit Prize have deliberately selected the Acme retirement plan, rather than having had it chosen for them by their employers.

(E) It presumes, without providing justification, that each of the Economic Merit Prize winners has retirement plan needs that are identical to the advertisement's intended audience's retirement plan needs.

PrepTest 117, Section 4, Question 20

Here's How to Crack It

Step 1: Assess the question Here's the question again.

The advertisement's argumentation is most vulnerable to criticism on which one of the following grounds?

This is a classic Flaw question. You're asked to describe what's wrong with the author's reasoning.

Step 2: Analyze the argument Again, you're reading for the conclusion and the premises, and you should think about the purpose structure and the assumptions the author makes. Here's the argument again.

> Advertisement: Each of the Economic Merit Prize winners from the past 25 years is covered by the Acme retirement plan. Since the winners of the nation's most prestigious award for economists have thus clearly recognized that the Acme plan offers them a financially secure future, it is probably a good plan for anyone with retirement needs similar to theirs.

What is the purpose structure of this argument? The author is interpreting the fact that all Economic Merit Prize winners have an Acme retirement plan to mean that they must recognize the plan provides a secure future, and thus the Acme plan is good for anyone with similar retirement needs.

Think about this for a moment. Remember that the conclusion for an argument with an Interpret purpose structure is often unwarranted by the evidence, and that the general assumption is that there is no other way to interpret the data. The author goes from a premise that all the winners *have* a particular retirement plan to the winners *clearly recognize* the benefits of the plan. The author believes that the winners chose the plan for its benefits.

But what if the winners didn't choose the plan? The plan could have been the prize, or could just be a popular plan, or the only plan available. The author doesn't consider this possibility. Let's summarize.

- Author's conclusion: *Acme retirement plan is probably a good plan for anyone with retirement needs similar to those of Economic Merit Prize winners.*
- Author's premises: *The winners are covered by the plan and have recognized that it provides them a secure future.*
- Author's assumption: *The winners chose the plan.*

Step 3: Act Remember to jot a note about what you need the credited response to do. In this case, you need the answer that matches how the winners might not have chosen the retirement plan.

Step 4: Answer using Process of Elimination

It ignores the possibility that the majority of Economic Merit Prize winners from previous years used a retirement plan other than the Acme plan.

This doesn't seem to match what you're looking for. The ad concerns people whose needs are similar to winners from the past 25 years, so previous winners are not relevant. Eliminate it.

 It fails to address adequately the possibility that any of several retirement plans would be good enough for, and offer a financially secure future to, Economic Merit Prize winners. 

The issue is whether the plan is good for people whose needs are similar to those of the winners, not what's good for the winners themselves. Eliminate it.

 It appeals to the fact that supposed experts have endorsed the argument's main conclusion, rather than appealing to direct evidence for that conclusion. 

This one is confusing, so be sure to match it to the parts of the argument. Who would the supposed experts be? The winners? Maybe, but did the winners endorse (approve) the argument's main conclusion (the Acme retirement plan is probably good for anyone with retirement needs similar to those of the winners)? Not in the argument. The winners' supposed choice of plan is used to support the conclusion, so this choice doesn't match and you should get rid of it.

(D) It takes for granted that some winners of the Economic Merit Prize have deliberately selected the Acme retirement plan, rather than having had it chosen for them by their employers. 

This looks like a good match. The argument states that the winners recognize the plan's benefits, but it does not provide evidence that the winners had the opportunity to choose this plan for themselves. If the plan was chosen for them by their employers, it might not be the best plan for the winners or for people with needs similar to theirs. Keep this one for now.

 It presumes, without providing justification, that each of the Economic Merit Prize winners has retirement plan needs that are identical to the advertisement's intended audience's retirement plan needs. 

Watch the language on this one. The conclusion refers to people with similar, not identical, needs. Remember that one word can break an answer choice. That leaves (D) as the credited response.

Summary: Flaw Questions

The key to cracking Flaw questions is finding what's wrong with the argument before you go to the answer choices. Just remember that these questions are different from Weaken questions, in which new information is brought in to attack the argument, and are different from Reasoning questions, in which finding the key assumption won't be nearly as useful.

Sample Question Phrasings	Act
Which of the following indicates a flaw in the author's reasoning? *A criticism of the arguments would most likely emphasize that it...* *The reasoning in the argument is most vulnerable to criticism on the grounds that the argument...* *The argument above relies on which of the following questionable techniques?*	• Break down the argument into its parts; the flaw is usually related to the assumption. • State in your own words what the problem with the argument is. • With each answer, try to match the actions described in the answer choices with those of the argument itself. Look for the choice that has the same problem you found. • Eliminate the answers that don't match; look for the answer that addresses the assumption.

LESSON 10: PRINCIPLE MATCH QUESTIONS

You're nearing the home stretch. The last two question types we will cover are Principle Match and Parallel-the-Reasoning.

We've already covered questions that ask you to find a Principle that strengthens or justifies the conclusion. Principle Match questions, on the other hand, ask for a generalization or rule that "conforms," or is consistent with the argument's method. The analysis you need to do will be similar to Reasoning questions, but the answers may be broader than you might expect.

While many Principle questions are reasonable, some can get nasty, and it's hard to tell which is which until you're in the middle of them. Therefore, you might consider holding off on Principle Match questions until you've worked most of the other types.

Let's look at how one works.

The Argument

15. Statistics indicating a sudden increase in the incidence of a problem often merely reflect a heightened awareness of the problem or a greater ability to record its occurrence. Hence we should be wary of proposals for radical solutions to problems when those proposals are a reaction to new statistical data.

The argumentation conforms most closely to which one of the following principles?

(A) A better cognizance of a problem does not warrant the undertaking of a radical solution to the problem.

(B) Attempts to stop the occurrence of a problem should be preceded by a determination that the problem actually exists.

(C) Proposals for radical solutions to problems should be based on statistical data alone.

(D) Statistical data should not be manipulated to make a radical solution to a problem seem more justified than it actually is.

(E) Radical solutions to problems can cause other problems and end up doing more harm than good.

PrepTest 117, Section 4, Question 4

Here's How to Crack It

Step 1: Assess the question First, as always, you have to identify your task. Here it is again.

> The argumentation conforms most closely to which one of the following principles?

You are asked to find a principle among the answers with which the argument would be consistent. The choices will be generally worded statements—like a moral to a story that could apply to multiple situations—and what you need to do is pick the one to which the argument "conforms," or fits. If this reminds you of how you work a Reasoning question, then you're on the right track.

Assess
Be sure to assess where the general principle will be found. Some principles are in the answer ("the following principle"), but some principles are in the passage ("the principle above").

Step 2: Analyze the argument You need to have a clear understanding of what's happening in the argument. Not all Principle Match questions will be true arguments. Some are more like stories that simply describe a certain situation. If that is the case, be sure to paraphrase the situation. Since this argument has a conclusion and premise, start by noting them.

Analyze
There is no need to find a conclusion and premises on a Principle Match question!

- Author's conclusion: *We should be wary of proposals for radical solutions to problems when those proposals are a reaction to new statistical data.*
- Author's premises: *Statistics that indicate increased incidence of a problem may actually reflect increased awareness of the problem or increased ability to measure it.*

Step 3: Act Because you're going to be asked to identify the principle with which the argument would fit best, you should be able to state in basic terms what's going on. For this example, you might come up with something like "Greater awareness or better measurements alone are not a good reason for radical solutions to problems."

Step 4: Answer using Process of Elimination As you evaluate the answer choices, match the general descriptions in the answers to the specifics in the argument. Eliminate any that are not consistent with your paraphrase or that don't match the information presented in the argument.

A better cognizance of a problem does not warrant the undertaking of a radical solution to the problem. 

This sounds like a pretty close match to what you are looking for; it says that the statistics may reflect greater awareness (cognizance) of a problem rather than an actual increase in its incidence. Thus, taking radical action might not be warranted. Hold on to it.

 Attempts to stop the occurrence of a problem should be preceded by a determination that the problem actually exists. 

This does not match the argument. Radical solutions are not necessarily the same as stopping a problem. In addition, the author accepts that problems exist but questions whether their apparent increase in frequency is real. Get rid of it.

 Proposals for radical solutions to problems should be based on statistical data alone. 

Be sure to read this one carefully. It says that radical solutions *should* be based on data alone. This goes against your paraphrase and the author's suggestion. Eliminate it.

 Statistical data should not be manipulated to make a radical solution to a problem seem more justified than it actually is. 

This statement may seem reasonable, but does it match the argument? While the author might even agree with this statement, the passage made no mention of manipulating data and this doesn't match your paraphrase. Get rid of it.

 Radical solutions to problems can cause other problems and end up doing more harm than good. 

Again, this statement may be true, or at least seem reasonable, but it doesn't match the argument or your paraphrase. Eliminate it.

Now you're left with (A), the correct answer. Notice that once you understood that the author was suggesting that statistics alone are not a good reason for radical solutions, you were able to eliminate any answer that didn't match up with your paraphrase.

This question illustrates how there can be a pretty big difference between a Principle Match question that asks you to find a principle that conforms to the reasoning and a Principle Strengthen question that asks you to justify the reasoning. (See page 58 for Principle Strengthen questions.) Of course, the answer on both will go along with the conclusion of the argument. But a principle to which the argument "conforms" must also match the argument's method.

Sometimes, the question will ask you to find an answer choice that would conform to a principle contained in the argument. Your approach should stay the same. In this case, paraphrase the principle and then find the answer choice that matches it best piece by piece.

Try one.

The Argument

16. Etiquette firmly opposes both obscene and malicious talk, but this does not imply that speech needs to be restricted by law. Etiquette does not necessarily even oppose the expression of offensive ideas. Rather, it dictates that there are situations in which the expression of potentially offensive, disturbing, or controversial ideas is inappropriate and that, where appropriate, the expression and discussion of such ideas is to be done in a civil manner.

    Which one of the following judgments most closely corresponds to the principles of etiquette stated above?

(A) Neighbors should not be gruff or unfriendly to one another when they meet on the street.

(B) When prosecutors elicit testimony from a cooperative witness, they should do so without intensive questioning.

(C) There should be restrictions on speech only if a large majority of the population finds the speech offensive and hateful.

(D) The journalists at a news conference should not ask a politician potentially embarrassing questions about a controversial policy issue.

(E) The moderator of a panel discussion of a divisive moral issue should not allow participants to engage in name-calling.

PrepTest 118, Section 4, Question 21

Here's How to Crack It

Step 1: Assess the question First, as always, you have to identify your task. Here it is again.

> Which one of the following judgments most closely corresponds to the principles of etiquette stated above?

You are asked to find a situation among the answers that is consistent with the general rule in the argument. This time, the choices will be specific situations and you need to pick the one that fits most accurately and completely with the principle in the argument.

Step 2: Analyze the argument Again, you need to have a clear understanding of what's happening in the argument. This one does not have a clear conclusion and premise, so just start by reading the rule carefully. First, you are told that etiquette opposes obscene and malicious talk, but not the expression of offensive ideas as long as they are discussed when appropriate and in a civil (polite) manner.

Step 3: Act You need to identify the situation in the answers that best matches the argument, so start with a paraphrase of the principle. Here, you might come up with something like this: etiquette allows for polite discussion even if the topics being discussed are offensive or controversial.

Step 4: Answer using Process of Elimination As you evaluate the answer choices, match the specific descriptions in the answers to the general rule in the argument. Eliminate any that are not consistent with your paraphrase or that don't match the principle presented in the argument.

 Neighbors should not be gruff or unfriendly to one another when they meet on the street. 

Does this match your paraphrase? There is no mention of discussing offensive or controversial material, so this doesn't match. Get rid of it.

 When prosecutors elicit testimony from a cooperative witness, they should do so without intensive questioning. 

This does not match the argument. This addresses being polite, but not politely discussing something controversial. Eliminate it.

 There should be restrictions on speech only if a large majority of the population finds the speech offensive and hateful. 

So, the only reason for restricting speech is what the majority finds offensive? The principle is about how to discuss offensive material, not when to restrict it. This one has to go.

 The journalists at a news conference should not ask a politician potentially embarrassing questions about a controversial policy issue. 

This almost matches, but it is about being polite and not embarrassing a politician, not about how to discuss controversial topics. Get rid of it.

(E) The moderator of a panel discussion of a divisive moral issue should not allow participants to engage in name-calling. 

This sounds like a pretty close match to what you are looking for; a moderator not allowing name-calling during discussion of a divisive issue lines up with polite discussion of controversial topics. This is your best answer.

This may have felt like it was trickier or involved more work. These can often be time-consuming questions, which is one of the reasons they are best saved for later. Your best approach is to have a solid paraphrase of the principle in the argument and then to match each answer choice to your paraphrase and the argument very carefully.

Arguments Technique: Using Process of Elimination with Principle Match Questions

As we saw from these examples, you are looking for a principle among the answer choices that will match the conditions in the argument, or you might be asked to find an answer choice that would conform to a principle in the argument. Either way, your task stays the same: eliminate any answers that don't match up with your paraphrase.

The important thing to remember: you're looking for an answer choice that matches the decision or action in the principle. The principle will be more general, but will match all the parts in the situation.

Summary: Principle Match Questions

Refer to the chart below on how to approach Principle Match questions.

Sample Question Phrasings	Act
The reasoning above most closely conforms to which of the following principles? *Which of the following examples conforms most closely to the principle given in the argument above?*	• Make sure you know in which direction the argument flows. Are you being asked to find a principle that conforms to a situation, or a situation that conforms to a principle? • Once you're sure, look for an answer that most closely matches the general principle underlying the argument.

LESSON 11: PARALLEL-THE-REASONING QUESTIONS

We're finally at the end. And there is a reason we saved Parallel-the-Reasoning questions for last—because you should probably avoid them until you've worked all the other questions you can tackle. These questions are not necessarily more difficult, but they are certainly more time-consuming on average than most other question types. Don't forget that all of the questions are worth one point each; why spend more time for the same reward?

Hint:
Save Parallel-the-Reasoning questions for last or skip them altogether.

The reason that these take so long is that you have to perform Step 2 (Analyze the argument) for six arguments rather than just one! Each answer choice is another argument. Many arguments attached to Parallel-the-Reasoning questions can be diagrammed in some fashion. Your job is then to find the answer choice that has the same diagram.

There are two major types of Parallel-the-Reasoning questions. One type asks you to simply parallel (match) the reasoning, which means the argument and the credited response are not logically flawed. The other type asks you to parallel the "flaw" or "error," which means the argument and the answer will contain the same reasoning error. Use this to guide your Process of Elimination: eliminate flawed answers on a Parallel-the-Reasoning, and get rid of logically correct answers on a Parallel-the-Flaw.

Let's do a more diagrammable Parallel-the-Flaw first.

The Argument

17. Political scientist: All governments worthy of respect allow their citizens to dissent from governmental policies. No government worthy of respect leaves minorities unprotected. Thus any government that protects minorities permits criticism of its policies.

The flawed pattern of reasoning in which one of the following most closely parallels that in the political scientist's argument?

(A) Politicians are admirable if they put the interests of those they serve above their own interests. So politicians who sometimes ignore the interests of their own constituents in favor of the nation as a whole deserve admiration, for they are putting the interests of those they serve above their own.

(B) All jazz musicians are capable of improvising and no jazz musician is incapable of reading music. Therefore all musicians who can read music can improvise.

(C) Ecosystems with cool, dry climates are populated by large mammals. Ecosystems populated by large mammals have abundant and varied plant life. Thus ecosystems that do not have cool, dry climates have abundant and varied plant life.

(D) Some intellectuals are not socially active, and no intellectual is a professional athlete. Therefore any professional athlete is socially active.

(E) First-person narratives reveal the thoughts of the narrator but conceal those of the other characters. Some third-person narratives reveal the motives of every character. Thus books that rely on making all characters' motives apparent should be written in the third person.

PrepTest 117, Section 4, Question 19

Here's How to Crack It

Step 1: Assess the question Good, you've read the question. Here it is again.

> The flawed pattern of reasoning in which one of the following most closely parallels that in the political scientist's argument?

Careful!
Some Parallel-the-Reasoning questions are not about flawed arguments. Read the question carefully.

Okay, so it's a Parallel-the-Reasoning argument, and you know that you have to try to diagram the argument, if possible, and match that diagram against the diagrams for each of the answer choices. You also know that the reasoning itself is bad because the question asks for the "flawed" pattern of reasoning.

Step 2: Analyze the argument As always, read it through carefully, looking for conclusions and premises as well as any of the common flawed patterns of reasoning. Here it is again.

> Political scientist: All governments worthy of respect allow their citizens to dissent from governmental policies. No government worthy of respect leaves minorities unprotected. Thus any government that protects minorities permits criticism of its policies.

This looks eminently diagrammable. When you see quantities like "all" or "none," you can turn these statements into conditionals and diagram them. Don't forget to note the conclusion and premises, and since you're looking for a flaw, the assumption.

- Author's conclusion: *Any government that protects minorities permits criticism of its policies.*
- Author's premises: *All governments worthy of respect allow their citizens to dissent from government policies and no government worthy of respect leaves minorities unprotected.*
- Author's assumption: *The author takes two separate facts and concludes that if you have one, you must also have the other.*

Step 3: Act Here's what we get when we diagram.

All governments worthy of respect allow their citizens to dissent (A → B); no government worthy of respect leaves minorities unprotected (A → C). So, any government that protects minorities permits criticism of its policies (C → B).

The arguer didn't properly connect C (not protecting minorities) with B (allowing dissent). Just because a government worthy of respect has these two traits does not guarantee that these two traits are always together. Now all we have to do is eliminate any answer choice that doesn't exhibit the same flawed logic.

> The credited response to a Parallel-the-Reasoning question will be a new argument that matches the key features and structure of the original argument.

Step 4: Answer using Process of Elimination Now you're going to carry your diagram to the answer choices and eliminate anything that doesn't match.

 Politicians are admirable if they put the interests of those they serve above their own interests. So politicians who sometimes ignore the interests of their own constituents in favor of the nation as a whole deserve admiration, for they are putting the interests of those they serve above their own. 

Diagram it: politicians who put others' interests above their own are admirable (A → B). Politicians who put national interests above their own constituents' interests are admirable (A → B again). This doesn't match the argument, so it isn't the answer. Eliminate it.

 All jazz musicians are capable of improvising and no jazz musician is incapable of reading music. Therefore all musicians who can read music can improvise. 

Diagram it: jazz musicians can improvise (A → B) and jazz musicians can read music (A → C), so musicians who can read music can improvise (C → B). Bingo! This is the same type of flawed reasoning as that above since this argument fails to consider that some jazz musicians might be able to do one but not the other. Hold on to it.

 Ecosystems with cool, dry climates are populated by large mammals. Ecosystems populated by large mammals have abundant and varied plant life. Thus ecosystems that do not have cool, dry climates have abundant and varied plant life. 

Diagram it: a place with a cool, dry climate has large mammals (A → B). A place with large mammals has lots of plants (B → C). A place without a cool, dry climate has lots of plants (~A → C). This doesn't match the argument, so it isn't the answer. Get rid of it.

 Some intellectuals are not socially active, and no intellectual is a professional athlete. Therefore any professional athlete is socially active. 

This one works out to A → B for the first part, A → ~C for the middle, and C → B for the last sentence. This can be appealing because it is really close, and if you miss translating the middle as, "if one is an intellectual, one is not an athlete," you can fall for it. Get rid of this one.

First-person narratives reveal the thoughts of the narrator but conceal those of the other characters. Some third-person narratives reveal the motives of every character. Thus books that rely on making all characters' motives apparent should be written in the third person.

You have (A → B but ~C) in the first sentence, and then (D → B and C) in the second sentence. The final sentence becomes (B and C → D). It's not even close to the original. It's out.

This leaves you with (B) because it's the only one that matches the structure of the original.

Nice job! You got the right answer simply by diagramming the statement in the argument, and then diagramming each of the answer choices until you found the one that matched the original diagram. However, you probably noticed that it took a long time to do this question. Many times, Parallel-the-Reasoning questions are even longer than this one and could take you three minutes to do. If you spend your time doing these questions, you might get through only half of an Arguments section! Therefore, be sure to save these for the end.

The Argument

18. A small car offers less protection in an accident than a large car does, but since a smaller car is more maneuverable, it is better to drive a small car because then accidents will be less likely.

Which one of the following arguments employs reasoning most similar to that employed by the argument above?

(A) An artist's best work is generally that done in the time before the artist becomes very well known. When artists grow famous and are diverted from artistic creation by demands for public appearances, their artistic work suffers. So artists' achieving great fame can diminish their artistic reputations.

(B) It is best to insist that a child spend at least some time every day reading indoors. Even though it may cause the child some unhappiness to have to stay indoors when others are outside playing, the child can benefit from the time by learning to enjoy books and becoming prepared for lifelong learning.

(C) For this work, vehicles built of lightweight materials are more practical than vehicles built of heavy materials. This is so because while lighter vehicles do not last as long as heavier vehicles, they are cheaper to replace.

(D) Although it is important to limit the amount of sugar and fat in one's diet, it would be a mistake to try to follow a diet totally lacking in sugar and fat. It is better to consume sugar and fat in moderation, for then the cravings that lead to uncontrolled binges will be prevented.

(E) A person who exercises vigorously every day has less body fat than an average person to draw upon in the event of a wasting illness. But one should still endeavor to exercise vigorously every day, because doing so significantly decreases the chances of contracting a wasting illness.

PrepTest 117, Section 4, Question 21

Here's How to Crack It

Step 1: Assess the question Read the question first, as always. Here it is.

> Which one of the following arguments employs reasoning most similar to that employed by the argument above?

This question is asking us to parallel the reasoning, with no mention of any flaws. You'll have to diagram or summarize the argument as best you can, diagram each answer, and see if they match.

Step 2: Analyze the argument Read it carefully, keeping a sharp eye out for "all," "only," "some," or "most" wording, as well as conditional statements.

> A small car offers less protection in an accident than a large car does, but since a smaller car is more maneuverable, it is better to drive a small car because then accidents will be less likely.

This doesn't contain conditional statements, but it still has a clear argument structure that you can work with and map out. You are asked to match the reasoning, not the flaw, so don't worry about finding flaws or assumptions.

- Author's conclusion: *Driving a small car is better because of the lower likelihood of accidents.*
- Author's premises: *Even though small cars offer less protection than large cars, they are more maneuverable.*

Step 3: Act Summarize the argument in general terms to make it easier to match the answers to it. In general terms, the author chooses one option over another because the disadvantage (less protection) of the chosen option is outweighed by an advantage (maneuverability) that makes the disadvantage a non-issue (accidents less likely). Now we need to find an answer that has similar features.

Step 4: Answer using Process of Elimination Now analyze your answers and eliminate answers that don't match.

 An artist's best work is generally that done in the time before the artist becomes very well known. When artists grow famous and are diverted from artistic creation by demands for public appearances, their artistic work suffers. So artists' achieving great fame can diminish their artistic reputations. 

Does this match your summary? There is no choice of a better option in this argument, so it doesn't match. Eliminate it!

 It is best to insist that a child spend at least some time every day reading indoors. Even though it may cause the child some unhappiness to have to stay indoors when others are outside playing, the child can benefit from the time by learning to enjoy books and becoming prepared for lifelong learning. 

Does this match your summary? One option (read inside) is chosen over another (playing outside) because the disadvantage (unhappy) is outweighed by an advantage (lifelong learning), but where is the advantage making the disadvantage a non-issue? It's not. Get rid of it!

 For this work, vehicles built of lightweight materials are more practical than vehicles built of heavy materials. This is so because while lighter vehicles do not last as long as heavier vehicles, they are cheaper to replace. 

In mapping this one out, you have one option (lightweight materials) chosen over another (heavy materials) because the advantage (cheaper) outweighs the disadvantage (not last as long). It doesn't imply that the advantage of being cheaper to replace makes the disadvantage of not lasting as long a non-issue, but this choice is the closest to the original so far, so keep it.

 Although it is important to limit the amount of sugar and fat in one's diet, it would be a mistake to try to follow a diet totally lacking in sugar and fat. It is better to consume sugar and fat in moderation, for then the cravings that lead to uncontrolled binges will be prevented. 

How well does this one hold up? Here, the choice is not between two entirely different options, each with an advantage or disadvantage. It is about limiting the only option presented to prevent one negative consequence. It doesn't match, so this one is out.

 A person who exercises vigorously every day has less body fat than an average person to draw upon in the event of a wasting illness. But one should still endeavor to exercise vigorously every day, because doing so significantly decreases the chances of contracting a wasting illness. 

Does this match your summary? One option (exercise) is better than another (no exercise) because the advantage (not getting sick) is outweighed by the disadvantage (less body fat) by making the disadvantage a non-issue (getting sick less likely). So far so good! Let's keep it.

Now compare (C) and (E). Choice (C) arrives at the conclusion that lightweight vehicles are better not because they make replacement a non-issue—that's still going to happen—but because they are cheaper to replace. The heavier vehicles are a better option if you want to avoid having to replace the vehicle. Both the original argument and (E) endorse the option that reduces the likelihood of the disadvantage, while (C) does not. That makes (E) the credited response.

Wow. Good work! But notice again how long it took to map out each and every answer choice, which means you might want to skip this one altogether, or save it for the very end. Notice, also, how similar the answers were. You can save a little time and headache by eliminating an answer as soon as you find a part that doesn't match.

Arguments Technique: Using Process of Elimination with Parallel-the-Reasoning Questions

It's pretty straightforward—if you are able to diagram the argument, then you must go to the answer choices and diagram those as well. Write it out and then you've got proof that the choice either matches or doesn't match the argument.

Hint:
Whenever possible, diagram Parallel-the-Reasoning on scratch paper; then diagram the answer choices and compare the diagrams.

Sometimes you can't diagram Parallel-the-Reasoning questions. In these instances, try to describe the reasoning in the argument in general terms. Look for patterns that can be easily summed up (for example, we have two things that appear to be similar and then we note a difference, or one thing is attributed to be the cause of another). Try to find an answer that could be summed up in the same way. Start by matching up conclusions; then work backward through the argument to match up each piece. If you find any part of an answer choice that you can't match up with part of the original argument, eliminate it.

Summary: Parallel-the-Reasoning Questions

Refer to the chart below on how to approach Parallel-the-Reasoning questions.

Sample Question Phrasings	Act
Which one of the following is most similar in reasoning to the argument above? *The flawed pattern of reasoning exhibited by the argument above is most similar to that in which of the following?*	• Parallel-the-Reasoning questions will contain either flawed or valid reasoning, and the question will tip you off. • Try to diagram the argument and then diagram each of the answer choices, comparing each one to the diagram you came up with for the argument itself. • If the argument is flawed, be careful not to choose an answer that fixes it. • Save Parallel-the-Reasoning questions for LAST.

CRACKING ARGUMENTS: PUTTING IT ALL TOGETHER

Now you've learned how to approach every type of question the LSAT will throw at you in an Arguments section.

How do you integrate this knowledge into working a whole Arguments section?

Pace Yourself

You know that you have only 35 minutes to tackle an entire Arguments section. But you're also faced with the fact that to get the credited response, you have to invest a significant amount of time in each argument. Hopefully, you've seen that these questions are doable—with the right approach—but that you might fall for traps or miss key words if you rush through them too quickly.

Hint

Check out the pacing chart on page 211.

The bottom line on effective pacing is this: *don't rush!* There are questions in which you'll be able to analyze the argument easily, predict the answer accurately, and find the answer you predicted quickly. Keep moving through these questions. But there will be others in which the argument takes a little extra time to analyze, or in which two or more of the answer choices seem as if they have a shot—or, alternatively, in which none of the answer choices is what you were hoping for. In these cases, it's important to slow down. Take more time to understand the question, the argument, and the answer choices when you're struggling. This isn't wasted time; it's the real work of LSAT Arguments.

Of course, along with spending time where you need to spend it, you should also keep an overall sense of what target you need to hit. You can arrive at a rough pacing target for Arguments by looking at the percentage you get right on the section and dividing that number by 3; round up to get a sense of what number of questions you're aiming for. For example, if you're getting 60 percent right on Arguments sections, then you'll want to shoot for 20 questions on each Arguments section. You might not hit this number exactly, but if you're significantly short of that number, then chances are you'll need to work faster to improve; if, on the other hand, you're getting 60 percent right but more or less finishing the section, then the only way you're going to be able to improve is to work on your accuracy; that will most likely necessitate slowing down.

Choose Wisely

You know that you have to invest a certain amount of time into each type of Arguments question to get the credited response. But you also know that some types of Arguments take less time than others. For instance, compare the amount of time that a Main Point question takes to the amount of time that a Parallel-the-Reasoning question takes. You have a choice in how to spend your time with each question. Does it make sense to tackle a bunch of time-consuming questions when there are others that take much less time to do but give you the same number of points? As you do more practice problems and evaluate your performance on them, you should get a pretty clear sense of where your strengths and weaknesses lie. You'll benefit by making charts of your performance on each section, broken down by question type, so that you can see your progress. (See Chapter 5 for additional study tips and information on evaluating your progress.) To help you plan your approach, here's a chart of the proportion of questions of each type that have shown up on recently administered LSATs.

	Approximate Number Per Section	**Approximate % of Total Arguments**
Main Point	2	7%
Necessary Assumption	3	7%
Sufficient Assumption	3	7%
Weaken	3–4	13%
Strengthen	2	8%
Resolve/Explain	1–2	5%
Inference	4	14%
Reasoning	2	6%
Flaw	3–4	13%
Principle	2–3	10%
Parallel-the-Reasoning	2	7%
Other	1	3%

The bottom line is this: do the questions that take you the least amount of time and that you're most comfortable with first. Once you start the section, make a decision about each question before you invest time answering it. Go after the ones that look short, sweet, and to the point, and leave the longer ones for later. Give priority to the tasks that you know play to your strengths. Likewise, if you come to an argument that really stumps you, don't worry about it—just put a mark next to it and move on. You can always come back once you've gone through all of the other arguments in the section.

Finally...

Practice, practice, practice. There are a number of different tasks that you'll be asked to perform in the Arguments section. As we've seen, each task will vary slightly in how you approach the argument and what you need to get out of it. There's no substitute for experience here. Use those previously administered LSATs that you've ordered from LSAC to get plenty of practice.

And remember that it's not enough to just work all the Arguments questions under the Sun. You'll have to go back and carefully evaluate your work. Figure out *why* you missed a question rather than simply looking at the right answer to learn why that one works. Did you miss the question because you didn't understand the argument? Did you miss a key word? Did you fall for an attractive distractor? Was the credited response one that didn't look very good but didn't have any flaw? Did you misinterpret the task presented by the question?

This kind of detailed evaluation will take time, but it is well worth it. Do it for Arguments. Do it for Reading Comprehension. There are many places where errors can creep into the process. You'll be able to improve only if you know what your tendencies are and how you can go about changing those tendencies that negatively impact your performance.

Now you know what you need to do, so keep up the effort and you'll see the results.

YOU AND YOUR CHART

The chart on the following pages will help you on the Arguments section. Lucky for you, we have posted a PDF of this chart in your online Student Tools—you can print it from there, then you should become intimately familiar with this chart. Put it in a prominent place. Make another copy and carry it along with you so you can refer to it while you're working practice problems. You should know this chart like the back of your hand by the time you take the real LSAT.

Question Type	Sample Question Phrasings	Act
Main Point	*What is the author's main point?* *The main conclusion drawn in the author's argument is that...* *The argument is structured to lead to which one of the following conclusions?*	• Identify the conclusion and premises. • Use the Why Test and then match your conclusion against the five answer choices. • Be careful not to fall for a premise in the answer choices. • When down to two choices, look for extreme wording and relevance to eliminate one choice and be left with the credited response.
Necessary Assumption	*Which of the following is an assumption on which the argument relies?* *The argument above assumes which of the following?* *The writer's argument depends on assuming which of the following?*	• Identify the conclusion, premises, and assumptions of the author. • If you're having trouble finding the assumption, look for a gap between two different ideas in the argument. • The assumption will always at least mildly strengthen the author's conclusion and is NECESSARY for the conclusion to follow from the information provided. • When down to two choices, negate each statement to see if the argument falls apart. If it does, that's your answer.

Question Type	Sample Question Phrasings	Act
Sufficient Assumption	*Which one of the following, if assumed, would enable the conclusion to be properly drawn?* *The conclusion follows logically if which one of the following is assumed?*	• Identify the conclusion, premises, and assumptions of the author. • Look for language in the conclusion that is not accounted for in the premise. • Paraphrase an answer that would strongly connect the premises to the conclusion and shore up the language gap. • Eliminate answer choices that bring in new information.
Weaken	*Which one of the following, if true, would most undermine the author's conclusion?* *Which of the following statements, if true, would most call into question the results achieved by the scientists?*	• Identify the conclusion, premises, and assumptions of the author. • Read critically, looking for instances in which the author made large leaps in logic. • Then, when you go to the answer choices, look for a choice that has the most negative impact on that leap in logic. • Assume all choices to be hypothetically true.

Question Type	Sample Question Phrasings	Act
Strengthen	*Which one of the following statements, if true, would most support the author's conclusion?* *Which one of the following statements, if true, would strengthen the author's argument?* *Which of the following principles, if established, justifies the conclusion drawn in the argument above?*	• Identify the conclusion, premises, and assumptions of the author. • Read critically, looking for where the author made large leaps in logic. • Then, when you go to the answer choices, look for a choice that has the most positive impact on that gap. • Assume all choices to be hypothetically true.
Resolve/ Explain	*Which one of the following provides the best resolution to the apparent paradox described by the committee member?* *Which one of the following statements, if true, would explain the discrepancy found by the scientists?*	• Identify the apparent discrepancy or paradox. • Go to the answer choices and look for a piece of information that, when added to the argument, allows both facts from the argument to be true. • Assume all choices to be hypothetically true.

Question Type	Sample Question Phrasings	Act
Inference	*Which one of the following statements can be validly inferred from the information above?* *If the statements above are true, then which of the following must also be true?* *Which one of the following conclusions can be validly drawn from the passage above?* *Which one of the following conclusions is best supported by the passage above?*	• Read carefully, paying close attention to qualifying language, and then go to the answer choices. • Once there, eliminate any answer choices that are not directly supported by evidence in the passage. • Look for relevance and extreme language to eliminate answer choices. • Use the contrapositive if there are "if...then" statements contained in the passage and in the answer choices.
Reasoning	*The argument proceeds by...* *Leah responds to Kevin by doing which one of the following?* *The method the activist uses to object to the developer's argument is to...* *Dr. Jacobs does which of the following?* *Which one of the following most accurately describes the role played in the argument by the claim that...*	• Read the arguments carefully and then describe what is happening in your own words, focusing on the purpose structure and the author's conclusion and premises. • Take this description and rigorously apply it to all the answer choices. • Once you're at the answer choices, use the technique of comparing the actions described in the answer choices against those that actually occur in the arguments. • Eliminate anything that doesn't appear in the argument.

Question Type	Sample Question Phrasings	Act
Flaw	*Which of the following indicates a flaw in the author's reasoning?* *A criticism of the arguments would most likely emphasize that it...* *The reasoning in the argument is most vulnerable to criticism on the grounds that the argument...* *The argument above relies on which of the following questionable techniques?*	• Break down the argument into its parts; the flaw is usually related to an assumption. • State in your own words what the problem with the argument is. • With each answer, try to match the actions described in the answer choices with those of the argument itself. Look for the choice that has the same problem you found. • Eliminate the answers that don't match; look for the answer that addresses the assumption.
Principle Match	*The reasoning above most closely conforms to which of the following principles?* *Which one of the following examples conforms most closely to the principle given in the argument above?*	• Make sure you know in which direction the argument flows. Are you being asked to find a principle that conforms to a situation, or a situation that conforms to a principle? • Once you're sure, look for an answer that most closely matches the general principle underlying the argument.

Question Type	Sample Question Phrasings	Act
Parallel-the-Reasoning	*Which one of the following is most similar in reasoning to the argument above?* *The flawed pattern of reasoning exhibited by the argument above is most similar to that in which of the following?*	• Parallel-the-Reasoning questions will contain either flawed or valid reasoning, and the question will tip you off. • Try to diagram the argument and then diagram each of the answer choices, comparing each one to the diagram you came up with for the argument itself. • If the argument is flawed, be careful not to choose an answer that fixes it. • Save Parallel-the-Reasoning questions for LAST.

APPLY WHAT YOU'VE LEARNED

Now it's time to put everything you've learned in this chapter to work on the following 13 arguments. The goal of this drill is to see how well you've mastered the four steps and how accurately you can work, not to see how fast you can get through these arguments.

If you want, you can measure the time it takes you to do all 13 questions. By measure, we mean set your timer to count up, and then turn it away so that you can't see the clock as you work on the questions. Put the timer in a drawer or in another room if necessary. When you're done, stop the clock and note how long it took you to complete them and then see how accurate you were. You should be learning to balance speed and accuracy throughout your preparation for the LSAT, but when in doubt, slow down and work for accuracy.

Arguments Practice Drill

Answers can be found in Chapter 9.

1. Acme Corporation offers unskilled workers excellent opportunities for advancement. As evidence, consider the fact that the president of the company, Ms. Garon, worked as an assembly line worker, an entry-level position requiring no special skills, when she first started at Acme.

   Which one of the following statements, if true, most weakens the reasoning above?

(A) Acme's vice president of operations also worked as an assembly line worker when he first started at Acme.

(B) Acme regularly hires top graduates of business schools and employs them briefly in each of a succession of entry-level positions before promoting them to management.

(C) Acme promotes its own employees to senior management positions much more frequently than it hires senior managers from other companies.

(D) Ms. Garon worked at Acme for more than 20 years before she was promoted to president.

(E) Acme pays entry-level employees slightly higher wages than most other businesses in the same industry.

2. Gardener: Researchers encourage us to allow certain kinds of weeds to grow among garden vegetables because they can repel caterpillars from the garden. While it is wise to avoid unnecessary use of insecticides, the researchers' advice is premature. For all we know, those kinds of weeds can deplete the soil of nutrients and moisture that garden crops depend on, and might even attract other kinds of damaging pests.

   Which one of the following most accurately expresses the main conclusion of the gardener's argument?

(A) To the extent that it is possible to do so, we should eliminate the use of insecticides in gardening.

(B) Allowing certain kinds of weeds to grow in vegetable gardens may contribute to a net increase in unwanted garden pests.

(C) Allowing the right kinds of weeds to grow in vegetable gardens can help toward controlling caterpillars without the use of insecticides.

(D) We should be cautious about the practice of allowing certain kinds of weeds to grow among garden vegetables.

(E) We should be skeptical about the extent to which certain kinds of weeds can reduce the presence of caterpillars in gardens.

3. Economist: During a recession, a company can cut personnel costs either by laying off some employees without reducing the wages of remaining employees or by reducing the wages of all employees without laying off anyone. Both damage morale, but layoffs damage it less, since the aggrieved have, after all, left. Thus, when companies must reduce personnel costs during recessions, they are likely to lay off employees.

Which one of the following, if true, most strengthens the economist's reasoning?

(A) Employee morale is usually the primary concern driving companies' decisions about whether to lay off employees or to reduce their wages.

(B) In general, companies increase wages only when they are unable to find enough qualified employees.

(C) Some companies will be unable to make a profit during recessions no matter how much they reduce personnel costs.

(D) When companies cut personnel costs during recessions by reducing wages, some employees usually resign.

(E) Some companies that have laid off employees during recessions have had difficulty finding enough qualified employees once economic growth resumed.

4. Global surveys estimate the earth's population of nesting female leatherback turtles has fallen by more than two-thirds in the past 15 years. Any species whose population declines by more than two-thirds in 15 years is in grave danger of extinction, so the leatherback turtle is clearly in danger of extinction.

Which one of the following is an assumption that the argument requires?

(A) The decline in the population of nesting female leatherback turtles is proportional to the decline in the leatherback turtle population as a whole.

(B) If the global population of leatherback turtles falls by more than two-thirds over the next 15 years, the species will eventually become extinct.

(C) The global population of leatherback turtles consists in roughly equal numbers of females and males.

(D) Very few leatherback turtles exist in captivity.

(E) The only way to ensure the continued survival of leatherback turtles in the wild is to breed them in captivity.

5. Pure science—research with no immediate commercial or technological application—is a public good. Such research requires a great amount of financial support and does not yield profits in the short term. Since private corporations will not undertake to support activities that do not yield short-term profits, a society that wants to reap the benefits of pure science ought to use public funds to support such research.

The claim about private corporations serves which one of the following functions in the argument?

(A) It expresses the conclusion of the argument.

(B) It explains what is meant by the expression "pure research" in the context of the argument.

(C) It distracts attention from the point at issue by introducing a different but related goal.

(D) It supports the conclusion by ruling out an alternative way of achieving the benefits mentioned.

(E) It illustrates a case where unfortunate consequences result from a failure to accept the recommendation offered.

6. Throughout a certain nation, electricity has actually become increasingly available to people in urban areas while energy production has been subsidized to help residents of rural areas gain access to electricity. However, even with the subsidy, many of the most isolated rural populations still have no access to electricity. Thus, the energy subsidy has failed to achieve its intended purpose.

   The reasoning in the argument is most vulnerable to criticism on the grounds that the argument

   (A) takes for granted that the subsidy's intended purpose could have been achieved if the subsidy had not existed

   (B) takes for granted that if a subsidy has any benefit for those whom it was not intended to benefit, then that subsidy has failed to achieve its intended purpose

   (C) presumes, without providing justification, that the intended purpose of the subsidy was to benefit not only rural populations in the nation who have no electricity, but other people in the nation as well

   (D) overlooks the possibility that even many of the people in the nation who live in urban areas would have difficulty gaining access to electricity without the subsidy

   (E) fails to take into account that the subsidy could have helped many of the rural residents in the nation gain access to electricity even if many other rural residents in the nation were not helped in this way

7. The trees always blossom in May if April rainfall exceeds 5 centimeters. If April rainfall exceeds 5 centimeters, then the reservoirs are always full on May 1. The reservoirs were not full this May 1 and thus the trees will not blossom this May.

   Which one of the following exhibits a flawed pattern of reasoning most similar to the flawed pattern of reasoning in the argument above?

   (A) If the garlic is in the pantry, then it is still fresh. And the potatoes are on the basement stairs if the garlic is in the pantry. The potatoes are not on the basement stairs, so the garlic is not still fresh.

   (B) The jar reaches optimal temperature if it is held over the burner for 2 minutes. The contents of the jar liquefy immediately if the jar is at optimal temperature. The jar was held over the burner for 2 minutes, so the contents of the jar must have liquefied immediately.

   (C) A book is classified "special" if it is more than 200 years old. If a book was set with wooden type, then it is more than 200 years old. This book is not classified "special," so it is not printed with wooden type.

   (D) The mower will operate only if the engine is not flooded. The engine is flooded if the foot pedal is depressed. The foot pedal is not depressed, so the mower will operate.

   (E) If the kiln is too hot, then the plates will crack. If the plates crack, then the artisan must redo the order. The artisan need not redo the order. Thus, the kiln was not too hot.

8. Executive: We recently ran a set of advertisements in the print version of a travel magazine and on that magazine's website. We were unable to get any direct information about consumer response to the print ads. However, we found that consumer response to the ads on the website was much more limited than is typical for website ads. We concluded that consumer response to the print ads was probably below par as well.

The executive's reasoning does which one of the following?

(A) bases a prediction of the intensity of a phenomenon on information about the intensity of that phenomenon's cause

(B) uses information about the typical frequency of events of a general kind to draw a conclusion about the probability of a particular event of that kind

(C) infers a statistical generalization from claims about a large number of specific instances

(D) uses a case in which direct evidence is available to draw a conclusion about an analogous case in which direct evidence is unavailable

(E) bases a prediction about future events on facts about recent comparable events

9. On the basis of relatively minor morphological differences, some scientists suggest that Neanderthals should be considered a species distinct from Cro-Magnons, the forerunners of modern humans. Yet the fact that the tools used by these two groups of hominids living in different environments were of exactly the same type indicates uncanny behavioral similarities, for only if they faced the same daily challenges and met them in the same way would they have used such similar tools. This suggests that they were members of the same species, and that the morphological differences are due merely to their having lived in different environments.

If the statements above are true, then each of the following could be true EXCEPT:

(A) Morphological differences between the members of two populations do not guarantee that the two populations do not belong to the same species.

(B) The daily challenges with which an environment confronts its inhabitants are unique to that environment.

(C) There are greater morphological differences between Cro-Magnons and modern humans than there are between Cro-Magnons and Neanderthals.

(D) Use of similar tools is required if members of two distinct groups of tool-making hominids are to be considered members of the same species.

(E) Through much of their coexistence, Cro-Magnons and Neanderthals were geographically isolated from one another.

10. Conservation officers justified their decision to remove a pack of ten coyotes from a small island by claiming that the coyotes, which preyed on wild cats and plover, were decimating the plover population and would soon wipe it out. After the coyotes were removed, however, the plover population plummeted dramatically, and within two years plover could no longer be found on the island.

Which one of the following would, if true, most help explain the phenomenon described above?

(A) Plover are ground-nesting birds, which makes them easy prey for coyotes.

(B) Wild cat and plover populations tend to fluctuate together.

(C) Coyotes are not susceptible to any of the diseases that commonly infect plover or wild cats.

(D) The wild cat population on the island was once significantly larger than it is currently.

(E) The coyotes preyed mainly on wild cats, and wild cats prey on plover.

11. Jurist: A nation's laws must be viewed as expressions of a moral code that transcends those laws and serves as a measure of their adequacy. Otherwise, a society can have no sound basis for preferring any given set of laws to all others. Thus, any moral prohibition against the violation of statutes must leave room for exceptions.

Which one of the following can be properly inferred from the jurist's statements?

(A) Those who formulate statutes are not primarily concerned with morality when they do so. 

(B) Sometimes criteria other than the criteria derived from a moral code should be used in choosing one set of laws over another.

(C) Unless it is legally forbidden ever to violate some moral rules, moral behavior and compliance with laws are indistinguishable.

(D) There is no statute that a nation's citizens have a moral obligation to obey.

(E) A nation's laws can sometimes come into conflict with the moral code they express.

12. A summer day is "pleasant" if there are intermittent periods of wind and the temperature stays below 84°F (29°C) all afternoon. A summer day with high humidity levels is "oppressive" either if the temperature stays above 84°F (29°C) all afternoon or if there is no wind.

Which one of the following summer weather reports most closely conforms to the principles stated above?

(A) The temperature on Friday stayed below 82°F (28°C) all day, and there was no wind at all. It was a day of low humidity, and it was a pleasant day.

(B) On Monday, the temperature ranged from 85°F to 90°F (30°C to 32°C) from early morning until night. It was an oppressive day even though the humidity levels were low.

(C) On Tuesday, the temperature neither rose above nor fell below 84°F (29°C) throughout late morning and all afternoon. It was a pleasant day because there were occasional periods of wind.

(D) On Wednesday, a refreshing breeze in the early morning became intermittent by late morning, and the day's humidity levels were constantly high. It was an oppressive day, even though the temperature did not rise above 84°F (29°C) all day.

(E) On Thursday morning, the air was very still, and it remained windless for the whole day. Humidity levels for the day were high, and even though the temperature fell below 84°F (29°C) between early and late afternoon, it was an oppressive day.

13. Mariah: Joanna has argued that Adam should not judge the essay contest because several of his classmates have entered the contest. However, the essays are not identified by author to the judge and, moreover, none of Adam's friends are classmates of his. Still, Adam has no experience in critiquing essays. Therefore, I agree with Joanna that Adam should not judge the contest.

Which one of the following principles, if valid, most helps to justify Mariah's argument?

(A) A suspicion of bias is insufficient grounds on which to disqualify someone from judging a contest.

(B) Expertise should be the primary prerequisite for serving as a contest judge.

(C) The ability of a judge to make objective decisions is more important than that judge's content expertise.

(D) In selecting a contest judge, fairness concerns should override concern for the appropriate expertise.

(E) A contest judge, no matter how well qualified, cannot judge properly if the possibility of bias exists.

Summary

- Arguments make up half of the questions on the LSAT. You must work hard to improve in this section if you want to reach your potential on test day.
- Always understand the question task before you read the argument. Some questions require you to find the conclusion and the premises; others require a different analysis. Knowing the question types and what makes the credited response correct for that question type will help you get through the section with speed and accuracy.
- Start thinking about your pacing plan. Know how many arguments you will attempt on test day.
- As you practice, look for similarities among arguments. You'll find that many arguments follow recognizable patterns; understanding these patterns will help you analyze the argument, eliminate wrong answers, and select the credited response.

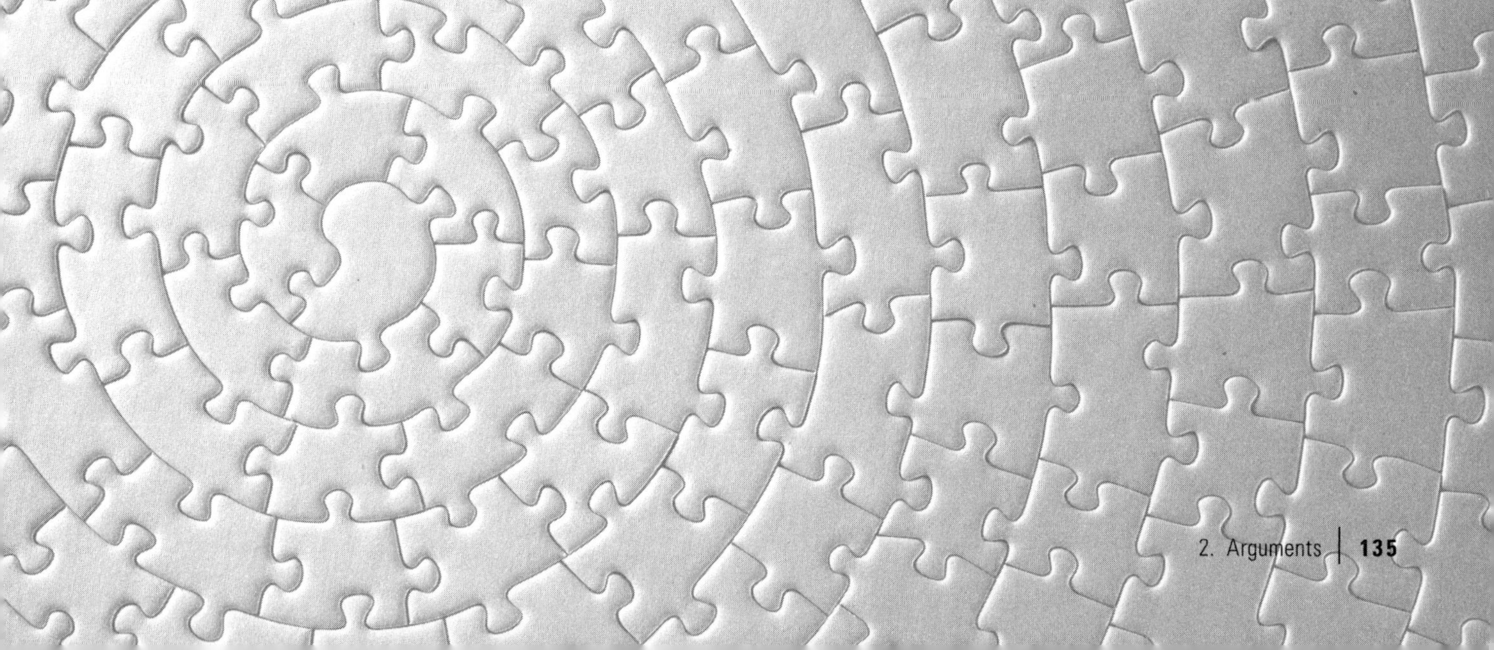

Chapter 3 Reading Comprehension

The Reading Comprehension section, as you might suspect, consists of long, fairly complex passages, each accompanied by a series of questions about that passage. The passages span quite a range in subject matter, but typically there's one from each of the following areas: arts/humanities, social sciences, natural sciences, and law. You do not need any prior knowledge of any of these areas to be able to answer the questions.

In this chapter, we will walk through the basics of taking apart Reading Comprehension passages and answering each type of Reading Comprehension question, with a special focus on the skills and techniques specific to the newer comparative question types.

WHAT IS READING COMPREHENSION?

"Reading Comprehension" sounds pretty straightforward, doesn't it? But, this is the LSAT, so it isn't quite as simple as it may seem. One way in which the test-writers make the section more challenging is how they construct the passage texts. Most of the time, the LSAT writers will take material from a book or journal and then adapt it to make it suitable for testing purposes. What does "adapt" mean? Because you're not supposed to need outside information to be able to understand the passage, the test-writers must remove any material that would require a deeper understanding of the subject beyond the limits of the passage. On one hand, this is a great advantage. Everything you need to know in order to answer the questions is right there in the passage. On the other hand, when they make these edits, much of the transitional material that made the original text more readable is taken out as well. What you're left with is often a pretty dense passage, chock full of details, with choppy or sometimes even nonexistent transitions from one subject to the next.

What's on This Section?

The Reading Comprehension section contains four passages (three single passages and one set of dual passages). Each passage has five to eight questions attached to it, for a total of 26 to 28 questions. The passages are typically between 55 and 65 lines long.

Before we begin, take a moment to read the instructions to this section.

> Directions: Each set of questions in this section is based on a single passage or a pair of passages. The questions are to be answered on the basis of what is **stated** or **implied** in the passage or pair of passages. For some questions, more than one of the choices could conceivably answer the question. However, you are to choose the **best** answer; that is, choose the response that most accurately and completely answers the question.

These are the directions that will appear on your LSAT. As usual on the LSAT, the official directions provide very little help. Review them now. They will not change. Don't waste time reading them in the test room.

What Does This Section Test?

Reading Comprehension tests your ability to not only find details scattered throughout the passage, but also to answer questions about the logic of the author's argument, or to apply new information given in the questions to what is already presented in the passage. And, because of the intense time pressure of the section, it also tests your ability to manage these tasks in the most efficient way possible.

Why Is This Section on the LSAT?

Reading Comprehension is on the LSAT to test your ability to read carefully and manage large amounts of information in a short period of time. This section also tests your ability to answer questions about a passage without bringing in any information from outside the passage.

READING COMPREHENSION: SECTION-WIDE STRATEGIES

First, let's go through the general strategies that will allow you to take control of the section as a whole. In the following portions of the chapter, we'll break down your step-by-step strategies for attacking each passage in the section.

It's Your Section: Prioritize

Choose Your Passages

The people who write this test are not your friends. Therefore, they may not give you the easiest passage first or the hardest passage last. Fortunately, you don't have to work the passages in the order that they appear. It is important to take a few seconds to assess the difficulty level of a passage before you dive in. Quickly read the first few sentences to get a sense of how tough the passage text will be, and glance over the questions. Abstract, theoretical language and ideas will make a passage hard to understand, while concrete and descriptive passages will be much easier to follow. Long question stems and answer choices, as well as questions that ask you to apply new information to the passage, will usually be much more challenging than short and straightforward questions. Don't overreact to unfamiliar topics; remember that all the information you need to answer the questions will be included right there in the passage text. Given that you're planning to apply to law school, a passage on some law-related theme might be of greater interest, but if it is written in a very abstract manner or about complicated legal theories, that doesn't necessarily mean that it will be easier to read and understand. Likewise, a science passage might not be familiar territory, but the language and ideas may be very direct and the questions themselves could be quite straightforward.

Here's What to Look for When You're Evaluating the Difficulty Level of a Passage

- Level of language and ideas: Passages that have clear, straightforward language and that have concrete, descriptive content will be easier to work than those that have abstract language and ideas.
- Sentence structure: Long, convoluted sentences don't bode well. Nor do long paragraphs, which probably contain multiple themes which will take some effort to separate from each other. Short, declarative sentences and shorter paragraphs will probably be easier to comprehend.
- Questions and answer choices: Scan the questions. Do you notice a lot of Reasoning questions? How long are the question stems and answer choices? Passages with long questions and lots of Reasoning questions will probably be more difficult to attack.

Some students also think that the number of questions a passage has should determine if and when they should attempt it. But if a really difficult passage has more questions, that doesn't mean that it will be any easier to get those questions right. In fact, you may end up sacrificing a lot of your time struggling through those questions, getting a high percentage of them wrong, causing you to miss out on an easier passage where you may be able to get all of those easier questions correct.

However, if two passages appear to be of equal difficulty, feel free to go for the one with more questions. All in all, if a passage looks especially formidable, nobody says that you have to do it now, or at all. Leave the hardest passage for last, or randomly guess on it and spend your time getting the other questions right.

Control Your Own Question Ordering

Just as you have control over which passages you do and when you do them, there is no need to complete the questions in the same order in which the test-writers happen to give them to you. Does the third question look especially formidable? Move past it and come back once you've worked the others on that passage. Are you having a horrible time deciding between two answer choices? Pick the one that looked right to you the first time, move on, and come back to that question one more time before going on to the next passage. You'd be amazed what a few minutes away from a question that's giving you trouble can do to clear your head. However, don't get bogged down on one question, reading it over and over. If you are really stuck, take your best shot and move on.

Your mantra: *I will remember that I am in control of the section. If a passage or question seems likely to be especially difficult, I will move past it. If a question frustrates me, I will work on a different one and return to it later with a fresh perspective. If I am still stuck, I will pick the most likely choice and move on.*

Take Control of the Passage: Read Actively

Reading Comprehension is probably the section of the test that feels the most familiar; you have been reading things and answering questions about those things for most of your life. However, doing well on LSAT Reading Comprehension requires reading in a way that is different from the way you handle material for school, work, personal enjoyment, or even for other standardized tests. Too many test-takers read the passage the first time through like a text book, scrutinizing every word and trying to remember all of the details. This approach uses up too much of your limited time. You gain points by correctly answering the questions, not by memorizing the passage. Going back to the passage to find details once you know that you need them to answer a question or to make a tough decision between two answer choices isn't wasted time; it's what Reading Comprehension is all about.

However, you do need to have a basic understanding of the author's argument in the passage in order to effectively address the questions. This involves knowing where key ideas are located, understanding the logical structure of the passage, and defining the purpose of the passage as a whole. Each passage has several big ideas, which will be illustrated or expanded upon. As you read, actively separate the core ideas, or claims, from the evidence used to support those claims. Focus your energy on identifying and understanding the claims, and leave the details for later (if and when they become necessary for answering the questions). The passage isn't going anywhere; if a question asks you for a detail that you skimmed over, you can always go back to find it. If you feel yourself getting bogged down, don't read troublesome text multiple times. Instead, push forward and keep an eye out for something else that helps you understand the content or purpose of that confusing part of the passage. Most fundamentally, as you read, you should think about how the major claims relate to each other and how they finally add up to the main point and purpose, or bottom line, of the entire passage.

Many people find it useful to quickly preview the questions before reading the passage. This can help you decide which parts of the passage to read more carefully and which sections you can skim through more quickly.

Your mantra: *I will get through the passage efficiently, concentrating on the big ideas and logical structure, leaving the details for later.*

Select an Answer on Every Question

Each question will appear on screen individually. When you're confident you've found the credited response, select your answer and move to the next screen. If you aren't sure of an answer, be sure to flag the question so you can return to answer it later. If you don't think you'll have time to return to the question, POE as many choices as you can and select one from the remaining choices. Flag it so you can return if you have time and move on to the next screen.

Your mantra: *I will select an answer for every question and flag questions that I skip for the time being.*

Breathe

After you've completed each passage, take three deep breaths. You've cleared your mind, and you're ready to push on to the next passage.

Your mantra: *I will take time after each passage I complete to take some deep breaths.*

Here Are Your Reading Comprehension Mantras

I will remember that I am in control of the section. If a passage or question is difficult, I will move past it to work on a different one. I'll come back later with a fresh perspective. If I am still stuck, I will pick the most likely choice and move on.

I will get through the passage efficiently, concentrating on the big ideas and logical structure, leaving the details for later.

I will select an answer for every question and flag questions that I skip for the time being.

I will take time after each passage I complete to take some deep breaths.

Pro Tip
Previewing the questions before working the passage is an optional step, but it works very well for many students. See the section on "Refining Your Skills" for some more guidance.

READING COMPREHENSION: A STEP-BY-STEP PROCESS

The next several sections of this chapter will give you a four-step process for attacking each Reading Comprehension passage. First, let's run through an overview of the steps, and then we will break down each step in detail, with guided practice so that you can see what each part of the process looks like in practice.

Step 1: Prepare the Passage

Here are the basics of preparing a passage:

A. Preview the questions, looking for lead words that tell you what parts of the passage will be especially relevant.
B. Work the passage efficiently, focusing on the main claims made by the author.
C. Annotate the passage, highlighting key words that relate to the question topics or that provide clues to the structure and tone of the author's argument, and making brief notes on scratch paper.
D. Define the Bottom Line of the passage as a whole: the main point, purpose, and tone of the text.

Step 2: Assess the Question

Translate exactly what each question is asking you to do with or to the passage.

Step 3: Act

Just as some Arguments questions are best answered by first identifying or analyzing certain aspects of the paragraph, most Reading Comprehension questions are most accurately and efficiently attacked by doing some work with the passage text before looking at a single answer choice.

Step 4: Answer

Use a combination of your understanding of the question and of the relevant part or parts of the passage to use Process of Elimination on the answer choices.

This probably all sounds a bit abstract so far, so now let's break down each step in more concrete and practical terms.

Step 1: Prepare the Passage

Why?

You would never try to answer an Arguments question without analyzing the argument first. The same applies to a Reading Comprehension passage. In your first read-through of the passage, you are laying the groundwork for the process of answering the questions. If you have little or no understanding of the passage text before you begin attacking the questions, your efficiency and accuracy will suffer. However, if you plod through the passage text, paying close attention to every single word, trying to understand and memorize every minor statement, you will be overwhelmed by the mass of information, not get what you really need out of the text, and take too much time away from the crucial process of actually answering the questions. Your goal is to spend 3–5 minutes on your first reading of the passage. Much more than that, and you won't have time to do the work you need to do while answering the questions.

Too many students fail to work on and refine their skills in working the passage. They keep making the same kinds of mistakes on the questions without realizing that those mistakes track back to problems with how they worked the passage in the first place. Remember—yes, this is essentially an open-book test in that all the information you need is there in the passage. But, you wouldn't go into an open-book test in a class without having a good sense of how your materials and notes are organized and where you will be able to find the relevant information you need to answer the questions.

How: Principles of Active Reading

Find the Main Point of Each Paragraph As you read through each paragraph for the first time, focus on separating out the major claims made by the author from the evidence used to support those claims. It is those main claims that will tell you what the author is trying to communicate in each paragraph and through the passage as a whole. Much of the supportive evidence will be unnecessary for answering the questions, but if you need it, when you have read the passage actively and with focus, you will know where to find it.

Authors use words purposefully to help you to understand what they are writing. Yes, the LSAC writers often edit passage texts to make them difficult to follow and understand, but they leave in a lot of clues as well. Use those clues to your advantage, and you will give yourself an excellent foundation for attacking the questions.

Let's take a look at a sample paragraph.

The classic defining work of social choice theory is Ken Arrow's careful investigation of voting through a series of thought experiments. The result—Arrow's Impossibility Theorem—indicated that no method of conducting a majority decision vote can be guaranteed to conform to the basic requirements of democracy. A simple example illustrates Arrow's idea: For an electorate of three voters—1, 2, and 3—there are three candidates—A, B, and C. Voter 1 prefers A to B, and B to C; voter 2 prefers B to C and C to A; voter 3 prefers C to A and A to B. In such an electorate, a runoff between A and B declares A the winner; a runoff between B and C is won by B, and a runoff between A and C is won by C. Therefore, whichever candidate wins, that candidate is actually less preferable to the electorate than the candidate that was not involved in the runoff.

What is really important here, in terms of getting a basic understanding of the author's main point in this paragraph? (And, was that example really so simple?) The main claims are (1) that Arrow's work is central to social choice theory, (2) that he suggested that this method of voting elects a candidate that no one actually prefers, and (3) that Arrow believes this is non-democratic. So, what wording tells you what to pay attention to, and what to move through more quickly on your first reading of the passage? The first sentence gives you your first clue: "The classic defining work of social choice theory." Right there, the author is telling you: "This is important, pay attention!" The second sentence tells you what the result of Arrow's investigation was, which is why his work was so important. But then the author says: "A simple example…," which alerts you to the fact that what follows will just be further illustration of what you already know: that Arrow believes that "no method of conducting a majority decision vote can be guaranteed to conform to the basic requirements of democracy." So, skim thorough all those complicated details—if a question asks you about the mechanics of the whole thing, you know exactly where to find them. Notice one more key word: "Therefore." This conclusion indicator tells you "slow down again, here comes something else important." And, this is the final main claim in the passage; it tells you why Arrow believes that the results are undemocratic—the winner of the election is not the one preferred by the electorate.

So, what is the author's main point in this paragraph? "Arrow's work suggesting the non-democratic nature of majority-decision voting is central to social choice theory." That's really all you need to get out of this paragraph before you move on to the next.

Fit the Pieces Together and Find the Bottom Line So, you now know what this paragraph is all about, but what about the passage as a whole? Do you know at this point that the main point of this paragraph is the central point of the entire passage? Of course not; you have to see what the author says next, and how it relates to what you just read.

Imagine that the next paragraph begins, "However, recent research has called the basic premises of Social Choice Theory into question." That word "However" and what follows tells you that now the passage may be going in a very different direction. As you read that next chunk of passage, then, go through the same process of finding the main claims and tracking the argument the author is making. Pay especially close attention to any words or phrases that indicate the author's attitude or opinion. From the first paragraph, you know that the author thinks Arrow's thought experiment was "careful," and that those who believe in Social Choice Theory agree with Arrow's results. Does that guarantee that the author agrees as well? Certainly not, and the beginning of this next paragraph indicates that the author may be about to describe some flaws in Arrow's work or ideas. If you keep tracking those main claims through the passage, you will know what the author's central point and purpose is: that is, the Bottom Line of the passage as a whole. That will give you an excellent basis on which to answer a variety of questions quickly and accurately, and to easily identify and avoid trap answers that misrepresent what the author has in fact claimed.

There are certain passage purposes that commonly appear on the LSAT, and being familiar with them can help you fit the pieces together as you read. So, as you read each paragraph and define the Bottom Line, ask yourself if the author is doing one of the following.

Telling a Story These are the passages that sound least like arguments; the author is often simply relating a series of events with a neutral tone. The passage may, for example, describe the development of an artistic style, or the process involved in a scientific discovery, or the progression of a political movement. However, these passages are still made up of "moving parts," each of which performs a particular function. Pay close attention to words that indicate a transition between one event or issue and another. When you are answering the questions, look out for wrong answers that misrepresent the sequence of events or that attribute an inappropriate tone to the author.

Comparing or Contrasting These passages often compare and/or contrast different theories or points of view. What distinguishes them from passages that defend, advocate, or criticize, is that the authors themselves do not take sides. In your annotation and analysis, pay close attention to the transitions between one side and the other, and to the differences or similarities described. When answering the questions, use your prep work to help you eliminate answers that describe the wrong position or side, or that mistake a similarity for a difference, or vice versa.

Defending or Advocating In these passages, the author will express a definitive point of view, either defending an idea or policy against its detractors, or making a recommendation about a particular point of view or course of action. As you work the passage, pay close attention to words that indicate the strength of the author's argument and make sure to carefully distinguish the author's position from any opposing positions that might be described. As you answer the questions, use this work to eliminate wrong answers that inaccurately describe the author's tone (often by making it stronger or more extreme) or that confuse the author's point of view with an opposing position.

Criticizing *Criticize* passages do just that; they say bad things about an idea, policy, or action. What distinguishes them from *Defend/Advocate* passages is that the author does not suggest or recommend an alternative. As you read and annotate the passage, pay close attention to exactly what is being criticized, and how strong the argument is (for example, is the author denouncing something, or rather just pointing out certain drawbacks). As you answer the questions, use your understanding of this logic to eliminate choices that describe supposed author recommendations that the author did not in fact make, answers that mix up what is and is not criticized, and choices that are inappropriate to the strength of the argument in the passage.

Highlight

The highlight and underline tools on the online test are most helpful on Reading Comprehension. Be sure to practice using these tools consistently!

A big part of active reading involves what your brain is doing as you read—mentally taking control over the material by focusing on what is important and avoiding getting caught up in the quicksand of potentially irrelevant or unnecessary details. Another part of active reading is using your online tools and pen to support your brain—mark up the passage in a way that helps you both to keep your focus and to find information you may need later as you answer the questions. There are two key forms of annotation you should be using:

- making concise notes indicating the main point of each paragraph and the Bottom Line of the passage as a whole on scratch paper
- highlighting or underlining logically important words and phrases

Let's take each of these and break them down further.

1. Notes

We have already talked about how to find the main points and identify the Bottom Line. It is a little too easy, however, to passively read through a passage and think "Yeah, got it" and only realize when you are done with the passage, or trying to answer the questions, that you really didn't "get it" after all, and all you have in your brain are a bunch of disconnected words and ideas. So, make yourself write down at least a few words for each paragraph and for the Bottom Line. And a few words is enough; you are not outlining every little thing that happened in each paragraph, but simply putting those central ideas into a short sentence or phrase. Even if you never look at those notes again, they will have served their main purpose of making you define those core ideas. However, if you are having trouble finding information later on as you answer the questions, those notes will come in very handy, as you can use them to figure out where that information may be hiding.

2. Symbols

There are a few things that deserve extra emphasis: indications of the author's attitude or opinion, any topic sentences or thesis statements that express the main point of a paragraph or of the passage as a whole (keeping in mind that not every paragraph or passage will have one), and, if you are previewing the questions, locations of question topics. Pick a single color of highlighter to mark opinions, thesis statements, or questions topics. If you have previewed the questions, highlight a relevant word or two when you find those topics in the passage. Don't jump out of the passage and answer the question before reading the rest of the passage; by highlighting them, you make them easy to find once you do get to that question.

3. Underline text

Use the underline tool to mark text within the passage. Underlining should be limited to things that you have good reason to think are logically important to the author's central points. Here are the key things to underline and why.

A. Conclusion indicators
Words like "therefore," "thus," "hence," or "in conclusion" tell you "this is what all that stuff I was just telling you leads up to." That is, what follows conclusion indicators tend to be major claims that are important for the main points and Bottom Line.

B. Attitude indicators
Tracking and identifying the author's tone is crucial to understanding the author's real position (and to avoiding wrong answers that misrepresent it). Many passages are neutral in tone; the author is simply describing or analyzing something without offering any positive or negative judgment. But, if you see words like "unfortunately" or "sadly" or "thankfully" or "brilliantly," or any other word or phrase that indicates similar ideas, they deserve your close attention.

C. Changes in direction
Difficult passages often have twists and turns, and the questions on these passages will very purposefully test if you have been able to track them accurately. So, if you see words like "however," "but," "on the other hand," "yet," or "in contrast," underline them and think carefully about how what came before that word or phrase logically relates to what comes after, and how it connects to the author's argument as a whole.

4. Continuations
Often authors will make a series of connected points, and to answer the questions, you need to see that they are, in fact, connected and how. So, when you see words like "furthermore," "additionally," or "moreover," underline them and think about what larger point or claim all those segments of the author's argument relate to. And, when you are going back to the passage to find that part of the argument, use your annotations to make sure that you are taking into account all of the relevant parts of the author's argument.

5. **Lists or sequence indicators**
   Often when answering the questions, you should know what came first, or last, or sooner, or later. Or, you may need to find a particular item on a list. Underline words like "first, "next," before," and "after" to help you answer those questions quickly and accurately.
6. **Example or support indicators**
   We already discussed that examples and other kinds of support for larger claims are not particularly important to pay attention to the first time through a passage. But underlining words like "for example" or "because" or "since" has two functions. First, it reassures you that you can, in fact, find those details later on if you need them (and so helps you move through them more quickly in the moment), and second, it actually helps you find them later if you need them for the questions.

PUTTING IT ALL TOGETHER

So, let's see how it works in practice. Work the passage on the following page as we have just discussed: define the main points and the Bottom Line and make thoughtful and concise annotations. Then turn the page and compare your work to the marked-up passage. That passage will not only have sample annotations, but also explanations of how you ideally should have read through the passage: what questions you should ask yourself as you read, and what deserves more or less attention in the text.

One of the most prolific authors of all time, Isaac Asimov was influential both in science fiction and in the popularization of science during the twentieth century, but he is also justly famous for the scope of his interests. Although the common claim that Asimov is the only author to have written a book in every category of the Dewey decimal system is untrue, its spirit provides an accurate picture of the man: a dedicated humanist who lauded the far-reaching power of reason. His most famous work, the *Foundation* trilogy, can be read as an illustration of Asimov's belief in reason and science, but even while he expressed that belief, science itself was calling it into question.

Foundation describes a time in which a vast empire spanning the galaxy is on the verge of collapse. Its inevitable doom is a consequence not of its size, but of the shortsightedness of its leaders. In this environment, a scientist named Hari Seldon devises an all-encompassing plan to help human civilization recover from the trauma of the empire's coming collapse. Using mathematics, Seldon is able to predict the future course of history for thousands of years, and he takes steps that are geared toward guiding that future in a beneficial direction. The trope of the benevolent and paternalistic scientist shaping existence from behind the scenes, present in much of Asimov's fiction, is never more explicit than in the *Foundation* series, which describes with an epic sweep the course and progress of the Seldon Plan.

As naïve and, perhaps, self-serving as the conceit of *Foundation* may seem to contemporary readers, it retains to some degree its ability to comfort by offering an antidote to the complex and unpredictable nature of experience. Science in Asimov's time was, in popular conceptions, engaged in just this pursuit: discerning immutable laws that operate beneath a surface appearance of contingency, inexplicability, and change. But even while Asimov wrote, science itself was changing. In physics, the study of matter at the subatomic level showed that indeterminacy was not a transitory difficulty to be overcome, but an essential physical principle. In biology, the sense of evolution as a steady progress toward better-adapted forms was being disturbed by proof of a past large-scale evolution taking place in brief explosions of frantic change. At the time of Asimov's death, even mathematics was gaining popular notice for its interest in chaos and inexplicability. Usually summarized in terms of the so-called "butterfly effect," chaos theory showed that perfect prediction could take place only on the basis of perfect information, which was by nature impossible to obtain. Science had dispensed with the very assumptions that motivated Asimov's idealization of it in the Seldon Plan. Indeed, it was possible to see chaos at work in *Foundation* itself: As sequels multiplied and began to be tied into narrative threads from Asimov's other novels, the urge to weave one grand narrative spawned myriad internal inconsistencies that were never resolved.

One of the most prolific authors of all time, Isaac Asimov was influential both in science fiction and in the popularization of science during the twentieth century, but he is also justly famous for the scope of his interests. Although the common claim that Asimov is the only author to have written a book in every category of the Dewey decimal system is untrue, its spirit provides an accurate picture of the man: a dedicated humanist who lauded the far-reaching power of reason. His most famous work, the *Foundation* trilogy, can be read as an illustration of Asimov's belief in reason and science, but even while he expressed that belief, science itself was calling it into question.

Foundation describes a time in which a vast empire spanning the galaxy is on the verge of collapse. Its inevitable doom is a consequence not of its size, but of the shortsightedness of its leaders. In this environment, a scientist named Hari Seldon devises an all-encompassing plan to help human civilization recover from the trauma of the empire's coming collapse. Using mathematics, Seldon is able to predict the future course of history for thousands of years, and he takes steps that are geared toward guiding that future in a beneficial direction. The trope of the benevolent and paternalistic scientist shaping existence from behind the scenes, present in much of Asimov's fiction, is never more explicit than in the *Foundation* series, which describes with an epic sweep the course and progress of the Seldon Plan.

Possible attitude toward IA

Disagreement with common claim

Back to positive

Key change in direction, and introduction of new theme

Description—Don't get bogged down in these details. Keep focus on purpose of author.

Question: "So is the passage likely to be all about the greatness of Asimov's work?"

Answer: "No—there is some inconsistency between Asimov's beliefs and the reality of science."

Main Point: *"IA's work expressed a belief about science and reason that may not be true."*

Question: "Why is the author giving me all of these details about IA's work and themes?"

Answer: "Given the end of P. 1, it's likely that the author will tell me later that they are unrealistic."

Main Point: *"Theme of IA's work—scientists can help save society."*

As naïve and, perhaps, self-serving as the conceit of *Foundation* may seem to contemporary readers, it retains to some degree its ability to comfort by offering an antidote to the complex and unpredictable nature of experience. Science in Asimov's time was, in popular conceptions, engaged in just this pursuit: discerning immutable laws that operate beneath a surface appearance of contingency, inexplicability, and change. But even while Asimov wrote, science itself was changing. In physics, the study of matter at the subatomic level showed that indeterminacy was not a transitory difficulty to be overcome, but an essential physical principle. In biology, the sense of evolution as a steady progress toward better-adapted forms was being disturbed by proof of a past large-scale evolution taking place in brief explosions of frantic change. At the time of Asimov's death, even mathematics was gaining popular notice for its interest in chaos and inexplicability. Usually summarized in terms of the so-called "butterfly effect," chaos theory showed that perfect prediction could take place only on the basis of perfect information, which was by nature impossible to obtain. Science had dispensed with the very assumptions that motivated Asimov's idealization of it in the Seldon Plan. Indeed, it was possible to see chaos at work in *Foundation* itself: As sequels multiplied and began to be tied into narrative threads from Asimov's other novels, the urge to weave one grand narrative spawned myriad internal inconsistencies that were never resolved.

Mildly negative wording, but then back to some positive

Crucial change in direction, and back to theme of end of P. 1

Thesis statement for paragraph

Examples of major claim just made—keep focus on purpose and how this relates to previous paragraphs, not details themselves

Thesis paragraph

Negative about an aspect of IA's work

Question: "So, what does the author really think about Asimov's work and relationship to science?"

Answer: "Science was evolving toward recognition of lack of control, which Asimov himself may have been realizing."

Main Point: *Changes in science in IA's time undermined assumptions of his work.*

Bottom Line of passage: *IA's main work expressed belief that science could be controlled for the good, but new scientific ideas in his own time cast doubt on that assumption.*

Steps 2 and 3: Assess and Act

Once you have prepared the passage, you are ready to assess the questions. Read each question **word for word** to understand exactly what that question is asking you to do. The LSAT writers are quite skilled at finding complicated ways to phrase what could have been a very straightforward question. Always take a moment to paraphrase the question before you take the next step.

Think of the question as setting out a task for you to accomplish. Identifying the question task allows you to define what the correct answer needs to do, and what you need to do with or to the passage, in order to find that correct answer as efficiently as possible.

If you can't identify the exact question type in the moment, don't panic; paraphrase the question and define for yourself what that question is asking you to do. However, most LSAT questions fall neatly into particular categories, and those categories are easy to learn and then apply. So, it is worth some work and time on your part to learn the types, keep the type and its logic clearly in mind as you are attacking the question, and then evaluate after having completed a passage or practice test if you did, in fact, correctly identify, translate, and address the question (and how you might have been able to do it even better).

Different types of questions require different kinds of actions on your part before you begin to evaluate the answer choices. So, it makes sense to talk about Assess and Act together for each of the question types.

LSAT Reading Comprehension questions fall into four basic categories. Here are those four categories, the question subtypes that fall under each, and the essential process to go through for each question type before you have read a single answer choice.

Big Picture Questions

Assess These questions require you to take the passage (or, in some cases for a Comparative Reading passage, both passages) as a whole into account.

There are three subtypes of Big Picture Questions.

- Main Point

  These questions are often worded as follows:

  Which of the following most accurately expresses the main point of the passage?

  Which title best describes the contents of the passage?

- Primary Purpose

  These questions are usually phrased as follows:

  The primary purpose of the passage is to

  In the passage, the author is primarily concerned with doing which of the following?

- Overall Attitude

  These questions may be phrased as follows:

  Which of the following most accurately describes the author's attitude in the passage?

  The author's opinion regarding the ideas described in the passage can best be described as

Purpose and Attitude questions may also ask you about the author's purpose in, or opinion about, a more specific or limited part of the passage rather than about the passage as a whole. Make sure that you define the relevant scope of the question as part of translating the question task.

Act Think about the work you did to Prepare the passage. What was your last step of that part of the process? You defined the Bottom Line, based on the author's central point and overall purpose and attitude. Therefore, in most cases, you will not need to go back to the passage before you start evaluating the answer choices. However, you may well need to refer back to the text at some point before you make a final choice, especially if you are stuck between two answers. Remember that even on a Big Picture question, one word can be enough to invalidate an answer choice.

Extract Questions

Assess Extract questions are asking you to find and select the answer choice that is best supported by the information in (and only in) some particular part or parts of the passage.

There are two subtypes of Extract questions.

- Fact

  These questions are often worded as follows:

  According to the passage

  The author states that

  Which of the following is mentioned in the passage?

- Inference

  These questions are phrased as some variation of the following:

  It can most reasonably be inferred from the passage that

  Which of the following is implied/suggested/assumed?

Which of the following conclusions is best supported by the passage?

With which of the following would the author be most likely to agree?

Which of the following can be most reasonably concluded from the passage?

As it is used in the passage, X refers most specifically to

Which of the following does the author appear to value most?

Act The answers to *Extract: Fact* questions will tend to be close paraphrases of something stated in the passage. *Extract: Inference* questions will sometimes require you to do a bit more work; the correct answer will be directly supported by one or more statements in the passage, but may not be stated outright in the text.

Tip:
If the question stem has no lead words referring to the passage, go back to the passage as you evaluate the answer choices.

However, the approach to any *Extract* question is the same. Don't rely only on your memory! Use the passage actively, and whenever possible, before you look at a single answer choice. The test-writers will give you plenty of wrong answers that "sound good" but that have something wrong with them that you will catch only if you go back to see exactly what the author actually said. If the question stem gives you lead words or directs you to a specific location in the passage, go back to the passage first and read at least 5 lines above and below that reference. Be sure to reread all of the relevant information. If the author's discussion of that topic begins earlier or continues longer (including situations in which the topic is discussed in more than one section of the passage), you will need to read more than those 10 or 11 lines. Once you have read and paraphrased the passage information, generate an answer in your own words (based on what the passage says), defining what the correct answer needs to do. Regardless of the exact form of the question, this is when previewing the questions and annotation really pays off; if you have already highlighted or underlined the relevant words in the passage, your task becomes much easier. Also, use your annotations that indicated key transitional points and claims equally actively. For example, if you have read 5 lines below, but the next sentence begins with a word like "however," keep reading. What comes after that shift is highly likely to be relevant to the question and to the correct answer.

Structure Questions

Assess There are two subtypes of Structure questions.

Occasionally, a Structure Organization question may ask you to describe the structure of a paragraph rather than the whole passage. As always, make sure to carefully define the scope of the question task.

- Organization

  Structure Organization questions ask you to describe the passage as a whole, piece by piece. These questions may be phrased as follows:

  Which one of the following most accurately states the organization of the passage?

- Function

  Structure Function questions ask you to describe WHY the author made a particular statement or included a particular paragraph. That is, they are testing to see if you understood the logical function or purpose of some part of the larger whole of the author's argument. These questions will be phrased with some variation of the following:

  The primary function of the second paragraph is to

  The main function of the reference to X is to

  The author mentions X in order to

Act For both versions of *Structure* questions, go back to the passage and use your annotation actively. Words like *therefore, for example, in contrast,* and so on tell you a lot about the purpose and function of that part of the passage.

Structure: Organization questions require you to describe the passage as a whole. They differ from *Big Picture* questions in that the correct choice will describe the logical structure of the passage step by step, rather than summarizing the content of the passage in a single statement. To answer these questions, break down each choice into pieces and check each piece against the passage. At this point, your preparation of the passage in defining the main point of each paragraph in succession will be especially useful, as the correct answer will follow the same progression.

Structure: Function questions have a more narrow focus. Because they ask you to define why the author included a particular paragraph or made a specific claim, go back to that part of the passage first. If it asks for the purpose of a paragraph, use your definition of the main point of that chunk, but also think about how it fits into the author's overall argument in the passage. If it asks for the purpose of a specific claim, go back to that part of the passage, read above and below the claim (just as you would for an Extract question), and paraphrase the claim being made. However, you have to take one more step before going to the answer choices: think not just about WHAT the author said but also WHY the author said it. That requires defining how that claim or statement relates to the rest of the paragraph and potentially to the passage as a whole.

Application

Occasionally, Application questions will give you the new information in the question stem rather than in the answer choices. In that case, define the theme of the new information and how it relates to the relevant part of the passage before evaluating the answer choices.

Assess Most Application questions involve using new information, that is, information that is not already provided in the passage, and applying it to what the author of the passage has already argued or stated. The majority of Application questions will fit into one of two subtypes:

- Strengthen/Weaken

  Strengthen questions may be phrased as follows, with the "X" in the sample question referring to a particular claim made in the passage:

  Which of the following would most clearly support the author's contention that "X"?

  The author's reasoning in support of her claim that "X" is justified would be most strengthened if which of the following were true?

  Conversely, a Weaken question may be phrased something like this:

  Which of the following, if true, would most undermine the author's claim that "X"?

Whether or not the question explicitly tells you to take the answer choices as true or valid, do so. That is, the question is not asking you to figure out what is already true based on the passage. Rather, it is asking you to **assume each answer choice to be a true statement**, to figure out how each would or would not apply or relate to the passage, and to find the one that either **most** strengthens or **most** weakens the cited claim or argument made by the author. These are the only LSAT Reading Comprehension questions that will ask you to essentially change (for better or worse) the logic of the author's argument, so it is especially crucial to understand the question task before taking your next steps.

- Analogy

  Analogy questions may be phrased something like this:

  Which of the following is most similar it its approach to the author's approach as it is described in the passage?

  Which of the following is most analogous to the situation described in the second paragraph?

  Which of the following describes a relationship that is most logically similar to the relationship between X and Y described in the passage?

Analogy questions are similar to Strengthen/Weaken questions in that they give you new information in the answer choices. However, they are very different in that they ask you not to make the author's argument better or worse, but rather to define the logic (not the topic or content) of the author's argument, and to find the answer choice that is most similar in its theme or logic.

Act Even though Application questions involve working with new information, this does not mean that you should go right to the choices without going back to the passage first. Nor does it mean that the correct answer will go beyond the scope of the passage. Any credited response (unless it is an Except question) still has to be directly relevant to an issue raised in the passage. Therefore, it is still crucial to go back to the passage, find and paraphrase the relevant claim or relationship, and define for yourself what the correct answer needs to look like. For a Strengthen/Weaken question, that means knowing ahead of time what issue and direction (with or against the passage) the correct answer needs to include. For an Analogy question, that means defining what theme or logical relationship the correct answer needs to describe or portray.

Step 4: Answer

Basics

As you evaluate the answer choices for each question, here are some essentials to keep in mind.

1. Always read each choice word for word the first time. This is no time to waste all of the good work you have done up to this point by skimming through the answers and making snap decisions based on what "sounds good" or "sounds bad." The test-writers will often write wrong answers in attractive ways, trying to distract you from the credited response. If you read the choices carelessly, you will fall for many of these traps.
2. Read all five choices before making a final decision. You are looking for the best answer, not the first one that sounds good.
3. Use Process of Elimination aggressively. Look for what is wrong with each choice, keeping in mind that one small part of the choice that doesn't match the passage and/or the question task means the whole choice is bad.
4. Use the passage and your own answer actively (especially when the nature of the question has made it possible to generate an answer in your own words first). Correct answers on LSAT Reading Comprehension questions almost always have solid support in the passage. Use that to your advantage, and don't assume that an answer that matches your expectations must be a trap!

Two Cuts

You will often find yourself going through the set of choices twice, eliminating the most obviously wrong choices the first time through, and then coming back to make a final decision between the two or three that you have left.

When you are down to two or three choices, don't panic and guess—this is a normal part of the process. Stay methodical, and go through the following final steps:

1. Reread the question stem, and make sure that you have correctly identified the question task.
2. Compare the remaining choices to each other, and identify relevant differences. That may be enough to alert you to the correct answer.
3. If not, go back to the passage one more time with the question task and the differences between the remaining choices in mind. Remember that you should still be using your main points, your Bottom Line, and your passage annotation actively to make sure that you are (1) going back to the correct section or sections of the text, and (2) correctly understanding what the relevant part of the passage is saying.
4. If you have eliminated four choices but aren't sure exactly why the remaining choice is correct, go ahead and pick it! That is the beauty of POE—if four choices are definitively wrong, you don't have to know exactly why the remaining choice is correct. And, while the correct answer may not exactly match what you were looking for, it will always be the one that has the least wrong with it.
5. If you have good support for one choice, but aren't sure exactly why one or more of the other four is wrong (and you have been through the process outlined above), go ahead and pick that well-supported answer and move on.

Attractive Distractors

These are common types of wrong answers that you will see over and over. The more familiar you are with how the test-writers often write wrong answers, the more quickly and accurately you will identify and eliminate them.

Wrong Part of the Passage Many of the wrong answer choices do contain content consistent with the passage. The problem is that this information is from a different part of the passage. For instance, if a passage is describing the properties of three different kinds of acids, and an Extract question asks about the properties of the second acid, many of the wrong choices will be properties of the first and third acids. As long as you focus on the information about the second acid only, you'll be able to eliminate any choices that talk about the first and third acids. Or, if a Structure Function question asks about the purpose of a particular statement, there will likely be a wrong answer that is about the purpose of some different statement made in the passage. Keep your focus on the purpose of the statement referenced in the question, and you will easily avoid the trap.

Extreme Language As we mentioned in the Arguments section, answer choices that make extreme claims or that use absolute wording often go beyond what can be supported by the passage. Because LSAT authors can have some strong opinions from time to time, however, you shouldn't simply eliminate choices with extreme language without checking that language against what was said in the passage. Think of extreme language as a red flag. When you see it, you should automatically look back to the passage to see whether the passage supports such a strong statement. If it doesn't, and the question hasn't asked you to strengthen or weaken the passage, then you can eliminate the answer choice. This is a particularly common trap on Extract and Big Picture questions.

Too Narrow or Too Broad Main Idea and Primary Purpose questions often have wrong answers that are either too narrow or too broad. Remember that the main idea or primary purpose should encompass the entire passage but not more or less than that. You'll see many wrong answers that either mention something that was contained in only a part of the passage or was accomplished in only a single paragraph, or others that would include not only the main topic of the passage, but also much more beyond that (for instance, the passage discusses dolphins, but the answer choice talks about all marine mammals).

Partially Wrong This is a popular type of wrong answer on LSAT Reading Comprehension. Your goal is to seek out and eliminate answer choices that contain anything at all that might make them wrong. No matter how good a choice may start out, if you see anything amiss, you have to get rid of the answer. Very often, a single word may be the cause of the problem (for example, use of the word *not* to turn the answer into the opposite of the credited response). In addition, it's possible that the problem with the answer choice may show up late in the choice—the test-writers are hoping to lull test-takers into a false sense of security. For this reason, it is imperative that you read each answer choice thoroughly and carefully all the way to its end. Don't allow the good part of a choice to cause you to overlook or ignore the bad part—part wrong means all wrong no matter how good the good part might be.

Not Supported by the Passage You must be able to prove your answer with information from the passage. Any answer choice that can't be proven in this way can't be right, even if you know it to be true from outside knowledge of a subject. Don't invent a connection between an answer choice and the passage if you can't find one already present.

PUTTING IT ALL TOGETHER

So, let's see how it works in practice. Work the passage on the following page as we have just discussed: define the main points and the Bottom Line and make thoughtful and concise annotations. Then turn the page and compare your work to the marked-up passage. That passage will have not only sample annotations, but also explanations of how you ideally should have read through the passage: what questions you should ask yourself as you read, and what deserves more or less attention in the text.

This Reading Passage and its questions are from PrepTest 117, Section 1, Questions 1–7.

Questions 1–7 are based on the following passage:

The Canadian Auto Workers' (CAW) Legal Services Plan, designed to give active and retired autoworkers and their families access to totally prepaid or partially reimbursed legal services, has been in operation since late 1985. Plan members have the option of using either the plan's staff lawyers, whose services are fully covered by the cost of membership in the plan, or an outside lawyer. Outside lawyers, in turn, can either sign up with the plan as a "cooperating lawyer" and accept the CAW's fee schedule as payment in full, or they can charge a higher fee and collect the balance from the client. Autoworkers appear to have embraced the notion of prepaid legal services: 45 percent of eligible union members were enrolled in the plan by 1988. Moreover, the idea of prepaid legal services has been spreading in Canada. A department store is even offering a plan to holders of its credit card.

While many plan members seem to be happy to get reduced-cost legal help, many lawyers are concerned about the plan's effect on their profession, especially its impact on prices for legal services. Some point out that even though most lawyers have not joined the plan as cooperating lawyers, legal fees in the cities in which the CAW plan operates have been depressed, in some cases to an unprofitable level. The directors of the plan, however, claim that both clients and lawyers benefit from their arrangement. For while the clients get ready access to reduced-price services, lawyers get professional contact with people who would not otherwise be using legal services, which helps generate even more business for their firms. Experience shows, the directors say, that if people are referred to a firm and receive excellent service, the firm will get three to four other referrals who are not plan subscribers and who would therefore pay the firm's standard rate.

But it is unlikely that increased use of such plans will result in long-term client satisfaction or in a substantial increase in profits for law firms. Since lawyers with established reputations and client bases can benefit little, if at all, from participation, the plans function largely as marketing devices for lawyers who have yet to establish themselves. While many of these lawyers are no doubt very able and conscientious, they will tend to have less expertise and to provide less satisfaction to clients. At the same time, the downward pressure on fees will mean that the full-fee referrals that proponents say will come through plan participation may not make up for a firm's investment in providing services at low plan rates. And since lowered fees provide little incentive for lawyers to devote more than minimal effort to cases, a "volume discount" approach toward the practice of law will mean less time devoted to complex cases and a general lowering of quality for clients.

1. Which one of the following most accurately expresses the main point of the passage?

(A) In the short term, prepaid legal plans such as the CAW Legal Services Plan appear to be beneficial to both lawyers and clients, but in the long run lawyers will profit at the expense of clients.

(B) The CAW Legal Services Plan and other similar plans represent a controversial, but probably effective, way of bringing down the cost of legal services to clients and increasing lawyers' clientele.

(C) The use of prepaid legal plans such as that of the CAW should be rejected in favor of a more equitable means of making legal services more generally affordable.

(D) In spite of widespread consumer support for legal plans such as that offered by the CAW, lawyers generally criticize such plans, mainly because of their potential financial impact on the legal profession.

(E) Although they have so far attracted many subscribers, it is doubtful whether the CAW Legal Services Plan and other similar prepaid plans will benefit lawyers and clients in the long run.

2. The primary purpose of the passage is to

(A) compare and contrast legal plans with the traditional way of paying for legal services

(B) explain the growing popularity of legal plans

(C) trace the effect of legal plans on prices of legal services

(D) caution that increased use of legal plans is potentially harmful to the legal profession and to clients

(E) advocate reforms to legal plans as presently constituted

3. Which one of the following does the author predict will be a consequence of increased use of legal plans?

(A) results that are largely at odds with those predicted by lawyers who criticize the plans

(B) a lowering of the rates such plans charge their members

(C) forced participation of lawyers who can benefit little from association with the plans

(D) an eventual increase in profits for lawyers from client usage of the plans

(E) a reduction in the time lawyers devote to complex cases

4. Which one of the following sequences most accurately and completely corresponds to the presentation of the material in the passage?

(A) a description of a recently implemented set of procedures and policies; a summary of the results of that implementation; a proposal of refinements in those policies and procedures

(B) an evaluation of a recent phenomenon; a comparison of that phenomenon with related past phenomena; an expression of the author's approval of that phenomenon

(C) a presentation of a proposal; a discussion of the prospects for implementing that proposal; a recommendation by the author that the proposal be rejected

(D) a description of an innovation; a report of reasoning against and reasoning favoring that innovation; argumentation by the author concerning that innovation

(E) an explanation of a recent occurrence; an evaluation of the practical value of that occurrence; a presentation of further data regarding that occurrence

5. The passage most strongly suggests that, according to proponents of prepaid legal plans, cooperating lawyers benefit from taking clients at lower fees in which one of the following ways?

(A) Lawyers can expect to gain expertise in a wide variety of legal services by availing themselves of the access to diverse clientele that plan participation affords.

(B) Experienced cooperating lawyers are likely to enjoy the higher profits of long-term, complex cases, for which new lawyers are not suited.

(C) Lower rates of profit will be offset by a higher volume of clients and new business through word-of-mouth recommendations.

(D) Lower fees tend to attract clients away from established, nonparticipating law firms.

(E) With all legal fees moving downward to match the plans' schedules, the profession will respond to market forces.

6. According to the passage, which one of the following is true of CAW Legal Services Plan members?

(A) They can enjoy benefits beyond the use of the services of the plan's staff lawyers.

(B) So far, they generally believe the quality of services they receive from the plan's staff lawyers is as high as that provided by other lawyers.

(C) Most of them consult lawyers only for relatively simple and routine matters.

(D) They must pay a fee above the cost of membership for the services of an outside lawyer.

(E) They do not include only active and retired autoworkers and their families.

7. Which one of the following most accurately represents the primary function of the author's mention of marketing devices in the last paragraph?

(A) It points to an aspect of legal plans that the author believes will be detrimental to the quality of legal services.

(B) It is identified by the author as one of the primary ways in which plan administrators believe themselves to be contributing materially to the legal profession in return for lawyers' participation.

(C) It identifies what the author considers to be one of the few unequivocal benefits that legal plans can provide.

(D) It is reported as part of several arguments that the author attributes to established lawyers who oppose plan participation.

(E) It describes one of the chief burdens of lawyers who have yet to establish themselves and offers an explanation of their advocacy of legal plans.

Explanations and Annotations

The Canadian Auto Workers' (CAW) Legal Services Plan, designed to give active and retired autoworkers and their families access to totally prepaid or partially reimbursed legal services, has been in operation since late 1985. Plan members have the option of using either the plan's staff lawyers, whose services are fully covered by the cost of membership in the plan, or an outside lawyer. Outside lawyers, in turn, can either sign up with the plan as a "cooperating lawyer" and accept the CAW's fee schedule as payment in full, or they can charge a higher fee and collect the balance from the client. Autoworkers appear to have embraced the notion of prepaid legal services: 45 percent of eligible union members were enrolled in the plan by 1988. Moreover, the idea of prepaid legal services has been spreading in Canada. A department store is even offering a plan to holders of its credit card.

Description of CAW plan and popularity

While many plan members seem to be happy to get reduced-cost legal help, many lawyers are concerned about the plan's effect on their profession, especially its impact on prices for legal services. Some point out that even though most lawyers have not joined the plan as cooperating lawyers, legal fees in the cities in which the CAW plan operates have been depressed, in some cases to an unprofitable level. The directors of the plan, however, claim that both clients and lawyers benefit from their arrangement. For while the clients get ready access to reduced-price services, lawyers get professional contact with people who would not otherwise be using legal services, which helps generate even more business for their firms. Experience shows, the directors say, that if people are referred to a firm and receive excellent service, the firm will get three to four other referrals who are not plan subscribers and who would therefore pay the firm's standard rate.

Lawyers worried about lower fees, while directors claim benefit from referrals

But it is unlikely that increased use of such plans will result in long-term client satisfaction or in a substantial increase in profits for law firms. Since lawyers with established reputations and client bases can benefit little, if at all, from participation, the plans function largely as marketing devices for lawyers who have yet to establish themselves. While many of these lawyers are no doubt very able and conscientious, they will tend to have less expertise and to provide less satisfaction to clients. At the same time, the downward pressure on fees will mean that the full-fee referrals that proponents say will come through plan participation may not make up for a firm's investment in providing services at low plan rates. And since lowered fees provide little incentive for lawyers to devote more than minimal effort to cases, a "volume discount" approach toward the practice of law will mean less time devoted to complex cases and a general lowering of quality for clients.

But these plans probably not good for either lawyers or clients

Bottom Line: *Legal Services plans like the CAW's are popular, but likely to negatively impact lawyers' profits and client satisfaction.*

Step 1: Prepare

Paragraph 1 Main Point: Description of CAW plan and its popularity.

This paragraph introduces the CAW plan and describes who it covers and how it works. You should notice, and mark with your annotation, that there are differences in ways that lawyers can participate and in how fee payment works. But, don't try to memorize all these variations—you know where to find the details if and when you need them later. The end of the paragraph tells you that this kind of plan appears to be popular and that the idea is spreading. Notice, however, that you don't know at this point if the author shares the positive point of view that others have about this type of plan. So far, the author isn't taking sides.

Paragraph 2 Main Point: Lawyers worried about lower fees, while directors claim benefit from referrals.

Notice the word "While" that starts this paragraph off. Already you get a hint that there may be those who are not as happy as others about these plans. (You might also notice that the author says that members "seem to be happy," but doesn't actually say that they are satisfied with the plan. You don't know yet why the author uses this kind of language, but keep it in mind as you read further into the passage.) And yes, the first part of this second paragraph introduces a contrast to the first paragraph: many lawyers think that such plans are already negatively affecting their profits. But now, with a "however," the passage moves back to a different and more positive point of view: the directors of the plans (whom you can identify as proponents of the plan) think lawyers and firms will benefit overall from increased business. Don't worry too much about the details of how; keep your focus on the directors' main claim.

The question to ask yourself at this point is "Do I know yet what the author thinks?" The answer is no. So far you have only contrasting points of view held by other people.

Paragraph 3 Main Point: But these plans are probably not good for either lawyers or clients.

Only now do you get definitive evidence about the author's own point of view. The passage states outright "But it is unlikely that increased use of such plans will result in long-term client satisfaction or in a substantial increase in profits for law firms." The word "Since" that begins the next sentence tells you that here comes the support for that judgment. So, while you do want to note (if you previewed the questions) that the reference to "marketing devices" is made in the context of the author's criticism, don't get too caught up in the explanation in the middle of the paragraph. As long as you get the two key ideas—the author thinks neither lawyers nor clients will get much benefit—you are good to go for the Bottom Line and to start on the questions.

Bottom Line: Legal Services plans like the CAW's are popular, but likely to negatively impact lawyers' profits and client satisfaction.

This is a "Criticize" passage, and in this case (but keep in mind this will not always be the case!), the author essentially expresses the Bottom Line through the main point of the last paragraph.

Steps 2–4: Attacking the Questions

Along with the explanations for each step of attacking each question, we have marked the questions up to show how you might do the same to help yourself to understand the question, evaluate each choice, and track your Process of Elimination.

1. Which one of the following most accurately expresses the main point of the passage?

(A) In the short term, prepaid legal plans such as the CAW Legal Services Plan appear to be beneficial to both lawyers and clients, but in the long run lawyers will profit at the expense of clients.

(B) The CAW Legal Services Plan and other similar plans represent a controversial, but probably effective, way of bringing down the cost of legal services to clients and increasing lawyers' clientele.

(C) The use of prepaid legal plans such as that of the CAW should be rejected in favor of a more equitable means of making legal services more generally affordable.

(D) In spite of widespread consumer support for legal plans such as that offered by the CAW, lawyers generally criticize such plans, mainly because of their potential financial impact on the legal profession.

(E) Although they have so far attracted many subscribers, it is doubtful whether the CAW Legal Services Plan and other similar prepaid plans will benefit lawyers and clients in the long run.

Here's How to Crack It

Step 2: Assess

This is a Big Picture: Main Point question. Therefore, it is asking you what the central point of the entire passage is.

Step 3: Act

Remind yourself of the Bottom Line you already defined: "Legal Services plans like the CAW's are popular, but likely to negatively impact lawyers' profits and client satisfaction."

Step 4: Answer

As you move through the choices, keep reminding yourself of the scope of the passage (the two aspects of the CAW and similar plans) and the negative attitude of the author.

The first part of (A) sounds okay, since it says "appear to be beneficial," but the second part goes wrong. The author indicates that lawyers may in fact not profit in the long run. This choice is half right but half wrong, and it misrepresents the author's attitude and opinion. So, (A) is out.

Choice (B) begins with suspicious wording with "controversial"; while there is debate regarding the value of the plan, the author doesn't go quite this far. However, if you are unsure about whether or not there is enough support for the word "controversial," there is an even more obvious reason to eliminate the choice: it is the opposite of the author's opinion. The author states clearly that they believe that such plans will be ineffective, not effective. Choice (B) is out.

Choice (C) may be momentarily tempting, given its negative tone. However, the author never goes so far as to claim such plans should be rejected or indicates that the problem is that they are inequitable or unfair. This choice is both too extreme and out of scope, so it should be eliminated.

You may have left (D) in contention the first time through the choices. "Widespread" and "generally" are a bit strong, based on the more moderate wording used by the author in paragraph 1, but at least some lawyers do in fact criticize such plans because of their financial impact on the profession. Let's imagine you left (D) in, and move on for the moment to the last answer.

Choice (E) matches your Bottom Line nicely. Yes, the plans have been popular and attracted subscribers, but no, the author does not think that such plans will benefit either lawyers or clients in the long run. And, if you go back and compare (E) and (D), you will see that (D) mentions only the lawyers' side and issue, leaving out the other key issue which is the potential negative impact on client satisfaction.

This leaves you with a clear decision: choice (E).

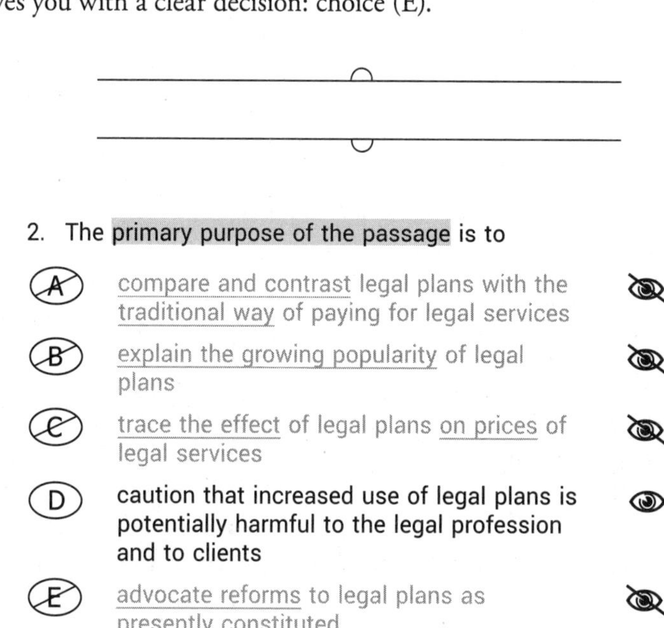

Here's How to Crack It

Step 2: Assess

The wording "primary purpose" makes it clear that this is a Big Picture: Primary Purpose question. So, the task is similar to that in question 1: find the answer that best represents the author's central goal in writing the passage as a whole.

Step 3: Act

Again, remind yourself of the Bottom Line you already defined: "Legal Services plans like the CAW's are popular, but likely to negatively impact lawyers' profits and client satisfaction." So, the purpose of the passage is to tell you that such plans may have these particular drawbacks.

Step 4: Answer

Choice (A) is problematic from the beginning. The author is not comparing and contrasting types of plans, nor are they spending much time at all describing how these legal services plans are different from traditional methods of payment. So, (A) is out of scope and out of contention.

Choice (B) may have tempted you for a moment, since the author does indicate in paragraph 1 that such plans are popular. However, does the author spend much time *explaining* that popularity? No. Is the passage as a whole about their popularity? No. Therefore, this choice is too narrow to have any chance of describing the author's primary purpose.

If you are attuned to this very common "too narrow" Attractive Distractor on Big Picture questions, you will have easily eliminated (C) as well. While the author does discuss effects on prices of legal services, they also discuss effects on client satisfaction. Therefore, (C) is out for a similar reason as (B) (as well as (D) in question 1).

Choice (D) nicely corresponds to the scope and tone of your Bottom Line. So, let's leave it in for now and consider (E).

Choice (E) is a trap for test-takers who think too far beyond the scope of the passage. Yes, the author indicates problems with legal services plans. However, do they take the further step of advocating changes or reforms? No. Remember, we defined the purpose of the passage as to criticize, not to advocate. Even if you are speculating that perhaps the author has this in mind, you can't point to any evidence of this in the passage.

This leaves you with (D) as the best representation of the author's primary purpose.

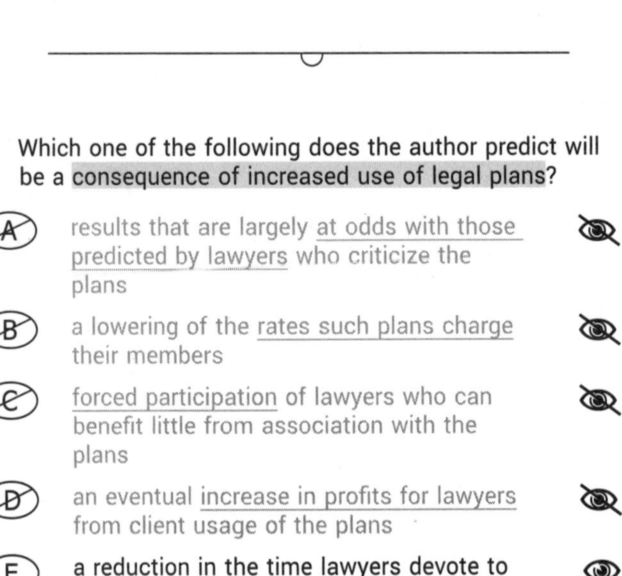

3. Which one of the following does the author predict will be a consequence of increased use of legal plans?

(A) results that are largely at odds with those predicted by lawyers who criticize the plans

(B) a lowering of the rates such plans charge their members

(C) forced participation of lawyers who can benefit little from association with the plans

(D) an eventual increase in profits for lawyers from client usage of the plans

(E) a reduction in the time lawyers devote to complex cases

Here's How to Crack It

Step 2: Assess

This is an Extract: Fact question. It is asking you what the author said will happen as a result of use of such plans.

Step 3: Act

This is the time to go back to the passage before POE. You know from your preparation of the passage that the author made two predictions in the last paragraph. One is that "downward pressure on fees" may hurt law firms' profits, and the other is that clients will receive lower quality service, in part because lawyers will spend less time on complicated cases. Go into the choices, then, with these two possible answers in mind.

Step 4: Answer

Read and paraphrase (A) carefully. It is using convoluted language to try to distract you from the fact that this is the exact opposite of what the author predicted. In paragraph 2, the author describes the fear of some lawyers that legal services plans will depress (and in some cases already have depressed) prices "in some cases to an unprofitable level." In paragraph 3, the author agrees that this may, in fact, occur. Therefore, the author predicts results that are consistent, not at odds with, these lawyers' prediction.

Choice (B) requires equally careful reading to see what it is really saying. Does the author predict a lowering of the rates *charged by the plans to their members*? No, they predict a lowering of fees paid to lawyers. This wrong answer is a trap set for test-takers who rely only on their memory, and/or who do not read the answer choices word for word.

Choice (C) immediately leaves the scope of the passage. The author never indicates that any lawyer will be forced to participate; paragraph 1 makes it pretty clear that lawyers join or cooperate voluntarily. So, (C) is gone.

Even though this is an Extract: Fact question, using your Bottom Line actively should allow you to eliminate (D) the first time through the answers. A major part of the author's criticism is that legal services plans may decrease, not increase, profits. This choice invalidates itself by contradicting the passage.

So, we are down to (E). Remember to read every choice carefully, even if you have eliminated (A)–(D). But all is good, as (E) is already one of the options you had in mind based on going back to the last paragraph before POE. This leaves you with (E) as the supported credited response.

4. Which one of the following sequences most accurately and completely corresponds to the presentation of the material in the passage?

(A) a description of a recently implemented set of procedures and policies;/a summary of the results of that implementation;/a proposal of refinements in those policies and procedures

(B) an evaluation of a recent phenomenon;/a comparison of that phenomenon with related past phenomena;/an expression of the author's approval of that phenomenon

(C) a presentation of a proposal;/a discussion of the prospects for implementing that proposal;/a recommendation by the author that the proposal be rejected

(D) a description of an innovation;/a report of reasoning against and reasoning favoring that innovation;/argumentation by the author concerning that innovation

(E) an explanation of a recent occurrence;/an evaluation of the practical value of that occurrence;/a presentation of further data regarding that occurrence

Here's How to Crack It

Step 2: Assess

The wording "sequences most accurately and completely corresponds to the presentation of the material in the passage" tells you that this is a Structure: Organization question. Therefore, it is asking you to find the choice that piece by piece follows and matches the main sections of the passage.

Step 3: Act

If you have prepared the passage well by defining the main point of each paragraph, you can move right into the choices, using that "outline" as your guide.

Step 4: Answer

Work actively to break down the pieces of each choice the first time through the answers; don't just read the whole choice as one big chunk and then ask "does anything sound wrong?" One useful technique is to visually break each answer up with a slash in between each section, making it easier for you to identify and check each individual chunk.

The first part of (A) is suspicious with the word "recently," but don't get stuck at this point trying to decide if 1985 can be called recent or not. Once you move on to the next two chunks of the choice, you can see where it goes definitively wrong. Paragraph 2 of the passage describes the positive and negative points of view regarding the eventual effects of the plan, not a summary of any actual results, and paragraph 3 presents the author's criticism with no proposals for reforms or refinements.

Choice (B) starts off wrong: you defined the purpose of paragraph 1 as describing, not evaluating, the plan. Chunk 2 is wrong as well: there is no comparison with related past phenomena, and chunk 3 seals the deal: the author disapproves, not approves of the plan. Recognizing any one of these three problems would be enough to eliminate the choice.

Choice (C) begins problematically—this is an existing plan, not a proposal. But, if you are unsure about that, there are plenty of other reasons to eliminate (C). Paragraph 2 does not discuss how likely the "proposal" is to be implemented but rather existing positive and negative views of the existing plans, and paragraph 3 expresses the author's criticism, but they do not go so far as to say the plans should be rejected.

Choice (D) nicely matches your main points piece by piece and in the correct order: description of the CAW and similar plans (which, since they began in 1985, can reasonably be called an "innovation"), arguments for and against such plans, and finally, the author's argument that such plans will likely have two types of negative effects.

Choice (E) begins okay (again, don't get stuck at this point trying to decide if 1985 qualifies as "recent"), but then goes wrong. Paragraph 2 presents contrasting points of view but not the author's evaluation of the practical value of the plans, and there is no actual data presented in paragraph 3.

This leaves you with (D) as the best piece by piece match to the passage presentation.

5. The passage most strongly suggests that, according to proponents of prepaid legal plans, cooperating lawyers benefit from taking clients at lower fees in which one of the following ways?

(A) Lawyers can expect to gain expertise in a wide variety of legal services by availing themselves of the access to diverse clientele that plan participation affords.

(B) Experienced cooperating lawyers are likely to enjoy the higher profits of long-term, complex cases, for which new lawyers are not suited.

(C) Lower rates of profit will be offset by a higher volume of clients and new business through word-of-mouth recommendations.

(D) Lower fees tend to attract clients away from established, nonparticipating law firms.

(E) With all legal fees moving downward to match the plans' schedules, the profession will respond to market forces.

Here's How to Crack It

Step 2: Assess

The wording "The passage most strongly suggests" tells you that this is an Extract: Inference question. Translate the rest of the question carefully, however! This question is NOT asking you what the author agrees with, but rather what the *proponents* of prepaid legal plans would think, and the author is definitively NOT a proponent.

Step 3: Act

You know from your passage prep that paragraph 2 describes the proponents' argument. Going back to that part of the passage, you see that their argument is that cooperating lawyers will come out ahead profit-wise when they get more business out of the deal: "if people are referred to a firm and receive excellent service, the firm will get three or four other referrals who are not plan subscribers and who would therefore pay the firms' standard rate." So, you are looking for something along these lines in a correct answer.

Step 4: Answer

Choice (A) is out of scope and therefore wrong. There is no discussion in the passage of greater diversity of clientele or of gaining greater expertise. The issue is volume and fees, not range of experience. Make sure not to speculate past the boundaries of the passage; even if you think that this could be a result, there is no evidence for it in the passage. If you left (A) in during your first cut through the choices, comparing it with (C) would alert you to what the real issue is in the passage.

Choice (B) may be momentarily attractive because it mentions profits. However, it introduces two comparisons—between experienced and new lawyers, and between fees for complex versus less complex cases—that are not supported. Note the trap; the author talks about inexperienced lawyers and complex cases later on in paragraph 3, but does not indicate any relevance of these issues to arguments made by proponents of the plans.

Choice (C) has the right issue (profiting through referrals and increased volume) and the right positive tone. So, leave it in and move on to (D).

Choice (D), like (A) and (B), brings in an issue that is not addressed in the passage. The author never indicates that proponents of the plans believe that cooperating lawyers will benefit through stealing clients away from other firms.

The trap in (E) is that it is not even clear what "respond to market forces" means. Probably that fees would decrease overall, which is definitely not in line with the proponents' argument, but why take the time to figure that out when you already have a choice that nicely matches what is directly discussed in the passage.

So, eliminate (E), pick (C), and move on!

---

6. According to the passage, which one of the following is true of CAW Legal Services Plan members?

(A) They can enjoy benefits beyond the use of the services of the plan's staff lawyers.

(B) So far, they generally believe the quality of services they receive from the plan's staff lawyers is as high as that provided by other lawyers.

(C) Most of them consult lawyers only for relatively simple and routine matters.

(D) They must pay a fee above the cost of membership for the services of an outside lawyer.

(E) They do not include only active and retired autoworkers and their families.

Here's How to Crack It

Step 2: Assess

"According to the passage" tells you that this is an Extract: Fact question. So, it is asking you to find the answer that is most directly supported by what is explicitly stated in the passage.

Step 3: Act

Paragraph 1 describes the CAW and who its members are. There are a variety of things in that paragraph that the correct answer might reference. So, it is reasonable, once you have identified the relevant section of the passage, to move into POE and then go back to the passage text as needed.

Step 4: Answer

Choice (A) may not immediately leap out at you, but when you go back to paragraph 1 you see the following: "Plan members have the option of using either the plan's staff lawyers, whose services are fully covered by the cost of membership in the plan, or an outside lawyer." If a plan member uses an outside lawyer, they would either pay the same as for a plan lawyer, or a reduced rate (whatever exceeds the plan's fee schedule). This definitely qualifies as a benefit beyond use of the plan's staff lawyers, so leave in (A).

Choice (B) is out of scope and therefore wrong. All you know from the passage is that "Autoworkers appear to have embraced the notion of prepaid legal services…." This tells you nothing about members' perceptions regarding the *quality of services* received from staff lawyers. Make sure not to over-speculate; if quality of service is not mentioned in this context, it cannot be in the correct answer to an Extract: Fact question.

Choice (C) is also out of scope. There is no discussion in the relevant part of the passage of what issues members consult lawyers about. This is a trap based on the last paragraph, where the author says that lawyers in the plan will have little incentive to devote lots of time to complex cases, which is a very different issue.

Choice (D) includes a word that should set off alarms in your POE brain: "must." Do members HAVE to pay additional fees? No, not if a cooperating lawyer "accept[s] the CAW's fee schedule as payment in full." Therefore, this choice is too extreme and should be eliminated.

Choice (E) requires careful, word-for-word reading. The passage states that the CAW plan is "designed to give active and retired autoworkers and their families access" to legal services. Therefore, the word "not" in this choice turns it into the opposite of what the author describes.

So, (E) is out, leaving you with (A) as the directly supported correct answer.

7. Which one of the following most accurately represents the primary function of the author's mention of marketing devices in the last paragraph?

(A) It points to an aspect of legal plans that the author believes will be detrimental to the quality of legal services.

(B) It is identified by the author as one of the primary ways in which plan administrators believe themselves to be contributing materially to the legal profession in return for lawyers' participation.

(C) It identifies what the author considers to be one of the few unequivocal benefits that legal plans can provide.

(D) It is reported as part of several arguments that the author attributes to established lawyers who oppose plan participation.

(E) It describes one of the chief burdens of lawyers who have yet to establish themselves and offers an explanation of their advocacy of legal plans.

Here's How to Crack It

Step 2: Assess

This question asks you for the "primary function" or purpose of a reference in the passage, making it a Structure: Function question. Your task, then, is to figure out WHY the author mentions marketing devices in that part of the passage.

Step 3: Act

You already know from preparing the passage that the third paragraph sets out the author's criticism of prepaid legal plans. Going back to that particular part of the paragraph, you see that the author states that the plans will function mostly as "marketing devices" for inexperienced lawyers, and that these lawyers "will tend to have less expertise and to provide less satisfaction to clients." So, your own answer to this question might be something like: "It is one of the problems with these legal plans."

Step 4: Answer

Choice (A) nicely matches the answer we just generated based on the question task and relevant part of the passage—leave it in!

The problem with (B) is clear if you have already identified the purpose of the reference. It is part of the author's criticism, not part of the proponents' defense of the plans.

Even though this is not a Big Picture question, your articulation of the Bottom Line eliminates (C). The author criticizes these legal plans, and nothing in the passage indicates any real benefit, including this "marketing device." Be careful not to use your own opinion; "marketing device" may sound like a positive thing to many people, but the author has the opposite opinion.

Choice (D) attributes this argument to the wrong people. Yes, there are lawyers who criticize the plans, but the "marketing device" argument is the author's, not these lawyers'. Your tracking of the structure of the passage, including the main points, helps you to eliminate this choice.

Choice (E) has a variety of problems. First, while the author does indicate that new lawyers would need to market themselves, the passage does not go so far as to describe this as "one of the chief burdens" of new lawyers. Even more importantly, the only lawyers' point of view described in the passage is in opposition to, not in support of, the plan; you are not told of any lawyers who are advocating legal plans.

This leaves you with (A) as the credited response.

READING COMPREHENSION: DUAL PASSAGES

One Reading Comprehension passage on each LSAT is a comparative reading set comprised of two shorter passages, each with a different treatment of a similar subject. These passages require the same skills as a regular Reading Comprehension passage; in fact, analyzing these passages is very similar to analyzing a single passage with multiple viewpoints. The difference is that the questions will often ask you to compare and contrast the structure, tone, and content of the two passages. Sometimes the questions will ask you to find differences or similarities between the two passages. You may also be asked how the author of one passage would respond to a part of the other author's passage. As you read, keep an eye out for these similarities and differences so you'll be ready to answer the questions. Part of your preparation should be to define not only the main points and Bottom Line of each passage, but also the relationship between the two. And, as you go through Assess, Act, and Answer on the questions, make sure that you carefully determine if the question is asking about only one of the two passages, or if it is asking what information appears in only one or the other or both, or if it is asking about some relationship between the two.

Let's work a comparative reading set together.

This Reading Passage and its questions are from PrepTest 130, Section 2, Questions 21–27.

Passage A

In music, a certain complexity of sounds can be expected to have a positive effect on the listener. A single, pure tone is not that interesting to explore; a measure of intricacy is required to excite human curiosity. Sounds that are too complex or disorganized, however, tend to be overwhelming. We prefer some sort of coherence, a principle that connects the various sounds and makes them comprehensible.

In this respect, music is like human language. Single sounds are in most cases not sufficient to convey meaning in speech, whereas when put together in a sequence they form words and sentences. Likewise, if the tones in music are not perceived to be tied together sequentially or rhythmically—for example, in what is commonly called melody—listeners are less likely to feel any emotional connection or to show appreciation.

Certain music can also have a relaxing effect. The fact that such music tends to be continuous and rhythmical suggests a possible explanation for this effect. In a natural environment, danger tends to be accompanied by sudden, unexpected sounds. Thus, a background of constant noise suggests peaceful conditions; discontinuous sounds demand more attention. Even soft discontinuous sounds that we consciously realize do not signal danger can be disturbing—for example, the erratic dripping of a leaky tap. A continuous sound, particularly one that is judged to be safe, relaxes the brain.

Passage B

There are certain elements within music, such as a change of melodic line or rhythm, that create expectations about the future development of the music. The expectation the listener has about the further course of musical events is a key determinant for the experience of "musical emotions." Music creates expectations that, if not immediately satisfied, create tension. Emotion is experienced in relation to the buildup and release of tension. The more elaborate the buildup of tension, the more intense the emotions that will be experienced. When resolution occurs, relaxation follows.

The interruption of the expected musical course, depending on one's personal involvement, causes the search for an explanation. This results from a "mismatch" between one's musical expectation and the actual course of the music. Negative emotions will be the result of an extreme mismatch between expectations and experience. Positive emotions result if the converse happens.

When we listen to music, we take into account factors such as the complexity and novelty of the music. The degree to which the music sounds familiar determines whether the music is experienced as pleasurable or uncomfortable. The pleasure experienced is minimal when the music is entirely new to the listener, increases with increasing familiarity, and decreases again when the music is totally known. Musical preference is based on one's desire to maintain a constant level of certain preferable emotions. As such, a trained listener will have a greater preference for complex melodies than will a naive listener, as the threshold for experiencing emotion is higher.

1. Which one of the following concepts is linked to positive musical experiences in both passages?

(A) continuous sound

(B) tension

(C) language

(D) improvisation

(E) complexity

2. The passages most strongly suggest that both are targeting an audience that is interested in which one of the following?

(A) the theoretical underpinnings of how music is composed

(B) the nature of the conceptual difference between music and discontinuous sound

(C) the impact music can have on human emotional states

(D) the most effective techniques for teaching novices to appreciate complex music

(E) the influence music has had on the development of spoken language

3. Which one of the following describes a preference that is most analogous to the preference mentioned in the first paragraph of passage A?

(A) the preference of some people for falling asleep to white noise, such as the sound of an electric fan

(B) the preference of many moviegoers for movies with plots that are clear and easy to follow

(C) the preference of many diners for restaurants that serve large portions

(D) the preference of many young listeners for fast music over slower music

(E) the preference of most children for sweet foods over bitter foods

4. Which one of the following most accurately expresses the main point of passage B?

(A) The type of musical emotion experienced by a listener is determined by the level to which the listener's expectations are satisfied.

(B) Trained listeners are more able to consciously manipulate their own emotional experiences of complex music than are naive listeners.

(C) If the development of a piece of music is greatly at odds with the listener's musical expectations, then the listener will experience negative emotions.

(D) Listeners can learn to appreciate changes in melodic line and other musical complexities.

(E) Music that is experienced by listeners as relaxing usually produces a buildup and release of tension in those listeners.

5. Which one of the following most undermines the explanation provided in passage A for the relaxing effect that some music has on listeners?

(A) The musical traditions of different cultures vary greatly in terms of the complexity of the rhythms they employ.

(B) The rhythmic structure of a language is determined in part by the pattern of stressed syllables in the words and sentences of the language.

(C) Many people find the steady and rhythmic sound of a rocking chair to be very unnerving.

(D) The sudden interruption of the expected development of a melody tends to interfere with listeners' perception of the melody as coherent.

(E) Some of the most admired contemporary composers write music that is notably simpler than is most of the music written in previous centuries.

6. Which one of the following would be most appropriate as a title for each of the passages?

(A) "The Biological Underpinnings of Musical Emotions"

(B) "The Psychology of Listener Response to Music"

(C) "How Music Differs from Other Art Forms"

(D) "Cultural Patterns in Listeners' Responses to Music"

(E) "How Composers Convey Meaning Through Music"

7. It can be inferred that both authors would be likely to agree with which one of the following statements?

(A) The more complex a piece of music, the more it is likely to be enjoyed by most listeners.

(B) More knowledgeable listeners tend to prefer music that is discontinuous and unpredictable.

(C) The capacity of music to elicit strong emotional responses from listeners is the central determinant of its artistic value.

(D) Music that lacks a predictable course is unlikely to cause a listener to feel relaxed.

(E) Music that changes from soft to loud is perceived as disturbing and unpleasant by most listeners.

Explanations and Annotations

Step 1: Prepare

As you prepare Comparative Reading passages, in most ways treat them the same as any passage: look for key logical clues, identify the main point of each paragraph, and define the Bottom Line of each passage, including the attitude and purpose of the author in the passage as a whole.

As you read passage B, already be on the lookout for similarities and differences with passage A. Keep in mind that while passage B is not written in direct response to passage A, there will be some relationship between them, including at least some similarities and at least some differences in content, scope, and/or attitude of the author.

<u>Passage A</u>

Paragraph 1 Main Point: While a simple musical sound is not likely to interest people, a certain complexity of sounds will.

Paragraph 2 Main Point: Just like with language, connection and coherence is important for understanding and appreciation.

Paragraph 3 Main Point: People find continuous sounds relaxing, in music and in general.

Passage A Bottom Line: Levels of complexity, coherence, and continuity affect the pleasure of listeners.

<u>Passage B</u>

As you read passage B, you see that it is very similar in content and purpose to passage A. Note where similar topics appear and what the author has to say about them, as well as where the author raises topics or issues that did not appear in passage A.

Paragraph 1 Main Point: In music, expectations create tension, and resolution of tension creates relaxation.

Paragraph 2 Main Point: When expectations match resolution, music can inspire positive emotions and vice versa.

Paragraph 3 Main Point: Also, the right level of complexity and familiarity makes music pleasurable for different listeners.

Passage B Bottom Line: Resolution of expectations, and complexity and familiarity, factor into the pleasure we find in music.

Relationship between Passages A and B: Both passages outline factors that affect our emotional response to music.

Steps 2–4: Attack the Questions

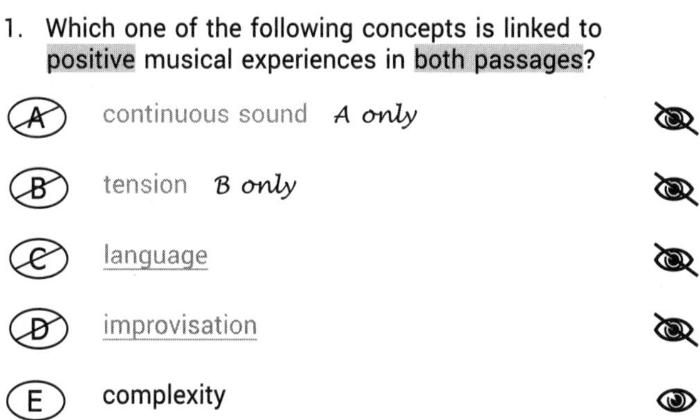

Here's How to Crack It

Step 2: Assess

This is an Extract: Fact question that asks about something that happens in BOTH passages.

Step 3: Act

Given that both passages mention a variety of things that can be linked to positive musical experiences, it is best to go directly to the answer choices first, and then go back to each passage and/or to your own passage prep notes as you evaluate the choices.

Step 4: Answer

Choice (A), "continuous sound," is mentioned only in passage A. This is a classic trap on a question that asks for something that happens in both passages.

Choice (B) is a similar trap. To the extent that it is linked to positive musical experiences, it is discussed only in passage B (paragraph 1). Don't spend too much time trying to decide if "tension" is close enough, or if it would need to say "resolution of tension" to answer the question; if it isn't addressed at all in the other passage, it has no chance of being the correct answer.

Choice (C), "language," is addressed only in passage A, and there it is as an analogy to music, not as a source of positive musical experiences. Similarly to (B), however, if you have seen that language is not discussed in passage B, this is enough to eliminate the choice.

Choice (D), "improvisation," is out of scope; it isn't discussed in either passage. Once you have figured out that it isn't in one of the passages, you can eliminate this choice without hunting through the other passage as well.

Choice (E), "complexity," is discussed in both passages in connection to positive musical experiences. You may well have enough information from preparing the passage, including the main points of each paragraph, to select this answer without going back to the passage text again. If not, you would go back to see that it is discussed in the first sentence of passage A and in the last paragraph of passage B.

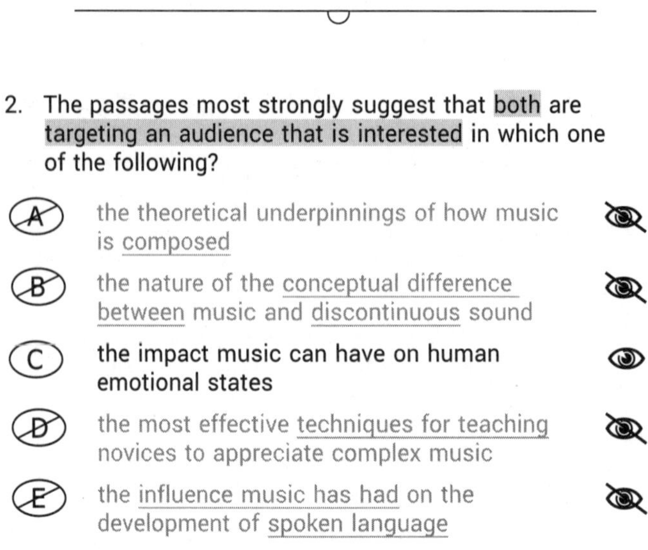

Here's How to Crack It

Step 2: Assess

This is an Extract: Inference question. However, in translating the question, you should notice that it is also very similar to a Big Picture: Primary Purpose question. By asking to whom each author is writing, it is essentially asking about the purpose of both authors.

Step 3: Act

You have already done enough preparation work in Step 1 to have a good answer to this question in mind: both passages are targeting an audience that is interested in the effects music has on the feelings of listeners.

Step 4: Answer

Choice (A) is out of scope for both passages; neither discusses how music is composed. Make sure not to take extra leaps to connect the effect of music to the reason why a piece of music was composed as it was. That connection would have to be made explicitly in both passages for this answer to be correct.

For (B), once you identify that continuous sounds are discussed only in passage A, this is enough to eliminate the answer choice. Even for passage A, this doesn't match, however, given that passage A is not talking about some conceptual *contrast* between music and discontinuous sound.

Choice (C) matches what you would have already defined as the relationship between the two passages: "Both passages outline factors that affect our emotional response to music." So, keep it in!

Choice (D) is beyond the scope of both passages; neither discusses *teaching* music appreciation. The trap is that the end of passage B mentions trained versus "naive" or novice listeners (although still not in the context of teaching music), and sometimes the last thing you read in a passage stands out in your mind.

Choice (E) is wrong for reasons similar to those for (D). Language is mentioned only in one passage (passage A), and even in that passage it is not discussed in the context of how one (music) influences the other (language).

This leaves you with (C) as the straightforwardly supported credited response.

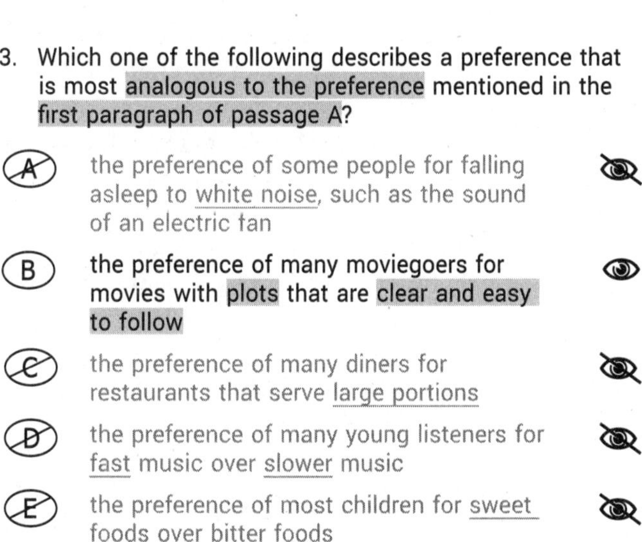

3. Which one of the following describes a preference that is most analogous to the preference mentioned in the first paragraph of passage A?

(A) the preference of some people for falling asleep to white noise, such as the sound of an electric fan

(B) the preference of many moviegoers for movies with plots that are clear and easy to follow

(C) the preference of many diners for restaurants that serve large portions

(D) the preference of many young listeners for fast music over slower music

(E) the preference of most children for sweet foods over bitter foods

Here's How to Crack It

Step 2: Assess

This is an Application: Analogy question. In translating it, note two key things. First, it asks only about passage A. Second, it asks for a preference logically similar to that mentioned in the first paragraph of that passage.

Step 3: Act

Go back to the passage and find the relevant preference: "a certain complexity of sound" that has "some sort of coherence, a principle that connects the various sounds and makes them comprehensible." So, you are looking for a preference, most likely for something other than music (given that this is an Analogy question) that is not too simple, but that is coherent and comprehensible.

Note that you can ignore passage B for this question, since it asks only about passage A.

Step 4: Answer

Choice (A) is wrong because it has no complexity to it. White noise, such as the sound of a fan, would be like a "single, pure tone," and the author says that such simple tones are not interesting to listeners.

Choice (B) has the right theme: a plot (which would involve different aspects linked together) that is comprehensible and easy to understand (which has the right type and level of complexity). So, leave it in!

Choice (C) is out of scope. Nothing in passage A or in this answer choice connects complexity or comprehensibility to size.

Choice (D) is also out of scope. It may be attractive because it mentions music, but remember that Analogy questions have nothing to do with the topic of the passage, only the logic, and choices that have the same topic may in fact be traps. Nothing in the passage connects speed to complexity or comprehensibility.

Choice (E), like (C), is out of scope. There is no evidence in the passage or in the answer choice that sweet foods would be any different than bitter foods in their "comprehensibility" (whatever that might mean in this context) or complexity.

This leaves you with (B) as the best logical match.

4. Which one of the following most accurately expresses the main point of passage B?

(A) The type of musical emotion experienced by a listener is determined by the level to which the listener's expectations are satisfied.

(B) Trained listeners are more able to consciously manipulate their own emotional experiences of complex music than are naive listeners.

(C) If the development of a piece of music is greatly at odds with the listener's musical expectations, then the listener will experience negative emotions.

(D) Listeners can learn to appreciate changes in melodic line and other musical complexities.

(E) Music that is experienced by listeners as relaxing usually produces a buildup and release of tension in those listeners.

Here's How to Crack It

Step 2: Assess

This is a Big Picture: Main Point question. Note that it asks for the main point of passage B, so passage A is irrelevant to this question.

Step 3: Act

You have already answered this question in your own words when you prepared the passages: resolution of expectations, and complexity and familiarity, factor into the pleasure we find in music. Make sure that you keep the scope of your own answer and of passage B in mind as you go through POE.

Step 4: Answer

Choice (A) may not perfectly match your own answer; the last paragraph goes a bit beyond expectations of the listener to bring in complexity and novelty (although they are not completely separate issues). But, this choice is definitely close enough to keep in during your first cut through the choices.

Choice (B) is both too narrow and inaccurate. The author discusses trained listeners only in the last paragraph (so, too narrow) and does not talk about how they can consciously manipulate their emotional experience (so, inaccurate). Therefore, (A) is the best match so far.

Choice (C) is very attractive because yes, the author does indicate this to be true in the second paragraph of the passage. But, it is only one theme within the discussion of satisfaction of expectations (for example, it mentions only the negative side). So, (A) is still a better match for the scope of the passage as a whole.

Choice (D) is the same kind of trap as (C): too narrow. You can infer it from the last paragraph, but this is not an Extract: Inference question. It says nothing about a major theme of the passage (resolution of expectations as it relates to emotion), and therefore is significantly more narrow than (A), and so deserves elimination.

Choice (E) is also a "too narrow trap," and it is much more narrow in scope than (A). Choice (E) is a major point within the first paragraph of the passage, but compare it with (A), which also includes the main point of the second paragraph of the passage and at least some connection to the final paragraph.

This leaves you with (A) as the best answer, even if you weren't completely satisfied with it when you first read it.

---

5. Which one of the following most undermines the explanation provided in passage A for the relaxing effect that some music has on listeners?

(A) The musical traditions of different cultures vary greatly in terms of the complexity of the rhythms they employ.

(B) The rhythmic structure of a language is determined in part by the pattern of stressed syllables in the words and sentences of the language.

(C) Many people find the steady and rhythmic sound of a rocking chair to be very unnerving.

(D) The sudden interruption of the expected development of a melody tends to interfere with listeners' perception of the melody as coherent.

(E) Some of the most admired contemporary composers write music that is notably simpler than is most of the music written in previous centuries.

Here's How to Crack It

Step 2: Assess

The word "undermines" alerts you that this is an Application: Weaken question. Note also that it references a particular explanation in passage A. So, you will be looking for an answer that most goes against that explanation (also be mindful that passage B is irrelevant to this question).

Step 3: Act

Go back to passage A and find the relevant explanation. Use your annotation and main points; the beginning of the third paragraph of that passage says "Certain music can also have a relaxing effect. The fact that such music tends to be continuous and rhythmical suggests a possible explanation for this effect."

Even though you can't predict exactly what new information the correct answer will bring in, you can still come up with a pretty good guideline for what that correct answer needs to indicate: "Continuous and/or rhythmical sounds may not be so relaxing."

Step 4: Answer

Choice (A) is out of scope. Notice that it doesn't tell you a variety of things that it would have to tell you in order to make it a correct answer. For example, it doesn't say that music that is less complex rhythmically is NOT rhythmic or continuous, or that the people in cultures with more rhythmic music find their music to be LESS relaxing.

Choice (B) also has no effect on the author's argument. What determines the rhythmic structure of language does not tell you anything about the *effect* of rhythmic sounds on the listener.

Choice (C) is going in the direction we already defined for the question. It describes a "steady and rhythmic sound" that, according to the author's argument, people should find relaxing. However, according to this choice (and remember, you take the choices on Weaken questions as true statements), people instead find it "very unnerving." So, this choice has the right issue and the right direction.

Choice (D) has part of the right issue (continuity) but the wrong direction; this is a classic type of wrong answer on a Weaken question. The answer describes a discontinuity that would interfere with a listener's perception of the melody as coherent. Aside from the fact that the issue of the question is relaxation, not coherence, this choice would be (if anything) consistent with the author's argument. This is the opposite of what you are looking for.

Choice (E), in part in a similar way to (A), introduces an irrelevant comparison. Simplicity is a different issue than continuity and rhythmic nature, and the answer choice does not suggest that this admired "simpler" music is non-rhythmic or non-continuous.

This leaves you with (C) as the answer that goes the furthest to undermine the author's argument.

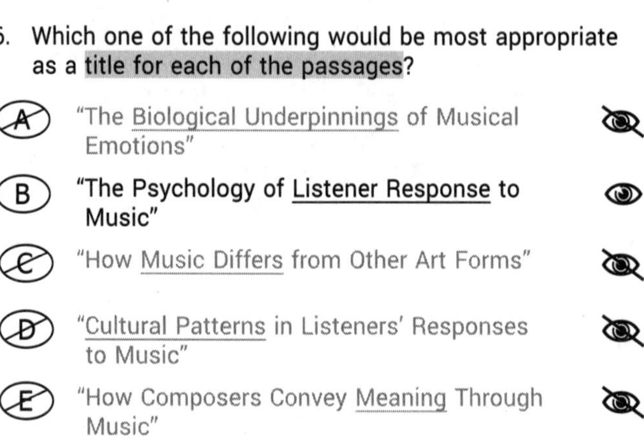

Here's How to Crack It

Step 2: Assess

This is a Big Picture: Main Point question (if you called it a Big Picture: Primary Purpose question, you were still on the right track). Note that it asks about "each of the passages," so the answer will have to fit with both.

Step 3: Act

Yet again, you have already done the necessary work in your preparation of the passages, with the Bottom Line of each and the relationship between the two.

Our Bottom Line of passage A is "Levels of complexity, coherence, and continuity affect pleasure of listener." Our Bottom Line of passage B is "Resolution of expectations, and complexity and familiarity, factor into the pleasure we find in music," and the relationship between passages A and B is "Both passages outline factors that affect our emotional response to music."

The correct answer has to be consistent with these Bottom Lines and this relationship.

Step 4: Answer

Choice (A) is out of scope. Neither passage says anything about biology. Be careful not to read too much into the fact that passage A mentions language or our brain's reaction to other types of sounds—you can't infer from this that the author is implying any common biological cause. (If you are unsure on that issue, you can still eliminate this choice based on passage B, which has no such references.) Along the same lines, you can't infer that either author attributes emotional reactions to biological causes.

Choice (B) is consistent with the Bottom Line of each passage and nicely matches our defined relationship between the two. "Pleasure" and "emotion" can definitely be directly connected to "psychology" without any outside knowledge or extra speculation, even if neither author explicitly uses that term.

Choice (C) is out of scope for both passages. Neither compares music to any other art form.

Choice (D) is also out of scope for both passage A and passage B. Neither passage talks about different cultures, nor how people in different cultures respond differently.

Choice (E) may be tempting, especially if you haven't defined the Bottom Lines and the relationship between the passages ahead of time. If you have, however, you will quickly see that neither is discussing meaning, but rather, emotional response of the listener.

This leaves you with (B) as the only possible answer.

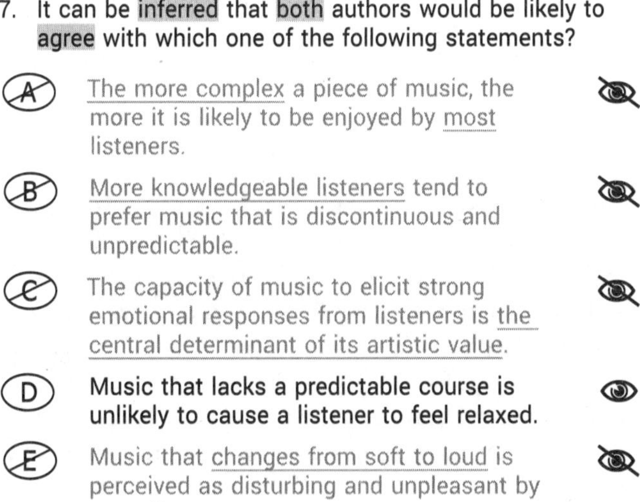
7. It can be inferred that both authors would be likely to agree with which one of the following statements?

(A) The more complex a piece of music, the more it is likely to be enjoyed by most listeners.

(B) More knowledgeable listeners tend to prefer music that is discontinuous and unpredictable.

(C) The capacity of music to elicit strong emotional responses from listeners is the central determinant of its artistic value.

(D) Music that lacks a predictable course is unlikely to cause a listener to feel relaxed.

(E) Music that changes from soft to loud is perceived as disturbing and unpleasant by most listeners.

Here's How to Crack It

Step 2: Assess

This is an Extract: Inference question. Note that it asks about both authors, meaning that it is asking for a statement that is supported by both passages, not just one or the other.

Step 3: Act

Because the question doesn't include any lead words referring to specific passage content, there is no work to be done with the texts before you move into POE.

Step 4: Answer

Notice the strength of language in (A). It indicates a linear relationship between complexity and enjoyment with no upper limit: the higher the complexity, the higher the enjoyment. This directly contradicts the first paragraph of passage A, in which the author states that "sounds that are too complex or disorganized, however, tend to be overwhelming" and therefore not enjoyable. And while the author of passage B does indicate in the last paragraph that trained listeners have a greater tolerance for and enjoyment of complexity, they do not go so far as to indicate that there is no upper limit even for these experienced listeners. Therefore, this choice is not supported by either passage.

The easiest way to eliminate (B) is that passage A never discusses how knowledgeable a listener might be. Furthermore, this choice is too extreme to be supported by the author of passage B. While the last paragraph indicates that knowledgeable listeners will have a greater preference and enjoyment of discontinuous and unpredictable music than "naive" or new listeners, they do not go so far as to say that knowledgeable listeners tend to prefer "discontinuous and unpredictable" music on the whole, but just that they have a "higher threshold" for these qualities.

Choice (C) starts off promisingly, with its reference to the ability of music to elicit emotional responses. However, it goes wrong when it states that this is "the central determinant of its artistic value." The strong wording "central determinant" should be a red flag, and neither author connects emotional response to artistic value of the music. Therefore, this choice is too extreme; if you called it "out of scope," you were also on the right track.

Choice (D) brings in an issue that you already know is discussed in both passages: the emotional effect of music on the listener and what kind of music will or will not be pleasurable. The main point of the last paragraph of passage A is that "People find continuous sounds relaxing, in music and in general," and the author directly stated in that last paragraph that people associate danger with "sudden, unexpected sounds." So, you can infer that the author of passage A would agree that unpredictable music will not relax the listener. As for passage B, the author states at the end of the first paragraph that when "resolution occurs, relaxation follows," and then goes on in the next paragraph to state that when what is expected does not occur, negative emotions result. Therefore, you can also infer that the author of passage B would agree with this choice. Leave it, and move on to (E).

Choice (E) is out of scope. Neither author makes any connection between change from soft to loud and the aspects of music that have an emotional effect on the listener. Be careful not to use outside knowledge or your own opinion to make a connection that is not made by the authors.

This leaves you with (D) as the only statement for which you have any evidence that both authors would accept it as true.

REFINING YOUR SKILLS

Now that you have learned and practiced the basic approach, here are some additional suggestions for further refining your strategy and continuing to improve your performance.

Previewing the Questions

As we mentioned earlier, many test-takers find it useful to preview the questions first, before reading the passage. What does previewing the questions entail? You quickly read through the question stems (not the answer choices), picking out references to passage content. Don't worry about identifying the question types in this stage; that comes later. Knowing what the questions are asking can help you to focus on the important information as you prepare the passage and to skim over the details that may or may not be important. If there is a reference in the question, go ahead and highlight that text in the passage (but don't jump in and read that section of the passage out of context). As you read the passage, when you come across a topic you recognize from the questions, pay special attention to that section, since you know that you will need it later on. An added benefit of previewing the questions is that having some context when you start to read the passage may well help you to better understand the author's argument the first time through.

Preview the Questions
Reading the questions first is an optional part of Step 1. Think of it like watching a preview before going to see a movie. You will already know some of the highlights and plot points, and will be better able to understand the story.

Try our four-step strategy—with and without previewing the questions—on two different sets of several passages. If you are not used to previewing, it will feel a bit strange at first. Practice it until you become comfortable with the approach, so that you can know for sure whether or not it is helpful for you. Once you have tried out both ways, choose the method that maximizes your efficiency and your accuracy, and use that approach consistently from then on.

There are a few things to keep in mind when previewing. First, it shouldn't take you more than 20–30 seconds per passage. You are not trying to memorize the questions, but rather to get a sense of what parts of the passage will be most important for answering the questions. Also, don't stop midway through the passage to answer questions, even if you think that you have the relevant information at that point. What the author says later on may affect the answer to that question. Also, for most of the questions it will be necessary to have a good understanding of the main point of the passage. If you stop reading in the middle of the process of preparing the passage, you will likely get distracted and have a harder time understanding the overall logic of the author's argument.

Pacing

Slowing Down

On most tests you have taken in your life, you can't get a good score without completing every question. The LSAT is not that kind of test! Many test-takers will maximize their overall percentage of correct answers on the Reading Comprehension section by randomly guessing on a certain number of questions and spending their time getting a high percentage of the rest of the questions correct. For many test-takers, that means pacing themselves such that they complete three of the four passages, filling in random guesses for all of the questions on one of the four. As you take more and more practice tests, evaluate your accuracy. If you are getting a high percentage of the questions wrong, and especially if a lot of those questions look fairly easy when you go back over them, that most likely means that you were working too fast and should slow down, at least at first until your accuracy improves, and perhaps even on the actual LSAT.

Speeding Up

On the other hand, if you are completing two or three passages with a high level of accuracy but can't get to a third or fourth passage, you may be going slower than you need, perhaps by reading the passage text much more carefully than necessary the first time through or by over-thinking the questions (which can actually also hurt your accuracy). If this is your situation, diagnose where you may be spending more time than necessary. Think about pushing yourself through the passage faster the first time through, not trying to read every word carefully or to understand every little detail. If you are moving through the passage quickly but bogging down in the questions, ask yourself if you are reading the question carefully the first time, getting what you need from the passage, and using that understanding to go through the choices (in more cases) no more than twice. Ask yourself how often you already had the right answer and then unnecessarily "triple-checked" it, or even spent more time talking yourself out of it and into a wrong answer. If this is often the case, push yourself through the choices more quickly, trusting your understanding and capacity to make accurate decisions.

Ordering The Questions

Many test-takers find it useful to do the questions in a particular order (within the set of questions attached to a passage). Some find it easier to first do the *Extract* or *Structure* questions that give you some concrete reference to the passage. By going back to the passage to answer these questions, they learn more about the author's argument and have more of a foundation for answering the rest of the set. Other test-takers prefer doing the *Big Picture* questions first, since they have just read the passage and defined the bottom line. Almost everyone does better by leaving the hardest questions within the set for last; these are often the *Application* questions, or any question that is long, convoluted, and hard to translate. Experiment with these different ordering strategies, find the one that works best for you, and use it consistently from that point on.

Self-Evaluation

Diagnosing the causes of your mistakes and refining your strategy based on that evaluation is crucial for continued improvement. Keep a self-evaluation journal or spreadsheet so that you can periodically review it and look for patterns in your own performance. For every question that you miss, or struggle with, ask and answer the following questions:

1. What was wrong with the answer I picked or seriously considered?
2. What attracted me to that wrong answer?
3. What led me to eliminate or just not select the correct answer?
4. What difference could I have seen between those two answers that would have helped me to get the question right or to get it right faster?
5. What will I do differently in the future?

Also look at questions you got right and passages you did well on, and ask yourself why, and what you can continue to do, and do more consistently, to reach that same high-performance level more consistently.

As you can see, there is not one specific characteristic that always makes a passage easier or harder. And the nature of the answer choices *can* significantly affect overall difficulty. As you work through the passages in this book and in the real LSATs you've ordered, note your impression of the passage's difficulty on the top of the page before you begin it. Afterward, check that impression against the reality of the passage—was your impression correct? If not, was there something you could have seen by reading the first few sentences and scanning the questions that would have led you to evaluate it more accurately? In this way, you will improve your skill in identifying which passages you should attempt and which you should avoid.

FINAL PASSAGE DRILL

As you do this passage, keep your main focus on strategy and accuracy, not on going as fast as you can. But, do keep track of the amount of time you spend on it so that you can begin to evaluate your pacing. Set a timer to count up but don't look at it while you work (put it in another room if you need to!). Once you are done, note your total time spent and go through the explanations that follow the passage. For every question that you missed, struggled with, or just spent too much time on, answer the self-evaluation questions outlined above.

This Passage and its questions are from PrepTest 124, Section 4, Passage 1, Questions 1–6.

Reading Comprehension Practice Drill

Answers can be found in Chapter 9.

Asian American poetry from Hawaii, the Pacific island state of the United States, is generally characterizable in one of two ways: either as portraying a model multicultural paradise, or as exemplifying familiar Asian American literary themes such as generational conflict. In this light, the recent work of Wing Tek Lum in *Expounding the Doubtful Points* is striking for its demand to be understood on its own terms. Lum offers no romanticized notions of multicultural life in Hawaii, and while he does explore themes of family, identity, history, and literary tradition, he does not do so at the expense of attempting to discover and retain a local sensibility. For Lum such a sensibility is informed by the fact that Hawaii's population, unlike that of the continental U.S., has historically consisted predominantly of people of Asian and Pacific island descent, making the experience of its Asian Americans somewhat different than that of mainland Asian Americans.

In one poem, Lum meditates on the ways in which a traditional Chinese lunar celebration he is attending at a local beach both connects him to and separates him from the past. In the company of new Chinese immigrants, the speaker realizes that while ties to the homeland are comforting and necessary, it is equally important to have "a sense of new family" in this new land of Hawaii, and hence a new identity—one that is sensitive to its new environment. The role of immigrants in this poem is significant in that, through their presence, Lum is able to refer both to the traditional culture of his ancestral homeland as well as to the flux within Hawaiian society that has been integral to its heterogeneity. Even in a laudatory poem to famous Chinese poet Li Po (701–762 A.D.), which partly serves to place Lum's work within a distinguished literary tradition, Lum refuses to offer a stereotypical nostalgia for the past, instead pointing out the often elitist tendencies inherent in the work of some traditionally acclaimed Chinese poets.

Lum closes his volume with a poem that further points to the complex relationships between heritage and local culture in determining one's identity. Pulling together images and figures as vastly disparate as a famous Chinese American literary character and an old woman selling bread, Lum avoids an excessively romantic vision of U.S. culture, while simultaneously acknowledging the dream of this culture held by many newly arrived immigrants. The central image of a communal pot where each person chooses what she or he wishes to eat but shares with others the "sweet soup / spooned out at the end of the meal" is a hopeful one; however, it also appears to caution that the strong cultural emphasis in the U.S. on individual drive and success that makes retaining a sense of homeland tradition difficult should be identified and responded to in ways that allow for a healthy new sense of identity to be formed.

1. Which one of the following most accurately expresses the main point of the passage?

(A) The poetry of Lum departs from other Asian American poetry from Hawaii in that it acknowledges its author's heritage but also expresses the poet's search for a new local identity.

(B) Lum's poetry is in part an expression of the conflict between a desire to participate in a community with shared traditions and values and a desire for individual success.

(C) Lum writes poetry that not only rejects features of the older literary tradition in which he participates but also rejects the popular literary traditions of Hawaiian writers.

(D) The poetry of Lum illustrates the extent to which Asian American writers living in Hawaii have a different cultural perspective than those living in the continental U.S.

(E) Lum's poetry is an unsuccessful attempt to manage the psychological burdens of reconciling a sense of tradition with a healthy sense of individual identity.

2. Given the information in the passage, which one of the following is Lum most likely to believe?

(A) Images in a poem should be explained in that poem so that their meaning will be widely understood.

(B) The experience of living away from one's homeland is necessary for developing a healthy perspective on one's cultural traditions.

(C) It is important to reconcile the values of individual achievement and enterprise with the desire to retain one's cultural traditions.

(D) One's identity is continually in transition and poetry is a way of developing a static identity.

(E) One cannot both seek a new identity and remain connected to one's cultural traditions.

3. The author of the passage uses the phrase "the flux within Hawaiian society" (middle of the second paragraph) primarily in order to

(A) describe the social tension created by the mix of attitudes exhibited by citizens of Hawaii

(B) deny that Hawaiian society is culturally distinct from that of the continental U.S.

(C) identify the process by which immigrants learn to adapt to their new communities

(D) refer to the constant change to which the culture in Hawaii is subject due to its diverse population

(E) emphasize the changing attitudes of many immigrants to Hawaii toward their traditional cultural norms

4. According to the passage, some Asian American literature from Hawaii has been characterized as which one of the following?

(A) inimical to the process of developing a local sensibility

(B) centered on the individual's drive to succeed

(C) concerned with conflicts between different age groups

(D) focused primarily on retaining ties to one's homeland

(E) tied to a search for a new sense of family in a new land

5. The author of the passage describes *Expounding the Doubtful Points* as "striking" (second sentence of the first paragraph) primarily in order to

(A) underscore the forceful and contentious tone of the work

(B) indicate that the work has not been properly analyzed by literary critics

(C) stress the radical difference between this work and Lum's earlier work

(D) emphasize the differences between this work and that of other Asian American poets from Hawaii

(E) highlight the innovative nature of Lum's experiments with poetic form

6. With which one of the following statements regarding Lum's poetry would the author of the passage be most likely to agree?

(A) It cannot be used to support any specific political ideology.

(B) It is an elegant demonstration of the poet's appreciation of the stylistic contributions of his literary forebears.

(C) It is most fruitfully understood as a meditation on the choice between new and old that confronts any human being in any culture.

(D) It conveys thoughtful assessments of both his ancestral homeland tradition and the culture in which he is attempting to build a new identity.

(E) It conveys Lum's antipathy toward tradition by juxtaposing traditional and nontraditional images.

Summary

- Here's our step-by-step approach to the Reading Comprehension section:

  Step 1: Prepare

  Step 2: Assess

  Step 3: Act

  Step 4: Answer

- Although you may be more familiar with Reading Comprehension than the other sections of this test, LSAT-style Reading Comprehension brings its own unique challenges and requires a particular strategic approach.
- Proper pacing is the key to a strong performance, and it will come only with a little experimentation and a lot of practice.
- Adjusting your everyday reading habits can also benefit your Reading Comprehension performance. Until you take the test, skip the clickbait and listicles and seek out more challenging reading.

Chapter 4
LSAT Writing

LSAT Writing is a 50-minute ungraded essay with an assigned topic. The LSAT Writing test is administered online separately from the LSAT and must be completed within a calendar year of your LSAT administration. Copies of your essay will be sent to law schools, along with your LSAT score, as part of your official report, so you'll want to do the best you can with the assignment you receive.

Writing Sample
Give this section all the time that an unscored section deserves.

HOW MUCH WILL MY ESSAY AFFECT MY LSAT SCORE?

Not one bit.

Only three sections contribute to your LSAT score: two Arguments sections, and one Reading Comprehension section.

If the Writing Test Is So Unimportant, Why Discuss It?

Just for your own peace of mind. Once you have the other sections of the test under control, look over the rest of this chapter. If you are short on time, you'd be better off practicing Arguments.

There's also the possibility that an admissions officer will pass their eyes over what you have written. If your essay is ungrammatical, riddled with misspellings, off the topic, and wildly disorganized, the admissions officer may think less of you.

Now, we're going to assume that the Writing Test counts a little bit. You should assume the same thing, but don't lose sleep over it. No one ever got into law school because of the LSAT Writing, and it's doubtful that anyone ever got rejected because of it either. Besides, good writing requires surprisingly few rules, and the rules we'll review will help your writing in general.

WHO WILL READ MY ESSAY?

Possibly no one.

How well or poorly you do on the LSAT Writing will almost certainly not affect your admissions chances.

THEN WHY DO LAW SCHOOLS REQUIRE IT?

Law schools feel guilty about not being interested in anything about you other than your grades and LSAT scores. Knowing that you have spent 50 minutes writing an essay for them makes them feel better about having no interest in reading what you have written.

WILL THE TEST CHANGE?

Always be sure to check the LSAC website at www.lsac.org for any updates to the test.

WHAT ARE THEY LOOKING FOR?

The general directions to the Writing Test mention that law schools are interested in three things: essay organization, vocabulary, and writing mechanics. Presumably, writing mechanics covers grammar and style.

What They're Really Looking For

Researchers at Educational Testing Service (the folks responsible for the SAT and the GRE, among other tests) once did a study of essay-grading behavior. They wanted to find out what their graders really responded to when they marked papers, and which essay characteristics correlated most strongly with good scores.

The researchers discovered that the most important characteristic, other than "overall organization," is "essay length." Also highly correlated with good essay scores are the number of paragraphs, average sentence length, and average word length. The bottom line? *Students who filled in all the lines, indented frequently, and used big words earned higher scores than students who didn't.*

We will discuss these points in more detail later. Because organization is the most important characteristic, let's start with that.

THE PROMPT

The prompt will present you with a debatable issue along with several different perspectives on the issue. You'll be asked a key question to address in your essay, but the prompt also asks you to engage with at least one of the perspectives provided in your argument. You can practice writing an essay with a sample prompt on LawHub.

What Am I Trying to Do?

You're trying to make an argument that supports your position on the issue with evidence. You cannot *prove* that any one side is better; you can only make a case that it is. The test-writers deliberately come up with a highly debatable issue so that you can choose a position from a large set of possibilities.

Just choose a position and justify your choice.

Picking Sides

The writing test asks you to make an argument as part of an ongoing conversation on a debatable issue. This means that no position is "correct." It doesn't matter what position you choose, so go with one that gives you more to work with.

Another way to decide is to compile a little list of the pros and cons on your scratch paper. Then simply pick the position whose list of pros is longer.

Every LSAT prompt instructs you to make a decision and develop an argument for it. Use the skills you've honed from the Arguments section of the test to help!

First, list each perspective as a heading. Underneath each heading draw two columns, one for the pros and one for the cons. Spend the first couple of minutes brainstorming the advantages and disadvantages of each choice. The key to brainstorming is *quantity,* not quality. You can select and discard points later.

Having brainstormed for pros and cons, select the ones you intend to keep and arrange them in order of importance, from *least* to *most* important.

Don't Forget the Cons

Some students believe that if you're trying to make a case for something, you should bring up the advantages only. This is wrong.

To persuade readers that your position is the stronger one, you must show that you have considered the arguments for other perspectives and found each one unconvincing.

Your argument, in other words, must show that you have weighed the pros and cons of different perspectives. The more forceful the objections you counter, the more compelling your position becomes.

Can I Raise Other Perspectives?

You *must* address at least one other perspective on the issue, but nothing prevents you from introducing additional considerations.

You need not address the other perspectives, or raise additional considerations, but if your position relates to other perspectives, and you have the time, you should include them in your argument. If none occurs to you, mention in the conclusion that you have addressed only one (or two) other perspectives on the issue, acknowledging that other considerations may be important.

Brainstorming the Pros and Cons

Remember, brainstorm first. You can use the scratch area to put your ideas before you dive into writing the essay. Start by making some bullets about your perspective on the issue. It will be easier to write the essay if you believe what you are saying. Next, read through the different perspectives provided in the prompt. Your essay will need to include at least one of these perspectives so take notes about how they relate to your argument. Look for other opinions that provide support for your argument directly. Alternatively, your argument may offer a compelling counter to one of the perspectives. Use all the pre-writing time you have to read the perspectives and brainstorm ideas.

Beginning Your Essay: Restating the Problem

Having brainstormed the relationships of the perspectives with your own argument, you are ready to start writing your essay. Your first paragraph should do little more than state your argument. Try not to use a tedious grade school opening such as, "The purpose of the essay I am about to write is to...." There are several more interesting ways to introduce an argument. Which one you choose will influence how you organize the rest of your essay. Keep this in mind as you sketch your outline. We'll tell you more about this as we go along. One possibility for an opening is simply to restate concisely the problem you are to address. This type of introduction sets up the conflict rather than immediately taking a side. The second, third, and fourth paragraphs are then devoted to weighing specific points of the argument. In this format, the author's preference isn't stated explicitly until the final paragraph, although a clear case for one should emerge as the essay progresses.

An essay such as this is really just an organized written version of the mental processes you went through in deciding your own view of the controversial issue and interacting with each of the perspectives. In the first paragraph you say, in effect, "Here are the problems, some different perspectives, and my decision." In the second, third, and fourth paragraphs you say, "Here are the pros and cons I weighed." In the fifth and final paragraph you say, "So you can see why I believe as I do." Your hope is that the reader, by following your reasoning step by step, will decide the same thing. The great advantage of this kind of organization is that it *does* follow your mental processes. That makes it a natural and relatively easy method.

Beginning Your Essay: Putting Your Cards on the Table

It's also possible to write an essay in which you begin by announcing your opinion. You state your argument in the first paragraph, back it up in the middle paragraphs, and then restate your preference with a concluding flourish in the final paragraph.

By introducing your argument in this way, you leave yourself with a great deal of latitude for handling the succeeding paragraphs. For example, you might use the second paragraph to discuss one of the perspectives and how it relates to your own opinion on the issue, the third paragraph to discuss a second perspective, and the fourth and final paragraph to summarize your argument.

The Body of Your Argument

We've discussed the introductory and concluding paragraphs. Depending on your argument and on the essay topic you actually confront, we recommend two variations for the middle paragraphs.

Variation 1

Paragraph 2: Write about one of the perspectives and how it relates to your own view on the issue.

Paragraph 3: Write about a second perspective and how it relates to your own view on the issue.

Variation 2

Paragraph 2: Choose one part of your argument and show how different perspectives relate to that topic. Use evidence to show how the perspectives support your argument.

Paragraph 3: Choose another part of your argument and show how the perspectives relate to it. Use evidence to support your position over another.

If necessary, you can divide any one of the middle paragraphs into two paragraphs. Both variations do the job. Choose a variation you feel comfortable with and memorize it. The less thinking you have to do on the actual exam, the better.

The Princeton Review Thesaurus of Pretty Impressive Words

The following list of words is not meant to be complete, nor is it in any particular order. Synonyms or related concepts are grouped where appropriate.

- example, instance, precedent, paradigm, archetype
- illustrate, demonstrate, highlight, acknowledge, exemplify, embody
- support, endorse, advocate, maintain, contend, espouse, champion
- supporter, proponent, advocate, adherent
- dispute, dismiss, outweigh, rebut, refute
- propose, advance, submit, marshal, adduce
- premise, principle, presumption, assumption, proposition
- advantages, merits, benefits
- inherent, intrinsic, pertinent
- indisputable, incontrovertible, inarguable, unassailable, irrefutable, undeniable, unimpeachable
- unconvincing, inconclusive, dubious, specious
- compelling, cogent, persuasive
- empirical, hypothetical, theoretical

Rules to Write By

1. Write as if you were actually making the recommendation.
2. Write naturally, but don't use abbreviations or contractions.
3. Make sure your position is clear.
4. Write as neatly as possible.
5. Indent your paragraphs.

A Note on Diction

Make sure you don't spoil your display of verbal virtuosity by misusing or misspelling these or any other ten-dollar words. Also, get your idioms straight.

A note on a common diction error: if, as in our writing sample, your choice involves only two options, *former* refers to the first and *latter* refers to the second. You cannot use these words to refer to more than two options.

Another common diction error occurs when two or more things are compared. The first option is *better* than the second, but it is not the *best,* which is used when discussing three or more options.

One Final Reminder

Don't forget to use spell-check.

Summary

- Don't worry about the LSAT Writing test. As long as you spend a little time brainstorming and outlining your essay, this inconsequential section should be no problem.

Chapter 5
Putting It All Together

You've worked through four pretty arduous chapters of *LSAT Premium Prep*. How should you feel? Answer: CONFIDENT! Why? Because you've been given a specific process and approach for each section of the LSAT. You've got a good game plan—and the team with the good game plan usually wins the game. This chapter contains a quick review of your game plan for each section of the exam, as well as some pacing suggestions and tips for the day of the test.

ARGUMENTS

Step 1: Assess the question

Step 2: Analyze the argument

Step 3: Act

Step 4: Answer using Process of Elimination

Pretty simple, right? Well, many people begin to get anxious and they tend to skip Step 3. They want to get right to the answer choices so they can start getting confused and frustrated. However, Step 3 is the most important step in this process. If you come up with your own ideas about what should be the right answer before looking at any of the choices, you'll be misled less often by those appealing but wrong answer choices.

READING COMPREHENSION

Step 1: Prepare

Step 2: Assess

Step 3: Act

Step 4: Answer

Well, here we've once again highlighted Step 3 because it's the most important step and it's the one students tend to skip most often. Again, nervousness about time is the culprit. But as you learned in the Reading Comprehension chapter, pinpointing the correct answer choice becomes much easier when you've already got an idea of what you should be looking for. Don't let the answer choices confuse you—approach the test questions by being ready for them as much as possible.

PACING

The most important principle to keep in mind when you're planning your pacing is balance. Remember that there are two things that determine effective pacing: your speed (the number of questions you attempt) and your accuracy (the chance that, when you attempt a question, you will get it right). Generally, as your speed increases, your accuracy decreases. The challenge is to find the peak pacing strategy for yourself on each section.

The only way to do this effectively is through practice, practice, practice, and analysis, analysis, analysis. Most test-takers do not perform optimally if they charge through at maximum speed. Similarly, dawdling and second-guessing yourself will not get you the most points. You need to adopt a strategy that allows you to slow down in the places you need to, but at the same time keeps you pushing through the questions that come more easily to you so you can devote time where it's needed.

The ideal way to strike this balance differs from section to section and is determined by the different natures of the questions. We have some more specific pacing guidelines for you below, but of course, knowing what target you have to hit is different from knowing how it feels to hit that target. To that end, here are some general pacing thoughts on each of the sections of the exam.

Arguments

On Arguments, the initial investment for a question is relatively small; and on many Arguments questions, there are things you can do to decide between close answer choices—but only up to a point.

The best approach here is to value speed and accuracy equally. On an easy Arguments question (there are usually many of these toward the beginning of the section), you should be able to proceed through POE and spot one that definitely looks best. In that case, pick it and go.

On a medium Arguments question, you may have two or three answer choices that seem possible. In that case, slow down—look at the conclusion of the argument, review the question if you're uncertain what it's asking you to do, look at the choices carefully, and make close comparisons. Making smart decisions in the down-to-two situation is how you make your money on the Arguments sections.

On difficult Arguments questions (many of these will be near the end of the section), mistrust answers that look extremely attractive. Keep an open mind as you look at the others, and if you're down to two here, follow the same process you use for medium questions. Look for subtle problems. If you can't find them, then go with the choice you thought was right at first and move on. However, if an answer looks too good to be true on a hard question, it probably is.

Pacing
Trust your gut.
You know the difference between chipping away at a difficult question and spinning your wheels trying to comprehend what you are reading.

If you begin an Arguments question and it baffles you right away, move on. You can always come back to it, and you haven't lost much if you spend just a little time and then decide to do something else. Similarly, if you've done everything you can in that down-to-two situation and have nothing else to go on, pick the answer you like better and move on. It takes only one or two questions that eat up a lot of time to hurt you on an Arguments section. Be willing to slow down, but don't ever stop.

Reading Comprehension

Speed and efficiency are important on Reading Comprehension. Remember that you don't get points for memorizing the passage; you're reading it to find the answers to the questions. Get through the initial preparation of the passage fairly quickly without getting bogged down in the details; you can always come back for them later. In this stage, avoid reading parts of the passage over and over; keep moving and come back to difficult sections of the passage only if necessary when answering the questions. However, you *do* need to get a basic understanding of the bottom line of the author's argument. Don't read the passage so quickly that you get little or nothing out of it.

Don't just skim the questions or answer choices in the Assess, Act, and Answer steps; read them carefully, word for word. Always go back to the passage when you are answering the questions. Read for context; don't answer the questions based on only a quick glance at isolated words or phrases from the passage. When you are down to two answer choices, compare them with each other and look for relevant differences. You may need to go back to the passage again at this stage to make a final choice. If you are still stuck, take your best shot, remembering how the test-writers create attractive wrong answers, and continue on. You can come back one more time before you move on to the next passage; sometimes getting a little distance from the question helps you to see what you didn't understand at first. However, don't spend a large percentage of your valuable time on a single question.

Evaluate each passage and the questions very quickly before diving in. If it looks nasty from the outset, then move to another passage; otherwise, start the passage and stick with it.

Here's a chart to help you assess your performance on the practice tests.

Pacing Yourself			
If you received...	**Your first goal is...**	**Your intermediate goal is...**	**Your final goal is...**
25–45% correct on Arguments	Work 12–15 Arguments and try to get 10–12 right in 35 minutes	Work 15–18 Arguments and try to get 12–15 right in 35 minutes	Work 18–21 Arguments and try to get 15–18 right in 35 minutes
45–65% correct on Arguments	Work 15–18 Arguments and try to get 12–15 right in 35 minutes	Work 18–21 Arguments and try to get 15–18 right in 35 minutes	Work 21–24 Arguments and try to get 18–21 right in 35 minutes
65–85% correct on Arguments	Work 18–21 Arguments and try to get 15–18 right in 35 minutes	Work 21–24 Arguments and try to get 18–21 right in 35 minutes	Work all the Arguments and try to get 20–23 right in 35 minutes
20–35% correct on Reading Comprehension	Do two Reading Comprehension passages in 35 minutes, trying to miss only one question per passage	Do two full Reading Comprehension passages and get halfway through a third passage in 35 minutes	Do three full Reading Comprehension passages in 35 minutes
35–50% correct on Reading Comprehension	Do two full Reading Comprehension passages and get halfway through a third passage in 35 minutes	Do three full Reading Comprehension passages in 35 minutes	Do three full Reading Comprehension passages and get halfway through the fourth passage in 35 minutes
50–80% correct on Reading Comprehension	Do three Reading Comprehension passages in 35 minutes, trying to miss only one question per passage	Do three full Reading Comprehension passages and get halfway through the fourth passage in 35 minutes	Do four full Reading Comprehension passages in 35 minutes

This is a general chart. Don't worry about being so exact here.

EVALUATING YOUR PERFORMANCE

One of the most important things you can do to continue to improve your score is to analyze the work you do in order to better gauge both the areas in which you're making errors and the amount of time you need to spend on a given question or group of questions to ensure a high level of accuracy. Here we'll discuss several ways to accomplish this.

As we recommended for the practice drills that accompany each of the chapters on Arguments and Reading Comprehension, it's a good idea to measure how long it takes you to do a passage or set of arguments accurately. There's no point rushing to get to questions (and wasting brain power) if you're not going to give yourself the opportunity to get those questions right. Remember, your score is based on how many questions you answer correctly, not on how many questions you actually get to attempt (and of course you're still choosing answers for those you don't attempt). By measuring how long it takes, on average, to work accurately through a passage or group of, say, eight arguments, you can build realistic expectations of how much you'll be able to do on a given timed section. This is important because it can help you set reachable goals for each area of the LSAT—for example, you can't expect to get to all four passages if you generally need to spend 15 minutes on just one of them.

To measure your work time, set your timer to count up, not down, and then don't look at it while you're working. Put it face down, in a drawer, or even in another room if necessary. When you've finished working, stop the clock and note the time elapsed. Then check your answers to see how accurate you were. If you missed half or more, you're definitely going too quickly. If, however, you got almost all of them correct, then you can start to think about where you might be able to speed up. Did you linger at an answer choice to convince yourself that it was really right, although you knew the other four choices were unequivocally wrong? As you continue to work questions, you'll eventually find that you hit your optimal speed for each section—if you go any slower, you won't get to the number of questions you know you need to answer to reach your goal, but if you work any faster, your careless errors will increase sharply.

Once you have an idea of how many questions you can reasonably expect to get to, you can start to figure out how you're going to get the score you want. Let's say you're aiming for a 160. You'd need approximately 75 correct answers to achieve that score. (You should use the conversion chart from the most recent LSAT you've ordered when making these estimates.) Perhaps Reading Comprehension is one of your strengths, so you can count on 23 out of 27 questions. Or maybe you average about 18 correct on an Arguments section. That leaves 16 that you'll need to pick up in the other Arguments section. Are you stronger in Arguments? Then your goal might be 20 on each Arguments section, with a Reading Comprehension goal of 17. Is your goal a 150? That's about 56 questions. How you break that down will be up to you, based on your own strengths and weaknesses.

As with all things on the LSAT, however, it's important not to overanalyze. Not all Arguments or Reading Comprehension sections are the same, which means you shouldn't expect to do the same on every one of them you work. Keep this in mind while you're planning your pacing adjustments and also while you're taking your test. If you came up a little short on Reading Comprehension, don't panic; chances are that you'll be able to pick up the slack on Arguments as long as you give yourself the chance. Setting goals is important, and it's important to have a plan for achieving them, but always be willing to improvise. Focus on what you can control, and take the test as it comes.

Okay, you've figured out how many more questions you need to get right to achieve your goal score. How do you go about fixing your errors? You want to keep track of your progress, preferably in a notebook, on each drill or timed section you do. Analysis is the key to better performance. After each drill or timed section, write down the drill or section number, and for each question you did, note the question number, question type, whether you got it right or wrong, and what happened if you did indeed miss it. After a while, you may begin to see patterns emerge. Maybe you always miss questions that ask what "must be false" because you forget the "false," or you constantly pick answer choices that go beyond the scope of a passage; or you lose focus when tackling EXCEPT questions. Or maybe there's a particular question type you keep misidentifying, or you're not picking the best questions for you to attempt. Whatever the problem is, you have to be able to diagnose it before you can fix it. Keeping track of your progress and reviewing the notes you make about questions you miss will help you further structure your preparation.

ADDITIONAL PRACTICE TIPS

Here are a few final, extra things to think about.

- Try to time your LSAT practice to the time of day you'll be taking the real thing. At the very least, start your practice tests at the same time that the real test will be given. For an afternoon test administration, this means you'll want to concentrate your study time during the afternoon; for all other administrations of the test, you'll want to practice in the morning.
- If you're taking a practice test with only three sections, it's a really good idea to take an extra section from one of the real LSATs you've ordered and use it as an experimental section when taking full-length practice tests. It will build your stamina, and it will give you a chance to practice with an extra section of each type of question because you never know what question type you could see as an experimental section on test day. Even when doing individual timed sections, try to do a couple of sections back-to-back before checking your answers. Get used to focusing for longer periods of time.
- Don't forget to check out our free online tools at PrincetonReview.com/prep. You just need to have this book handy when you log in for the first time.

Up-to-date Information: Check out www.lsac.org for more information about specifics: locations, dates, and restrictions.

THE DAY OF THE TEST

There is probably just as much bad advice as good advice dispensed about what to do on test day. A lot of the good advice is just common sense, but we're going to give it to you here just in case you're a bit distracted.

Visit Your Test Location Before Test Day

Why worry on test day about the best way to get to your test location? If you don't plan to take the test at home, visit your test location a few weeks or days before the test so you know exactly where to go on test day. Better yet, go there with a practice LSAT and try to get into the room where you're going to take the LSAT. Work the test in that room, if possible, so you're on familiar ground the day of the test. This will do wonders for your comfort and confidence. You'll know if the room is hot or cold, what the lighting is like, whether you'll be working at an individual desk or a long table, and so on. Use the Boy Scout motto here: be prepared.

Eat and Drink What You Normally Eat and Drink

People have many different ideas about what to eat and drink on the morning of the test. The most important thing is not to vary dramatically from what you normally ingest. Don't eat a big, heavy breakfast that will leave you sluggish. Don't skip breakfast completely. Eat a reasonable meal that will prepare you for a grueling three-and-a-half-hour test. And don't experiment with caffeine. If you don't normally have coffee in the morning, don't start on test day. If you do normally have coffee in the morning, don't skip it on test day. The same advice applies if you get your caffeine from soda or any other caffeinated beverage.

Take a Snack

You can leave the testing room and have a snack during the 10-minute break if you choose to. Be prepared by having a bottle of water and a granola bar or a banana ready to go. You're not allowed to eat in the testing room, but you can always go outside and fuel up for the second half of the test.

Use the Timer

LSAC does not permit the use of digital timers, but there is a timer built into the online exam. You can turn off the timer if you want to, but we recommend using the timer or an analog watch to track your time. You'll get a digital five-minute warning, so be sure to answer any remaining questions before the time is up.

Take Everything You'll Need

Yes, you will need to log into the testing website and present proper identification. Some allowed items you may want to have ready are a pen or pencil, five blank sheets of scratch paper, a highlighter, tissues, and a bottle of water. Refer to the registration instructions and follow the procedures outlined there. Don't leave any room for the unexpected.

Get There Nice and Early and Warm Up Your Brain

You're going to be stressed out enough on test day without worrying that you'll be late for the test. Get to wherever you plan to take the test nice and early and warm up your brain by running through a few arguments. And don't bother to check the answers; the purpose is warming up, not diagnosis. That way, you'll already be in gear by the time you open up the first section. You want to hit the ground running so you won't be warming up on questions that count toward your score.

Some Stress Is Good; Too Much Stress Is Bad

We know you're going to be stressed the day of the exam, and a little stress is not a bad thing—it will keep you on your toes. But if you tend to get *really* stressed by standardized tests, try a yoga or meditation class, or some other type of relaxation therapy, preferably starting a month before the test. This way, you'll have some techniques to calm you down, taught to you by people who know what they're doing. One Princeton Review student had a dream about test day—she went into the test, and the bubbles were about five feet in diameter. She hadn't even finished bubbling in one bubble before the proctor called time. If you're having dreams like this, relaxation therapy might help.

Wear Layered Clothing

If you plan to take the test somewhere other than your home, who knows how cold or how warm the test location will be on test day? Wear your most comfortable layered clothing so you can put more layers on if you're cold or take layers off if you're hot.

Be Confident and Be Aggressive

When we talk to students after they've taken the LSAT, they often say, "By the time I got to section 4, I just didn't care anymore. I just filled in whatever." Don't say that; don't think that—section 4 will probably count because the experimental section could be any of the four sections. When you begin section 4, keep in mind that it's most likely a real section that will count toward your score. Your goal is to take three deep breaths and to fight your way through that last section, and approach it just as aggressively as you approached the other sections of the exam. It's going to count—don't lose your confidence and your energy here because it's almost over!

Here is another problem students have reported: "I was doing fine until I hit section 3. I really struggled with the Reading passages, and I couldn't concentrate on the last two sections of the test." Well, guess what? That was probably the experimental section! Don't let a complex or tough section get you down, especially if it's early in the test. Remember that they are using the experimental sections to test new questions—some of them invariably will be a bit strange. And even if it is a section that ultimately counts toward your score, getting stressed out over it will only hurt your performance on that section and potentially on subsequent scored sections as well. Just roll with the punches.

Your Test Day "Top Ten"

Here are the tips mentioned above in a handy numbered list. Find some room on the fridge.

1. Visit your test location before test day.
2. Eat and drink what you normally eat and drink.
3. Take a snack.
4. Use the timer.
5. Take everything you'll need.
6. Get there nice and early and warm up your brain.
7. Some stress is good; too much stress is bad.
8. Wear layered clothing.
9. Be confident and be aggressive.
10. Always keep your cursor moving.

Good luck on test day!

Always Keep Your Cursor Moving

Actively using your online tools and scratch paper will help you to stay engaged. Eliminate all the wrong answer choices; highlight and underline key words in Reading Comprehension and Arguments passages. By constantly keeping your cursor moving, you'll be keeping your brain moving as well.

If you find that you're losing focus, stop working for a second and regroup. Never waste time working on a question if your mind has gone astray or if you find that you can't focus on the task at hand. The few seconds you invest in a short break will pay off in the long run.

And remember that you can always come back to a question that is giving you grief. Just flag it so that you can find it later if you have time to come back to it. Don't spend too much time on any one question. It will only lead to frustration and lost points.

Summary

- As you practice, your approach will become more intuitive. Until then, be sure to focus on the steps we've outlined so that you have a systematic approach for every section of the test. Most important, do not forget to do a little work before rushing to the answer choices.
- Make sure you are totally prepared for test day. You can't control the questions you will see that day, but you can make sure that you are in the best position to answer those questions.

Chapter 6
Law School Admissions

The process of applying to law school, although simple enough in theory, is viewed by many to be about as painful as a root canal. The best way to avoid the pain is to start early. If you're reading this in December, hoping to get into a law school for the following year, and haven't done anything about it, you're in big trouble. If you've got an LSAT score that you're happy with, you're in less trouble. However, your applications will get to the law schools after the optimum time and the applications themselves, even with the most cursory glance by an admissions officer, may appear rushed. The best way to think about applying is to start early in the year, take care of one thing at a time, and be totally finished by December.

This chapter is mainly a nuts-and-bolts manual on how to apply to law school and when to do it. A checklist, information about Law School Forums, fee waivers, the Credential Assembly Service (CAS), and several admissions calendars, which will show you when you need to take which step, are included.

LSAC, LSAT, CAS

The Law School Admission Council (LSAC), headquartered in Newtown, Pennsylvania, is the governing body that oversees the creation, testing, and administration of the LSAT (Law School Admission Test). The LSAC also runs the Credential Assembly Service (CAS), which provides information (in a standard format) on law school applicants to the schools themselves. All American Bar Association, or ABA-approved, law schools are members of LSAC.

LSAT SCORE DISTRIBUTION

Most test-takers are interested in knowing where their LSAT scores fall within the distribution of all scores. This chart should help you determine how well you did in comparison to fellow test takers over the last few years. Please be aware, however, that percentiles are not fixed values that remain constant over time. Unlike an LSAT score, a percentile rank associated with a given test score may vary slightly depending on the year in which it is reported. This chart is just to give you a roughly accurate idea where you rank compared to those competing for the same spot in law school.

Score	% Below	Score	% Below	Score	% Below	Score	% Below
180	99.9	165	93.2	150	44.9	135	5.3
179	99.9	164	91.4	149	41.0	134	4.4
178	99.9	163	89.7	148	37.0	133	3.5
177	99.8	162	87.3	147	33.4	132	2.9
176	99.7	161	84.9	146	29.6	131	2.3
175	99.6	160	82.2	145	26.4	130	1.9
174	99.5	159	79.1	144	23.3	129	1.5
173	99.3	158	76.5	143	20.2	128	1.2
172	99.0	157	72.6	142	17.7	127	0.9
171	98.5	156	68.7	141	15.2	126	0.7
170	98.1	155	65.7	140	12.9	125	0.6
169	97.5	154	61.5	139	10.9	124	0.5
168	96.7	153	57.3	138	9.2	123	0.4
167	95.7	152	53.2	137	7.8	122	0.3
166	94.6	151	49.1	136	6.5	121	0.3
						120	0.0

WHEN TO APPLY

Consider these application deadlines for fall admission: Yale Law School, on or about February 15; New York University (NYU) Law School, on or about February 15; Loyola University Chicago School of Law, on or about May 1. Although some of this information may make starting the application process in December seem like a viable option, remember that law schools don't wait until they've received every application to start selecting students. In fact, the longer you wait to apply to a school, the worse your chances are of getting into that school. Maybe your chances will go only from 90 percent to 85 percent, but you shouldn't take an unnecessary risk by waiting.

Additionally, some schools have "early admissions decisions" options, so that you may know by December if you've been accepted (for instance, NYU's early admission deadline is on or about November 15). This option is good for a few reasons: it can give you an indication of what your chances are at other schools; it can relieve the stress of waiting until April to see where you're going to school; and if you're put on the waiting list the first time around, you might be accepted a bit later on in the process—i.e., when everyone else is hearing from law schools for the first time. However, not every school has an early admission option, and not every school's option is the same, so check with your prospective institutions' policies before you write any deadlines on your calendar.

Law School Forums

Law School Forums are an excellent way to talk with representatives and gather information on almost every law school in the country simultaneously. More than 150 schools send admissions officers to these forums, which take place in major cities around the country between February and October. If at all possible, GO. For information about forum dates and locations, check the LSAC website at www.lsac.org.

Let's take a look at the major steps in the application process.

- **Take the LSAT.** All ABA-approved and most non-ABA-approved law schools in the United States and Canada accept an LSAT score from each applicant. The LSAT is offered multiple times each year. Some schools may accept a GRE score from students who have not taken the LSAT.
- **Register for CAS.** You can register online for the Credential Assembly Service at the same time you register to take the LSAT.
- **Select approximately seven schools.** After you've selected your schools, you'll be able to see which schools want what types of things on their applications—although almost all of them will want three basic things: a personal statement, recommendations, and a résumé. Each applicant should be thinking about putting law schools into three categories: (1) "reach" schools, (2) schools where you've got a good chance of being accepted, and (3) "safety" schools. At a minimum, each applicant should apply to two to three schools in each category. (Most admissions experts will say either 2-2-3 or 2-3-2.) It is not uncommon for those with extremely low grades or low LSAT scores (or both) to apply to 15 or 20 schools.
- **Write your personal statement(s).** It may be that you'll need to write only one personal statement (many schools will ask that your personal statement be about why you want to obtain a law degree), but you may need to write several—which is why you need to select your schools fairly early.
- **Obtain two or three recommendations.** Some schools will ask for two recommendations, at least one of which should be academic (both if you are a recent graduate). Others want more than two recommendations and want at least one of your recommenders to be someone who knows you outside traditional academic circles.

- **Update/create a résumé.** Most law school applications ask that you submit a résumé. Make sure yours is up to date and suitable for submission to an academic institution.
- **Get your academic transcripts sent to CAS.** A minor administrative detail, seemingly, but then again, if you forget to do this, CAS will not send your information to the law schools. CAS helps the law schools by acting as a clearinghouse for information—CAS, not you, sends the law schools your undergraduate and graduate school transcripts, your LSAT score(s), and an undergraduate academic summary.

Those are the major steps in applying to law school. From reading this chapter, you might discover that there are other steps you need to take—such as preparing an addendum to your application, asking for application fee waivers, applying for a special administration of the LSAT, and so on. If you sense that you might need to do anything special, start your application process even earlier than what is recommended. One LSAC sample schedule recommends taking the June LSAT for fall admission the following year. This schedule allows you to focus on the LSAT in the spring and early summer and then start the rest of your application process rolling. That's good advice—as mentioned in the LSAT portion of this book, the LSAT is one of the most important factors in getting into the best law school possible.

The sample schedule also indicates that you should research schools in late July/early August. While you are doing this, go ahead and subscribe to CAS and send your transcript request forms to your undergraduate and any other educational institutions—there's no reason to wait until September to do this (you should pay CAS for seven law school applications, unless you're positive you want to apply to only a few schools). Why do this? Because undergraduate institutions can and will make mistakes and delay the transcript process—even when you go there personally and pay them to provide your records. This is essential if you're applying for early decision at some law schools—the transcript process can be a nightmare.

Finally, you should send your applications to law schools between late September and early November. Naturally, if you bombed the LSAT the first time around, you're still in good shape to take the test again in October. Another good piece of news on that front is that more and more law schools are now just simply taking the highest LSAT score that each applicant has, rather than averaging multiple scores. If you have to take the LSAT again, this is good news—but with proper preparation, you can avoid having to spend too much quality time with the LSAT.

A Simple Checklist

The following is a simple checklist for the major steps of the application process. Each shaded box indicates the recommended month during which you should complete that action.

	Jan.	Feb.	Mar.	Apr.	May	June	July	Aug.	Sept.	Oct.	Nov.	Dec.
Take practice LSAT	■											
Research LSAT prep companies		■										
Obtain Registration Information Book			■									
Register for June LSAT				■								
Take LSAT prep course				■	■	■						
Take LSAT						■						
Register for Credential Assembly Service (CAS)—formerly known as the Law School Data Assembly Service							■					
Research law schools							■					
Obtain law school applications								■				
Get transcripts sent to CAS								■				
Write personal statement(s)									■			
Update/create résumé									■			
Get recommendations									■			
Send early decision applications										■		
Finish sending all applications											■	
Relax												■

HELPFUL HINTS ON PERSONAL STATEMENTS, RECOMMENDATIONS, RÉSUMÉS, AND ADDENDA

Although your LSAT score is one of the most important factors in the admissions process, you should still present a professional résumé, get excellent recommendations, and hone your personal statement when preparing your law school applications.

Many law schools still employ the "three-pile" system in the application process.

Pile 1 contains applicants with high enough LSAT scores and GPAs to admit them pretty much automatically.

Pile 2 contains applicants who are "borderline"—decent enough LSAT scores and GPAs for that school but not high enough for automatic admission. Admissions officers look at these applications thoroughly to sort out the best candidates.

Pile 3 contains applicants with "substandard" LSAT scores and GPAs for that school. These applicants are usually rejected without much further ado. There are circumstances in which admissions officers will look through pile 3 for any extraordinary applications, but it doesn't happen very often.

What does this mean? Well, if you're lucky, you are in pile 2 (and not pile 3!) for at least one of your "reach" schools. And if you are, there's a good possibility that your application will be thoroughly scrutinized by the admissions committee. Consequently, make sure the following four elements of your application are as strong as you can possibly make them.

Personal Statement

Ideally, your personal statement should be two pages long. Often, law schools will ask you to identify exactly why you want to go to law school and obtain a law degree. "I love *How To Get Away with Murder*" is not the answer to this question. There should be some moment in your life, some experience that you had, or some intellectual slant that you are interested in that is directing you to law school. Identify that reason, write about it, and make it compelling.

Then you should have three or four people read your personal statement and critique it. You should select people whom you respect intellectually, not people who will merely give it a cursory read and tell you it's fine. Also, your personal statement is not the place to make excuses, get on your soapbox, or try your hand at alliterative verse. Make it intelligent, persuasive, short, and powerful—those are the writing and analytical qualities law schools look for.

Recommendations

Most law schools ask for two or three recommendations. Typically, the longer it has been since you've graduated, the tougher it is to obtain academic recommendations. However, if you've kept your papers and if your professors were tenured, chances are you'll still be able to find them and obtain good recommendations—just present your prof of choice with your personal statement and a decent paper you did in their course. That way, the recommender has something tangible to work from. And that's the simple secret to great recommendations—if the people you're asking for recommendations don't know anything specific about you, how can the recommendation possibly be compelling? Getting the mayor of your town or a state senator to write a recommendation helps only if you have a personal and professional connection to them in some way. That way, the recommender will be able to present to the admissions committee actual qualities and accomplishments you have demonstrated.

Fee Waivers

Even though the cost of taking the LSAT, subscribing to CAS, paying for LSAT prep materials, and paying application fees will probably be one-hundredth of your total law school outlay, it's still not just a drop in the bucket. The LSAT is $220, CAS is $200 (includes one report sent to a CAS-requiring law school and three letters of recommendation), plus $45 for each additional school you are applying to. And law school applications themselves are typically around $50 each. As a result, LSAC, as well as most law schools, offers a fee waiver program. If you're accepted into the LSAC program, you get two free LSATs per year, one LSAT Writing, one CAS subscription, and four CAS law school reports. With proper documentation, you can also waive a good portion of your law school application fees. You can apply for a fee waiver through your LSAC.org account.

If you've been out of school for some time and are having trouble finding academic recommendations, choose people from your workplace, from the community, or from any other area of your life that is important to you. You should respect the people you choose—you should view them as quality individuals who have in some way shaped your life. If they're half as good as you think they are, they will know, at least intuitively, that they in some way were responsible for part of your development or education, and they will then be able to talk intelligently about it. Simply put, these people should know who you are, where you live, what your background is, and what your desires and motivations are—otherwise, your recommendations will not distinguish you from the 10-foot-high pile that's on an admissions committee desk.

Résumés

Résumés are a fairly simple part of your application, but make sure yours is updated and proofed correctly. Errors on your résumé (and, indeed, anywhere on your application) will make you look as if you don't really care too much about going to law school. Just remember that this should be a more academically oriented résumé, because you are applying to an academic institution. Put your academic credentials and experiences first—no matter what they are.

Addenda

If your personal and academic life has run fairly smoothly, you shouldn't need to include any addenda with your application. Addenda are brief explanatory letters written to explain or support a "deficient" portion of your application. Some legitimate addenda topics are academic probation, low/discrepant GPA, low/discrepant LSAT score, arrests/convictions, DUI/DWI suspensions, a leave of absence or other "time gaps," and other similar circumstances.

The addenda are not the place to go off on polemics about standardized testing—if you've taken the LSAT two or three times and simply did not do very well, after spending time preparing with a test prep company or private tutor, merely tell the admissions committee that that's what you've done—you worked as hard as you could to achieve a high score and explored all possibilities to help you achieve that goal. Then let them draw their own conclusions. Additionally, addenda should be brief and balanced—do not go into detailed descriptions of things. Explain the problem and state what you did about it. Simply put, do not whine.

GATHERING INFORMATION AND MAKING DECISIONS

There are some key questions that you should ask before randomly selecting law schools around the country or submitting your application to someone or other's list of the "top ten" law schools and saying, "If I don't get in to one of these schools, I'll go to B-School instead." Here are some questions to think about.

Where Would You Like to Practice Law?

For instance, if you were born and bred in the state of Nebraska, care deeply about it, wish to practice law there, and want to someday be governor, then it might be a better move to go to the University of Nebraska School of Law than, say, the University of Virginia, even though UVA is considered a "top ten" law school. A law school's reputation is usually greater on its home turf than anywhere else (except for Harvard and Yale). Apply to the schools in the geographic area where you wish to practice law. You'll be integrated into the community, you may gain some experience in the region doing clinics during law school, and it should be easier for you to get more interviews and position yourself as someone who already knows, for instance, Nebraska.

What Type of Law Would You Like to Practice?

Law schools *do* have specialties. For instance, if you are very interested in environmental law, it might be better to go to Vermont Law School than to go to NYU. Vermont Law School is one of the most highly regarded schools in the country when it comes to environmental law; so look at what you want to do in addition to where you want to do it.

Can You Get In?

Many people apply to Harvard. Very few get in. Go right ahead and apply, if you wish, but unless you've got killer scores and/or have done some very outstanding things in your life, your chances are, well, *slim*. Apply to a few reach schools, but make sure they are schools you really want to go to.

Did You Like the School When You Went There?

What if you decided to go to Stanford, got in, went to Palo Alto, California, and decided that you hated it? The weather was horrible! The architecture was mundane! There's nothing to do nearby! Well, maybe Stanford wasn't the best example—but you get the point. Go to the school and check it out. Talk to students and faculty. Walk around. *Then* make a decision.

Summary

- The application process, although detailed, is much easier than taking the extremely stressful LSAT, which in turn will be much easier than your first year of law school—no matter where you go. However, you've still got to *want* to go to law school. Applying to law school is a demanding process, and if you're not committed to doing it well, it will almost certainly come across in your applications. Be as thorough in preparing your applications as you were in preparing for the LSAT; otherwise you run the risk of turning in applications that are late or contain errors, thereby hurting your chances of getting accepted by the schools to which you really want to go.
- If all this administrative stuff seems overwhelming (i.e., you're the type of person who dreads filling out a deposit slip), the major test-prep companies have designed law school application courses that force you to think about where you want to go and make sure you've got all your recommendations, résumés, personal statements, addenda, and everything else together.
- Whatever your level of administrative faculty, the choice of where you want to go to school is yours. You'll probably be paying a lot of money to go, so you should really make sure you go to the place that's best for you. Take the time to research the schools because you'll be paying for law school for a long, long time.

Chapter 7
Arguments Practice

The questions in this section are from PrepTest 125, Section 2, Questions 1–26.

Arguments Practice

Answers can be found in Chapter 9.

1. Executive: Our company is proud of its long history of good relations with its employees. In fact, a recent survey of our retirees proves that we treat our employees fairly, since 95 percent of the respondents reported that they had always been treated fairly during the course of their careers with us.

The executive's argument is flawed in that it

(A) presents as its sole premise a claim that one would accept as true only if one already accepted the truth of the conclusion

(B) relies on evidence that cannot be verified

(C) equivocates on the word "fairly"

(D) bases a generalization on a sample that may not be representative

(E) presumes, without providing justification, that older methods of managing employees are superior to newer ones

2. Many of those who are most opposed to cruelty to animals in the laboratory, in the slaughterhouse, or on the farm are people who truly love animals and who keep pets. The vast majority of domestic pets, however, are dogs and cats, and both of these species are usually fed meat. Therefore, many of those who are most opposed to cruelty to animals do, in fact, contribute to such cruelty.

Which one of the following is an assumption made by the argument?

(A) Loving pets requires loving all forms of animal life.

(B) Many of those who are opposed to keeping dogs and cats as pets are also opposed to cruelty to animals.

(C) Some people who work in laboratories, in slaughterhouses, or on farms are opposed to cruelty to animals.

(D) Many popular pets are not usually fed meat.

(E) Feeding meat to pets contributes to cruelty to animals.

3. Statistics from the National Booksellers Association indicate that during the last five years most bookstores have started to experience declining revenues from the sale of fiction, despite national campaigns to encourage people to read more fiction. Therefore, these reading campaigns have been largely unsuccessful.

   Which one of the following statements, if true, most seriously weakens the argument?

(A) Mail order book clubs have enjoyed substantial growth in fiction sales throughout the last five years.

(B) During the last five years the most profitable items in bookstores have been newspapers and periodicals rather than novels.

(C) Fierce competition has forced booksellers to make drastic markdowns on the cover price of best-selling biographies.

(D) Due to the poor economic conditions that have prevailed during the last five years, most libraries report substantial increases in the number of patrons seeking books on changing careers and starting new businesses.

(E) The National Booksellers Association statistics do not include profits from selling novels by mail to overseas customers.

4. People who consume a lot of honey tend to have fewer cavities than others have. Yet, honey is high in sugar, and sugar is one of the leading causes of tooth decay.

   Which one of the following, if true, most helps to resolve the apparent paradox described above?

(A) People who eat a lot of honey tend to consume very little sugar from other sources.

(B) Many people who consume a lot of honey consume much of it dissolved in drinks.

(C) People's dental hygiene habits vary greatly.

(D) Refined sugars have been linked to more health problems than have unrefined sugars.

(E) Honey contains bacteria that inhibit the growth of the bacteria that cause tooth decay.

5. Byrne: One of our club's bylaws specifies that any officer who fails to appear on time for any one of the quarterly board meetings, or who misses two of our monthly general meetings, must be suspended. Thibodeaux, an officer, was recently suspended. But Thibodeaux has never missed a monthly general meeting. Therefore, Thibodeaux must have failed to appear on time for a quarterly board meeting.

   The reasoning in Byrne's argument is flawed in that the argument

(A) fails to consider the possibility that Thibodeaux has arrived late for two or more monthly general meetings

(B) presumes, without providing justification, that if certain events each produce a particular result, then no other event is sufficient to produce that result

(C) takes for granted that an assumption required to establish the argument's conclusion is sufficient to establish that conclusion

(D) fails to specify at what point someone arriving at a club meeting is officially deemed late

(E) does not specify how long Thibodeaux has been an officer

6. Manufacturers of writing paper need to add mineral "filler" to paper pulp if the paper made from the pulp is to look white. Without such filler, paper products look grayish. To make writing paper that looks white from recycled paper requires more filler than is required to make such paper from other sources. Therefore, barring the more efficient use of fillers in paper manufacturing or the development of paper-whitening technologies that do not require mineral fillers, if writing paper made from recycled paper comes to replace other types of writing paper, paper manufacturers will have to use more filler than they now use.

Which one of the following is an assumption on which the argument depends?

(A) Certain kinds of paper cannot be manufactured from recycled paper.

(B) The fillers that are used to make paper white are harmful to the environment.

(C) Grayish writing paper will not be a universally acceptable alternative to white writing paper.

(D) Beyond a certain limit, increasing the amount of filler added to paper pulp does not increase the whiteness of the paper made from the pulp.

(E) The total amount of writing paper manufactured worldwide will increase significantly in the future.

7. Environmentalist: The excessive atmospheric buildup of carbon dioxide, which threatens the welfare of everyone in the world, can be stopped only by reducing the burning of fossil fuels. Any country imposing the strict emission standards on the industrial burning of such fuels that this reduction requires, however, would thereby reduce its gross national product. No nation will be willing to bear singlehandedly the costs of an action that will benefit everyone. It is obvious, then, that the catastrophic consequences of excessive atmospheric carbon dioxide are unavoidable unless ______.

Which one of the following most logically completes the argument?

(A) all nations become less concerned with pollution than with the economic burdens of preventing it

(B) multinational corporations agree to voluntary strict emission standards

(C) international agreements produce industrial emission standards

(D) distrust among nations is eliminated

(E) a world government is established

8. A clear advantage of digital technology over traditional printing is that digital documents, being patterns of electronic signals rather than patterns of ink on paper, do not generate waste in the course of their production and use. However, because patterns of electronic signals are necessarily ephemeral, a digital document can easily be destroyed and lost forever.

The statements above best illustrate which one of the following generalizations?

(A) A property of a technology may constitute an advantage in one set of circumstances and a disadvantage in others.

(B) What at first appears to be an advantage of a technology may create more problems than it solves.

(C) It is more important to be able to preserve information than it is for information to be easily accessible.

(D) Innovations in document storage technologies sometimes decrease, but never eliminate, the risk of destroying documents.

(E) Advances in technology can lead to increases in both convenience and environmental soundness.

9. Museum visitor: The national government has mandated a 5 percent increase in the minimum wage paid to all workers. This mandate will adversely affect the museum-going public. The museum's revenue does not currently exceed its expenses, and since the mandate will significantly increase the museum's operating expenses, the museum will be forced either to raise admission fees or to decrease services.

Which one of the following is an assumption required by the museum visitor's argument?

(A) Some of the museum's employees are not paid significantly more than the minimum wage.

(B) The museum's revenue from admission fees has remained constant over the past five years.

(C) Some of the museum's employees are paid more than the current minimum wage.

(D) The annual number of visitors to the museum has increased steadily.

(E) Not all visitors to the museum are required to pay an admission fee.

10. Helen: Reading a book is the intellectual equivalent of investing money: you're investing time, thereby foregoing other ways of spending that time, in the hope that what you learn will later afford you more opportunities than you'd get by spending the time doing something other than reading that book.

Randi: But that applies only to vocational books. Reading fiction is like watching a sitcom: it's just wasted time.

Which one of the following most accurately describes the technique Randi uses in responding to Helen's claims?

(A) questioning how the evidence Helen uses for a claim was gathered

(B) disputing the scope of Helen's analogy by presenting another analogy

(C) arguing that Helen's reasoning ultimately leads to an absurd conclusion

(D) drawing an analogy to an example presented by Helen

(E) denying the relevance of an example presented by Helen

11. Contrary to recent speculations, no hardware store will be opening in the shopping plaza. If somebody were going to open a store there, they would already have started publicizing it. But there has been no such publicity.

Which one of the following most accurately expresses the conclusion drawn in the argument?

(A) Some people have surmised that a hardware store will be opening in the shopping plaza.

(B) A hardware store will not be opening in the shopping plaza.

(C) If somebody were going to open a hardware store in the shopping plaza, that person would already have started publicizing it.

(D) It would be unwise to open a hardware store in the shopping plaza.

(E) There has been no publicity concerning the opening of a hardware store in the shopping plaza.

12. Ethicist: Although science is frequently said to be morally neutral, it has a traditional value system of its own. For example, scientists sometimes foresee that a line of theoretical research they are pursuing will yield applications that could seriously harm people, animals, or the environment. Yet, according to science's traditional value system, such consequences do not have to be considered in deciding whether to pursue that research. Ordinary morality, in contrast, requires that we take the foreseeable consequences of our actions into account whenever we are deciding what to do.

The ethicist's statements, if true, most strongly support which one of the following?

(A) Scientists should not be held responsible for the consequences of their research.

(B) According to the dictates of ordinary morality, scientists doing research that ultimately turns out to yield harmful applications are acting immorally.

(C) Science is morally neutral because it assigns no value to the consequences of theoretical research.

(D) It is possible for scientists to both adhere to the traditional values of their field and violate a principle of ordinary morality.

(E) The uses and effects of scientifically acquired knowledge can never be adequately foreseen.

13. Consumers seek to purchase the highest quality at the lowest prices. Companies that do not offer products that attract consumers eventually go bankrupt. Therefore, companies that offer neither the best quality nor the lowest price will eventually go bankrupt.

The conclusion above follows logically if which one of the following is assumed?

(A) No company succeeds in producing a product that is both highest in quality and lowest in price.

(B) Products that are neither highest in quality nor lowest in price do not attract consumers.

(C) Any company that offers either the highest quality or the lowest price will avoid bankruptcy.

(D) Some consumers will not continue to patronize a company purely out of brand loyalty.

(E) No company is driven from the market for reasons other than failing to meet consumer demands.

14. The number of serious traffic accidents (accidents resulting in hospitalization or death) that occurred on Park Road from 1986 to 1990 was 35 percent lower than the number of serious accidents from 1981 to 1985. The speed limit on Park Road was lowered in 1986. Hence, the reduction of the speed limit led to the decrease in serious accidents.

Which one of the following statements, if true, most weakens the argument?

(A) The number of speeding tickets issued annually on Park Road remained roughly constant from 1981 to 1990.

(B) Beginning in 1986, police patrolled Park Road much less frequently than in 1985 and previous years.

(C) The annual number of vehicles using Park Road decreased significantly and steadily from 1981 to 1990.

(D) The annual number of accidents on Park Road that did not result in hospitalization remained roughly constant from 1981 to 1990.

(E) Until 1986 accidents were classified as "serious" only if they resulted in an extended hospital stay.

15. Humans are supposedly rational: in other words, they have a capacity for well-considered thinking and behavior. This is supposedly the difference that makes them superior to other animals. But humans knowingly pollute the world's precious air and water and, through bad farming practices, deplete the soil that feeds them. Thus, humans are not rational after all, so it is absurd to regard them as superior to other animals.

The reasoning above is flawed in that it

(A) relies crucially on an internally contradictory definition of rationality

(B) takes for granted that humans are aware that their acts are irrational

(C) neglects to show that the irrational acts perpetrated by humans are not also perpetrated by other animals

(D) presumes, without offering justification, that humans are no worse than other animals

(E) fails to recognize that humans may possess a capacity without displaying it in a given activity

16. "Good hunter" and "bad hunter" are standard terms in the study of cats. Good hunters can kill prey that weigh up to half their body weight. All good hunters have a high muscle-to-fat ratio. Most wild cats are good hunters, but some domestic cats are good hunters as well.

If the statements above are true, which one of the following must also be true?

(A) Some cats that have a high muscle-to-fat ratio are not good hunters.

(B) A smaller number of domestic cats than wild cats have a high muscle-to-fat ratio.

(C) All cats that are bad hunters have a low muscle-to-fat ratio.

(D) Some cats that have a high muscle-to-fat ratio are domestic.

(E) All cats that have a high muscle-to-fat ratio can kill prey that weigh up to half their body weight.

17. Ethicist: The penalties for drunk driving are far more severe when the drunk driver accidentally injures people than when no one is injured. Moral responsibility for an action depends solely on the intentions underlying the action and not on the action's results. Therefore, legal responsibility, depending as it does in at least some cases on factors other than the agent's intentions, is different than moral responsibility.

The claim that the penalties for drunk driving are far more severe when the drunk driver accidentally injures people than when no one is injured plays which one of the following roles in the ethicist's argument?

(A) It is a premise offered in support of the claim that legal responsibility for an action is based solely upon features of the action that are generally unintended by the agent.

(B) It is offered as an illustration of the claim that the criteria of legal responsibility for an action include but are not the same as those for moral responsibility.

(C) It is offered as an illustration of the claim that people may be held morally responsible for an action for which they are not legally responsible.

(D) It is a premise offered in support of the claim that legal responsibility depends in at least some cases on factors other than the agent's intentions.

(E) It is a premise offered in support of the claim that moral responsibility depends solely on the intentions underlying the action and not on the action's result.

18. Columnist: Taking a strong position on an issue makes one likely to misinterpret or ignore additional evidence that conflicts with one's stand. But in order to understand an issue fully, it is essential to consider such evidence impartially. Thus, it is best not to take a strong position on an issue unless one has already considered all important evidence conflicting with that position.

The columnist's reasoning most closely conforms to which one of the following principles?

(A) It is reasonable to take a strong position on an issue if one fully understands the issue and has considered the evidence regarding that issue impartially.

(B) To ensure that one has impartially considered the evidence regarding an issue on which one has taken a strong position, one should avoid misinterpreting or ignoring evidence regarding that issue.

(C) Anyone who does not understand an issue fully should avoid taking a strong position on it.

(D) One should try to understand an issue fully if doing so will help one to avoid misinterpreting or ignoring evidence regarding that issue.

(E) It is reasonable to take a strong position on an issue only if there is important evidence conflicting with that position.

19. The coach of the Eagles used a computer analysis to determine the best combinations of players for games. The analysis revealed that the team has lost only when Jennifer was not playing. Although no computer was needed to discover this information, this sort of information is valuable, and in this case it confirms that Jennifer's presence in the game will ensure that the Eagles will win.

The argument above is most vulnerable to criticism on the grounds that it

(A) infers from the fact that a certain factor is sufficient for a result that the absence of that factor is necessary for the opposite result

(B) presumes, without providing justification, that a player's contribution to a team's win or loss can be reliably quantified and analyzed by computer

(C) draws conclusions about applications of computer analyses to sports from the evidence of a single case

(D) presumes, without providing justification, that occurrences that have coincided in the past must continue to coincide

(E) draws a conclusion about the value of computer analyses from a case in which computer analysis provided no facts beyond what was already known

20. Of the various food containers made of recycled Styrofoam, egg cartons are among the easiest to make. Because egg shells keep the actual food to be consumed from touching the Styrofoam, used Styrofoam need not be as thoroughly cleaned when made into egg cartons as when made into other food containers.

Which one of the following is most strongly supported by the information above?

(A) No food containers other than egg cartons can safely be made of recycled Styrofoam that has not been thoroughly cleaned.

(B) There are some foods that cannot be packaged in recycled Styrofoam no matter how the Styrofoam is recycled.

(C) The main reason Styrofoam must be thoroughly cleaned when recycled is to remove any residual food that has come into contact with the Styrofoam.

(D) Because they are among the easiest food containers to make from recycled Styrofoam, most egg cartons are made from recycled Styrofoam.

(E) Not every type of food container made of recycled Styrofoam is effectively prevented from coming into contact with the food it contains.

21. Most people who become migraine sufferers as adults were prone to bouts of depression as children. Hence it stands to reason that a child who is prone to bouts of depression is likely to suffer migraines during adulthood.

The flawed pattern of reasoning in the argument above is most parallel to that in which one of the following?

(A) Most good-tempered dogs were vaccinated against rabies as puppies. Therefore, a puppy that is vaccinated against rabies is likely to become a good-tempered dog.

(B) Most vicious dogs were ill-treated when young. Hence it can be concluded that a pet owner whose dog is vicious is likely to have treated the dog badly when it was young.

(C) Most well-behaved dogs have undergone obedience training. Thus, if a dog has not undergone obedience training, it will not be well behaved.

(D) Most of the pets taken to veterinarians are dogs. Therefore, it stands to reason that dogs are more prone to illness or accident than are other pets.

(E) Most puppies are taken from their mothers at the age of eight weeks. Thus, a puppy that is older than eight weeks is likely to have been taken from its mother.

22. Student: The publications of Professor Vallejo on the origins of glassblowing have reopened the debate among historians over whether glassblowing originated in Egypt or elsewhere. If Professor Vallejo is correct, there is insufficient evidence for claiming, as most historians have done for many years, that glassblowing began in Egypt. So, despite the fact that the traditional view is still maintained by the majority of historians, if Professor Vallejo is correct, we must conclude that glassblowing originated elsewhere.

Which one of the following is an error in the student's reasoning?

(A) It draws a conclusion that conflicts with the majority opinion of experts.

(B) It presupposes the truth of Professor Vallejo's claims.

(C) It fails to provide criteria for determining adequate historical evidence.

(D) It mistakes the majority view for the traditional view.

(E) It confuses inadequate evidence for truth with evidence for falsity.

23. At Southgate Mall, mattresses are sold only at Mattress Madness. Every mattress at Mattress Madness is on sale at a 20 percent discount. So every mattress for sale at Southgate Mall is on sale at a 20 percent discount.

Which one of the following arguments is most similar in its reasoning to the argument above?

(A) The only food in Diane's apartment is in her refrigerator. All the food she purchased within the past week is in her refrigerator. Therefore, she purchased all the food in her apartment within the past week.

(B) Diane's refrigerator, and all the food in it, is in her apartment. Diane purchased all the food in her refrigerator within the past week. Therefore, she purchased all the food in her apartment within the past week.

(C) All the food in Diane's apartment is in her refrigerator. Diane purchased all the food in her refrigerator within the past week. Therefore, she purchased all the food in her apartment within the past week.

(D) The only food in Diane's apartment is in her refrigerator. Diane purchased all the food in her refrigerator within the past week. Therefore, all the food she purchased within the past week is in her apartment.

(E) The only food that Diane has purchased within the past week is in her refrigerator. All the food that she has purchased within the past week is in her apartment. Therefore, all the food in her apartment is in her refrigerator.

24. There are 1.3 billion cows worldwide, and this population is growing to keep pace with the demand for meat and milk. These cows produce trillions of liters of methane gas yearly, and this methane contributes to global warming. The majority of the world's cows are given relatively low-quality diets even though cows produce less methane when they receive better-quality diets. Therefore, methane production from cows could be kept in check if cows were given better-quality diets.

Which one of the following, if true, adds the most support for the conclusion of the argument?

(A) Cows given good-quality diets produce much more meat and milk than they would produce otherwise.

(B) Carbon and hydrogen, the elements that make up methane, are found in abundance in the components of all types of cow feed.

(C) Most farmers would be willing to give their cows high-quality feed if the cost of that feed were lower.

(D) Worldwide, more methane is produced by cows raised for meat production than by those raised for milk production.

(E) Per liter, methane contributes more to global warming than does carbon dioxide, a gas that is thought to be the most significant contributor to global warming.

25. To face danger solely because doing so affords one a certain pleasure does not constitute courage. Real courage is manifested only when a person, in acting to attain a goal, perseveres in the face of fear prompted by one or more dangers involved.

Which one of the following statements can be properly inferred from the statements above?

(A) A person who must face danger in order to avoid future pain cannot properly be called courageous for doing so.

(B) A person who experiences fear of some aspects of a dangerous situation cannot be said to act courageously in that situation.

(C) A person who happens to derive pleasure from some dangerous activities is not a courageous person.

(D) A person who faces danger in order to benefit others is acting courageously only if the person is afraid of the danger.

(E) A person who has no fear of the situations that everyone else would fear cannot be said to be courageous in any situation.

26. The government will purchase and install new severe weather sirens for this area next year if replacement parts for the old sirens are difficult to obtain. The newspaper claims that public safety in the event of severe weather would be enhanced if new sirens were to be installed. The local company from which replacement parts were purchased last year has since gone out of business. So, if the newspaper is correct, the public will be safer during severe weather in the future.

    The argument's conclusion follows logically from its premises if which one of the following is assumed?

(A) If public safety in the event of severe weather is enhanced next year, it will be because new sirens have been purchased.

(B) The newspaper was correct in claiming that public safety in the event of severe weather would be enhanced if new sirens were purchased.

(C) The local company from which replacement parts for the old sirens were purchased last year was the only company in the area that sold them.

(D) Replacement parts for the old sirens will be difficult to obtain if the government cannot obtain them from the company it purchased them from last year.

(E) Because the local company from which replacement parts had been purchased went out of business, the only available parts are of such inferior quality that use of them would make the sirens less reliable.

Chapter 8
Reading Comprehension Practice

The passages and questions in this section are from PrepTest 125, Section 1, Questions 1–27.

Reading Comprehension Practice

Answers can be found in Chapter 9.

This passage was adapted from an article published in 1996.

The Internet is a system of computer networks that allows individuals and organizations to communicate freely with other Internet users throughout the world. As a result, an astonishing variety of information is able to flow unimpeded across national and other political borders, presenting serious difficulties for traditional approaches to legislation and law enforcement, to which such borders are crucial.

Control over physical space and the objects located in it is a defining attribute of sovereignty. Lawmaking presupposes some mechanism for enforcement, i.e., the ability to control violations. But jurisdictions cannot control the information and transactions flowing across their borders via the Internet. For example, a government might seek to intercept transmissions that propagate the kinds of consumer fraud that it regulates within its jurisdiction. But the volume of electronic communications crossing its territorial boundaries is too great to allow for effective control over individual transmissions. In order to deny its citizens access to specific materials, a government would thus have to prevent them from using the Internet altogether. Such a draconian measure would almost certainly be extremely unpopular, since most affected citizens would probably feel that the benefits of using the Internet decidedly outweigh the risks.

One legal domain that is especially sensitive to geographical considerations is that governing trademarks. There is no global registration of trademarks; international protection requires registration in each country. Moreover, within a country, the same name can sometimes be used proprietarily by businesses of different kinds in the same locality, or by businesses of the same kind in different localities, on the grounds that use of the trademark by one such business does not affect the others. But with the advent of the Internet, a business name can be displayed in such a way as to be accessible from any computer connected to the Internet anywhere in the world. Should such a display advertising a restaurant in Norway be deemed to infringe a trademark in Brazil just because it can be accessed freely from Brazil? It is not clear that any particular country's trademark authorities possess, or should possess, jurisdiction over such displays. Otherwise, any use of a trademark on the Internet could be subject to the jurisdiction of every country simultaneously.

The Internet also gives rise to situations in which regulation is needed but cannot be provided within the existing framework. For example, electronic communications, which may pass through many different territorial jurisdictions, pose perplexing new questions about the nature and adequacy of privacy protections. Should French officials have lawful access to messages traveling via the Internet from Canada to Japan? This is just one among many questions that collectively challenge the notion that the Internet can be effectively controlled by the existing system of territorial jurisdictions.

1. Which one of the following most accurately expresses the main point of the passage?

(A) The high-volume, global nature of activity on the Internet undermines the feasibility of controlling it through legal frameworks that presuppose geographic boundaries.

(B) The system of Internet communications simultaneously promotes and weakens the power of national governments to control their citizens' speech and financial transactions.

(C) People value the benefits of their participation on the Internet so highly that they would strongly oppose any government efforts to regulate their Internet activity.

(D) Internet communications are responsible for a substantial increase in the volume and severity of global crime.

(E) Current Internet usage and its future expansion pose a clear threat to the internal political stability of many nations.

2. The author mentions French officials in connection with messages traveling between Canada and Japan (second-to-last sentence of the passage) primarily to

(A) emphasize that the Internet allows data to be made available to users worldwide

(B) illustrate the range of languages that might be used on the Internet

(C) provide an example of a regulatory problem arising when an electronic communication intended for a particular destination passes through intermediate jurisdictions

(D) show why any use of a trademark on the Internet could be subject to the jurisdiction of every country simultaneously

(E) highlight the kind of international cooperation that made the Internet possible

3. According to the passage, which one of the following is an essential property of political sovereignty?

(A) control over business enterprises operating across territorial boundaries

(B) authority over communicative exchanges occurring within a specified jurisdiction

(C) power to regulate trademarks throughout a circumscribed geographic region

(D) control over the entities included within a designated physical space

(E) authority over all commercial transactions involving any of its citizens

4. Which one of the following words employed by the author in the second paragraph is most indicative of the author's attitude toward any hypothetical measure a government might enact to deny its citizens access to the Internet?

(A) benefits

(B) decidedly

(C) unpopular

(D) draconian

(E) risks

5. What is the main purpose of the fourth paragraph?

(A) to call into question the relevance of the argument provided in the second paragraph

(B) to provide a practical illustration that questions the general claim made in the first paragraph

(C) to summarize the arguments provided in the second and third paragraphs

(D) to continue the argument that begins in the third paragraph

(E) to provide an additional argument in support of the general claim made in the first paragraph

Passage A

Drilling fluids, including the various mixtures known as drilling muds, play essential roles in oil-well drilling. As they are circulated down through the drill pipe and back up the well itself, they lubricate the drill bit, bearings, and drill pipe; clean and cool the drill bit as it cuts into the rock; lift rock chips (cuttings) to the surface; provide information about what is happening downhole, allowing the drillers to monitor the behavior, flow rate, pressure, and composition of the drilling fluid; and maintain well pressure to control cave-ins.

Drilling muds are made of bentonite and other clays and polymers, mixed with a fluid to the desired viscosity. By far the largest ingredient of drilling muds, by weight, is barite, a very heavy mineral of density 4.3 to 4.6. It is also used as an inert filler in some foods and is more familiar in its medical use as the "barium meal" administered before X-raying the digestive tract.

Over the years individual drilling companies and their expert drillers have devised proprietary formulations, or mud "recipes," to deal with specific types of drilling jobs. One problem in studying the effects of drilling waste discharges is that the drilling fluids are made from a range of over 1,000, sometimes toxic, ingredients—many of them known, confusingly, by different trade names, generic descriptions, chemical formulae, and regional or industry slang words, and many of them kept secret by companies or individual formulators.

Passage B

Drilling mud, cuttings, and associated chemicals are normally released only during the drilling phase of a well's existence. These discharges are the main environmental concern in offshore oil production, and their use is tightly regulated. The discharges are closely monitored by the offshore operator, and releases are controlled as a condition of the operating permit.

One type of mud—water-based mud (WBM)—is a mixture of water, bentonite clay, and chemical additives, and is used to drill shallow parts of wells. It is not particularly toxic to marine organisms and disperses readily. Under current regulations, it can be dumped directly overboard. Companies typically recycle WBMs until their properties are no longer suitable and then, over a period of hours, dump the entire batch into the sea.

For drilling deeper wells, oil-based mud (OBM) is normally used. The typical difference from WBM is the high content of mineral oil (typically 30 percent). OBMs also contain greater concentrations of barite, a powdered heavy mineral, and a number of additives. OBMs have a greater potential for negative environmental impact, partly because they do not disperse as readily. Barite may impact some organisms, particularly scallops, and the mineral oil may have toxic effects. Currently only the residues of OBMs adhering to cuttings that remain after the cuttings are sieved from the drilling fluids may be discharged overboard, and then only mixtures up to a specified maximum oil content.

6. A primary purpose of each of the passages is to

(A) provide causal explanations for a type of environmental pollution

(B) describe the general composition and properties of drilling muds

(C) point out possible environmental impacts associated with oil drilling

(D) explain why oil-well drilling requires the use of drilling muds

(E) identify difficulties inherent in the regulation of oil-well drilling operations

7. Which one of the following is a characteristic of barite that is mentioned in both of the passages?

(A) It does not disperse readily in seawater.

(B) It is not found in drilling muds containing bentonite.

(C) Its use in drilling muds is tightly regulated.

(D) It is the most commonly used ingredient in drilling muds.

(E) It is a heavy mineral.

8. Each of the following is supported by one or both of the passages EXCEPT:

(A) Clay is an important constituent of many, if not all, drilling muds.

(B) At least one type of drilling mud is not significantly toxic to marine life.

(C) There has been some study of the environmental effects of drilling-mud discharges.

(D) Government regulations allow drilling muds to contain 30 percent mineral oil.

(E) During the drilling of an oil well, drilling mud is continuously discharged into the sea.

9. Which one of the following can be most reasonably inferred from the two passages taken together, but not from either one individually?

(A) Barite is the largest ingredient of drilling muds, by weight, and also the most environmentally damaging.

(B) Although barite can be harmful to marine organisms, it can be consumed safely by humans.

(C) Offshore drilling is more damaging to the environment than is land-based drilling.

(D) The use of drilling muds needs to be more tightly controlled by government.

(E) If offshore drilling did not generate cuttings, it would be less harmful to the environment.

10. Each of the following is supported by one or both of the passages EXCEPT:

(A) Drillers monitor the suitability of the mud they are using.

(B) The government requires drilling companies to disclose all ingredients used in their drilling muds.

(C) In certain quantities, barite is not toxic to humans.

(D) Oil reserves can be found within or beneath layers of rock.

(E) Drilling deep oil wells requires the use of different mud recipes than does drilling shallow oil wells.

11. Based on information in the passages, which one of the following, if true, provides the strongest support for a prediction that the proportion of oil-well drilling using OBMs will increase in the future?

(A) The cost of certain ingredients in WBMs is expected to increase steadily over the next several decades.

(B) The deeper an offshore oil well, the greater the concentration of barite that must be used in the drilling mud.

(C) Oil reserves at shallow depths have mostly been tapped, leaving primarily much deeper reserves for future drilling.

(D) It is unlikely that oil drillers will develop more efficient ways of removing OBM residues from cuttings that remain after being sieved from drilling fluids.

(E) Barite is a common mineral, the availability of which is virtually limitless.

12. According to passage B, one reason OBMs are potentially more environmentally damaging than WBMs is that OBMs

(A) are slower to disperse

(B) contain greater concentrations of bentonite

(C) contain a greater number of additives

(D) are used for drilling deeper wells

(E) cannot be recycled

Aida Overton Walker (1880–1914), one of the most widely acclaimed African American performers of the early twentieth century, was known largely for popularizing a dance form known as the cakewalk through her choreographing, performance, and teaching of the dance. The cakewalk was originally developed prior to the United States Civil War by African Americans, for whom dance was a means of maintaining cultural links within a slave society. It was based on traditional West African ceremonial dances, and like many other African American dances, it retained features characteristic of African dance forms, such as gliding steps and an emphasis on improvisation.

To this African-derived foundation, the cakewalk added certain elements from European dances: where African dances feature flexible body postures, large groups and separate-sex dancing, the cakewalk developed into a high-kicking walk performed by a procession of couples. Ironically, while these modifications later enabled the cakewalk to appeal to European Americans and become one of the first cultural forms to cross the racial divide in North America, they were originally introduced with satiric intent. Slaves performed the grandiloquent walks in order to parody the processional dances performed at slave owners' balls and, in general, the self-important manners of slave owners. To add a further irony, by the end of the nineteenth century, the cakewalk was itself being parodied by European American stage performers, and these parodies in turn helped shape subsequent versions of the cakewalk.

While this complex evolution meant that the cakewalk was not a simple cultural phenomenon—one scholar has characterized this layering of parody upon parody with the phrase "mimetic vertigo"—it is in fact what enabled the dance to attract its wide audience. In the cultural and socioeconomic flux of the turn-of-the-century United States, where industrialization, urbanization, mass immigration, and rapid social mobility all reshaped the cultural landscape, an art form had to be capable of being many things to many people in order to appeal to a large audience.

Walker's remarkable success at popularizing the cakewalk across otherwise relatively rigid racial boundaries rested on her ability to address within her interpretation of it the varying and sometimes conflicting demands placed on the dance. Middle-class African Americans, for example, often denounced the cakewalk as disreputable, a complaint reinforced by the parodies circulating at the time. Walker won over this audience by refining the cakewalk and emphasizing its fundamental grace. Meanwhile, because middle- and upper-class European Americans often felt threatened by the tremendous cultural flux around them, they prized what they regarded as authentic art forms as bastions of stability; much of Walker's success with this audience derived from her distillation of what was widely acclaimed as the most authentic cakewalk. Finally, Walker was able to gain the admiration of many newly rich industrialists and financiers, who found in the grand flourishes of her version of the cakewalk a fitting vehicle for celebrating their newfound social rank.

13. Which one of the following most accurately expresses the main point of the passage?

(A) Walker, who was especially well known for her success in choreographing, performing, and teaching the cakewalk, was one of the most widely recognized African American performers of the early twentieth century.

(B) In spite of the disparate influences that shaped the cakewalk, Walker was able to give the dance broad appeal because she distilled what was regarded as the most authentic version in an era that valued authenticity highly.

(C) Walker popularized the cakewalk by capitalizing on the complex cultural mix that had developed from the dance's original blend of satire and cultural preservation, together with the effects of later parodies.

(D) Whereas other versions of the cakewalk circulating at the beginning of the twentieth century were primarily parodic in nature, the version popularized by Walker combined both satire and cultural preservation.

(E) Because Walker was able to recognize and preserve the characteristics of the cakewalk as African Americans originally performed it, it became the first popular art form to cross the racial divide in the United States.

14. The author describes the socioeconomic flux of the turn-of-the-century United States in the third paragraph primarily in order to

(A) argue that the cakewalk could have become popular only in such complex social circumstances

(B) detail the social context that prompted performers of the cakewalk to fuse African and European dance forms

(C) identify the target of the overlapping parodic layers that characterized the cakewalk

(D) indicate why a particular cultural environment was especially favorable for the success of the cakewalk

(E) explain why European American parodies of the cakewalk were able to reach wide audiences

15. Which one of the following is most analogous to the author's account in the second paragraph of how the cakewalk came to appeal to European Americans?

(A) Satirical versions of popular music songs are frequently more popular than the songs they parody.

(B) A style of popular music grows in popularity among young listeners because it parodies the musical styles admired by older listeners.

(C) A style of music becomes admired among popular music's audience in part because of elements that were introduced in order to parody popular music.

(D) A once popular style of music wins back its audience by incorporating elements of the style of music that is currently most popular.

(E) After popular music begins to appropriate elements of a traditional style of music, interest in that traditional music increases.

16. The passage asserts which one of the following about the cakewalk?

(A) It was largely unknown outside African American culture until Walker popularized it.

(B) It was mainly a folk dance, and Walker became one of only a handful of people to perform it professionally.

(C) Its performance as parody became uncommon as a result of Walker's popularization of its authentic form.

(D) Its West African origins became commonly known as a result of Walker's work.

(E) It was one of the first cultural forms to cross racial lines in the United States.

17. It can be inferred from the passage that the author would be most likely to agree with which one of the following statements?

(A) Because of the broad appeal of humor, satiric art forms are often among the first to cross racial or cultural divisions.

(B) The interactions between African American and European American cultural forms often result in what is appropriately characterized as "mimetic vertigo."

(C) Middle-class European Americans who valued the cakewalk's authenticity subsequently came to admire other African American dances for the same reason.

(D) Because of the influence of African dance forms, some popular dances that later emerged in the United States featured separate-sex dancing.

(E) Some of Walker's admirers were attracted to her version of the cakewalk as a means for bolstering their social identities.

18. The passage most strongly suggests that the author would be likely to agree with which one of the following statements about Walker's significance in the history of the cakewalk?

(A) Walker broadened the cakewalk's appeal by highlighting elements that were already present in the dance.

(B) Walker's version of the cakewalk appealed to larger audiences than previous versions did because she accentuated its satiric dimension.

(C) Walker popularized the cakewalk by choreographing various alternative interpretations of it, each tailored to the interests of a different cultural group.

(D) Walker added a "mimetic vertigo" to the cakewalk by inserting imitations of other performers' cakewalking into her dance routines.

(E) Walker revitalized the cakewalk by disentangling its complex admixture of African and European elements.

19. The passage provides sufficient information to answer which one of the following questions?

(A) What were some of the attributes of African dance forms that were preserved in the cakewalk?

(B) Who was the first performer to dance the cakewalk professionally?

(C) What is an aspect of the cakewalk that was preserved in other North American dance forms?

(D) What features were added to the original cakewalk by the stage parodies circulating at the end of the nineteenth century?

(E) For about how many years into the twentieth century did the cakewalk remain widely popular?

In principle, a cohesive group—one whose members generally agree with one another and support one another's judgments—can do a much better job at decision making than it could if it were noncohesive. When cohesiveness is low or lacking entirely, compliance out of fear of recrimination is likely to be strongest. To overcome this fear, participants in the group's deliberations need to be confident that they are members in good standing and that the others will continue to value their role in the group, whether or not they agree about a particular issue under discussion. As members of a group feel more accepted by the others, they acquire greater freedom to say what they really think, becoming less likely to use deceitful arguments or to play it safe by dancing around the issues with vapid or conventional comments. Typically, then, the more cohesive a group becomes, the less its members will deliberately censor what they say out of fear of being punished socially for antagonizing their fellow members.

But group cohesiveness can have pitfalls as well: while the members of a highly cohesive group can feel much freer to deviate from the majority, their desire for genuine concurrence on every important issue often inclines them not to use this freedom. In a highly cohesive group of decision makers, the danger is not that individuals will conceal objections they harbor regarding a proposal favored by the majority, but that they will think the proposal is a good one without attempting to carry out a critical scrutiny that could reveal grounds for strong objections. Members may then decide that any misgivings they feel are not worth pursuing—that the benefit of any doubt should be given to the group consensus. In this way, they may fall victim to a syndrome known as "groupthink," which one psychologist concerned with collective decision making has defined as "a deterioration of mental efficiency, reality testing, and moral judgment that results from in-group pressures."

Based on analyses of major fiascoes of international diplomacy and military decision making, researchers have identified groupthink behavior as a recurring pattern that involves several factors: overestimation of the group's power and morality, manifested, for example, in an illusion of invulnerability, which creates excessive optimism; closed-mindedness to warnings of problems and to alternative viewpoints; and unwarranted pressures toward uniformity, including self-censorship with respect to doubts about the group's reasoning and a concomitant shared illusion of unanimity concerning group decisions. Cohesiveness of the decision-making group is an essential antecedent condition for this syndrome but not a sufficient one, so it is important to work toward identifying the additional factors that determine whether group cohesiveness will deteriorate into groupthink or allow for effective decision making.

20. Which one of the following most accurately expresses the main point of the passage?

(A) Despite its value in encouraging frank discussion, high cohesion can lead to a debilitating type of group decision making called groupthink.

(B) Group members can guard against groupthink if they have a good understanding of the critical role played by cohesion.

(C) Groupthink is a dysfunctional collective decision-making pattern that can occur in diplomacy and military affairs.

(D) Low cohesion in groups is sometimes desirable when higher cohesion involves a risk of groupthink behavior.

(E) Future efforts to guard against groupthink will depend on the results of ongoing research into the psychology of collective decision making.

21. A group of closely associated colleagues has made a disastrous diplomatic decision after a series of meetings marked by disagreement over conflicting alternatives. It can be inferred from the passage that the author would be most likely to say that this scenario

(A) provides evidence of chronic indecision, thus indicating a weak level of cohesion in general

(B) indicates that the group's cohesiveness was coupled with some other factor to produce a groupthink fiasco

(C) provides no evidence that groupthink played a role in the group's decision

(D) provides evidence that groupthink can develop even in some groups that do not demonstrate an "illusion of unanimity"

(E) indicates that the group probably could have made its decision-making procedure more efficient by studying the information more thoroughly

22. Which one of the following, if true, would most support the author's contentions concerning the conditions under which groupthink takes place?

(A) A study of several groups, each made up of members of various professions, found that most fell victim to groupthink.

(B) There is strong evidence that respectful dissent is more likely to occur in cohesive groups than in groups in which there is little internal support.

(C) Extensive analyses of decisions made by a large number of groups found no cases of groupthink in groups whose members generally distrust one another's judgments.

(D) There is substantial evidence that groupthink is especially likely to take place when members of a group develop factions whose intransigence prolongs the group's deliberations.

(E) Ample research demonstrates that voluntary deference to group opinion is not a necessary factor for the formation of groupthink behavior.

23. The passage mentions which one of the following as a component of groupthink?

(A) unjustified suspicions among group members regarding an adversary's intentions

(B) strong belief that the group's decisions are right

(C) group members working under unusually high stress, leading to illusions of invulnerability

(D) the deliberate use of vapid, clichéd arguments

(E) careful consideration of objections to majority positions

24. It can be inferred from the passage that both the author of the passage and the researchers mentioned in the passage would be most likely to agree with which one of the following statements about groupthink?

(A) Groupthink occurs in all strongly cohesive groups, but its contribution to collective decision making is not fully understood.

(B) The causal factors that transform group cohesion into groupthink are unique to each case.

(C) The continued study of cohesiveness of groups is probably fruitless for determining what factors elicit groupthink.

(D) Outside information cannot influence group decisions once they have become determined by groupthink.

(E) On balance, groupthink cannot be expected to have a beneficial effect in a group's decision making.

25. In the passage, the author says which one of the following about conformity in decision-making groups?

(A) Enforced conformity may be appropriate in some group decision situations.

(B) A high degree of conformity is often expected of military decision-making group members.

(C) Inappropriate group conformity can result from inadequate information.

(D) Voluntary conformity occurs much less frequently than enforced conformity.

(E) Members of noncohesive groups may experience psychological pressure to conform.

26. In the second sentence of the passage, the author mentions low group cohesiveness primarily in order to

(A) contribute to a claim that cohesiveness can be conducive to a freer exchange of views in groups

(B) establish a comparison between groupthink symptoms and the attributes of low-cohesion groups

(C) suggest that there may be ways to make both cohesive and noncohesive groups more open to dissent

(D) indicate that both cohesive and noncohesive groups may be susceptible to groupthink dynamics

(E) lay the groundwork for a subsequent proposal for overcoming the debilitating effects of low cohesion

27. Based on the passage, it can be inferred that the author would be most likely to agree with which one of the following?

(A) Highly cohesive groups are more likely to engage in confrontational negotiating styles with adversaries than are those with low cohesion.

(B) It is difficult for a group to examine all relevant options critically in reaching decisions unless it has a fairly high degree of cohesiveness.

(C) A group with varied viewpoints on a given issue is less likely to reach a sound decision regarding that issue than is a group whose members are unified in their outlook.

(D) Intense stress and high expectations are the key factors in the formation of groupthink.

(E) Noncohesive groups can, under certain circumstances, develop all of the symptoms of groupthink.

Chapter 9
Drill Answers and Explanations

CHAPTER 2: ARGUMENTS

Answers for Arguments Practice Drill (Pages 129–134)

1. **B** PrepTest 127, Section 2, Question 3
2. **D** PrepTest 127, Section 3, Question 5
3. **A** PrepTest 127, Section 3, Question 8
4. **A** PrepTest 124, Section 1, Question 9
5. **D** PrepTest 124, Section 1, Question 11
6. **E** PrepTest 127, Section 2, Question 12
7. **A** PrepTest 124, Section 1, Question 21
8. **D** PrepTest 127, Section 3, Question 6
9. **B** PrepTest 127, Section 3, Question 22
10. **E** PrepTest 127, Section 3, Question 7
11. **E** PrepTest 124, Section 1, Question 16
12. **E** PrepTest 127, Section 1, Question 23
13. **B** PrepTest 127, Section 3, Question 3

Explanations for Arguments Practice Drill (Pages 129–134)

1. **B** Weaken

The argument concludes that Acme Corporation offers unskilled workers excellent opportunities for advancement based on the example of Ms. Garon, who started as an assembly line worker, a position that requires no special skills, and is now the president of the company. However, you don't actually know that Ms. Garon had no special skills when she started. You need to find an answer choice that offers another explanation for how she attained her position as president even though she began as an assembly line worker.

A. No. If anything, this strengthens the argument by implying that Ms. Garon's career is representative of the path Acme employees take.

B. Yes. This suggests that she advanced to her position by virtue of her business degree; therefore, this casts doubt on the argument that unskilled workers have excelled opportunities for advancement at Acme.

C. No. This doesn't tell you whether unskilled workers are among those getting promoted, so it doesn't really impact the argument.

D. No. This is irrelevant. How long she worked at Acme is not important; the reason behind her promotion is, but this choice doesn't address that.

E. No. This is out of scope; there's no link between wages and skills here.

2. **D** Main Point

The gardener concludes that the researchers' advice—allow certain kinds of weeds to grow among garden vegetables so as to repel caterpillars—is premature. Why? Those kinds of weeds could deplete the soil of nutrients and moisture that garden crops depend on and might attract other kinds of damaging pests.

A. No. This is not the issue; the gardener doesn't say that the use of insecticides should be eliminated.

B. No. This is a premise.

C. No. This is part of the researchers' advice, with which the gardener disagrees.

D. Yes. This matches the tone of the gardener's conclusion, which is that the researchers' advice is premature.

E. No. The gardener doesn't dispute the fact that certain weeds could have the effect of reducing the presence of caterpillars; he is more concerned about what other unforeseen effects these weeds might have.

3. **A** Strengthen

The economist states that companies have two means by which they can cut personnel costs during a recession—laying off some employees without reducing the wages of remaining employees or reducing the wages of all employees without laying anyone off. While both damage morale, layoffs damage it less since those who are aggrieved have left. From all this, the economist concludes that when companies must reduce personnel costs during recessions, they are likely to lay off employees. To strengthen this argument, you need to show that morale is a significant factor in companies' decision-making during a recession.

A. Yes. If employee morale is the primary concern, this would strengthen the economist's conclusion that companies will choose the option that damages morale less—laying off employees.

B. No. Increasing wages is outside the scope of the argument.

C. No. Making a profit is outside the scope of the argument, which is concerned with cutting personnel costs.

D. No. The fact that some employees resign when companies resort to reducing wages to cut personnel costs doesn't tie in to the idea of employee morale, as others may not choose to resign.

E. No. Finding qualified employees after a recession is irrelevant to the economist's argument.

4. **A** Necessary Assumption

The argument concludes that the leatherback turtle is in danger of extinction, based on evidence about nesting female leatherback turtles. This population of turtles has fallen by more than two-thirds in the past 15 years. Any species whose population declines by that amount in that amount of time is in grave danger of extinction. There needs to be a connection between the statistics for nesting female leatherback turtles and the leatherback turtle population as a whole.

A. Yes. This connects the decline of nesting female leatherback turtles to a similar decline in the leatherback turtle population as a whole.

B. No. This is too strong. The argument never claims that the turtles will actually become extinct.

C. No. This is too general. The argument needs a connection between the numbers of nesting female leatherbacks and the leatherback population as a whole. This compares the numbers of females in general with the number of males.

D. No. The argument doesn't address turtles in captivity.

E. No. The argument doesn't attempt to solve the problem; it just points out the problem.

5. **D** Reasoning

The argument concludes that a society that wants to reap the benefits of pure science ought to use public funds to support such research. The argument defines pure science as research with no immediate commercial or technological application and claims that it is a public good. Because of its nature, pure science needs a lot of monetary support and doesn't make profits in the short term. The argument then eliminates another possible funding avenue for pure science by claiming that private corporations will not fund activities that do not yield short-term profits.

A. No. The claim about private corporations is not the conclusion.

B. No. The claim about private corporations does not help define "pure research."

C. No. The claim about private corporations does not address a different goal.

D. Yes. This claim eliminates another possible funding source for pure science, which benefits the public.

E. No. This claim is not an example, so it doesn't illustrate a case.

6. **E** Flaw

The argument concludes that the energy subsidy has failed to achieve its intended purpose. Why? Even with subsidized energy production, which was intended to help residents of rural areas gain access to electricity, many of the most isolated rural populations still have no access to electricity. Yet the argument doesn't seem to take into account the fact that the subsidy's intended purpose might still be achieved even if only some, not all, rural populations now have access to electricity.

A. No. The argument never claims the subsidy's intended purpose could have been arrived at by other means, only that it has not been fulfilled thus far.

B. No. There is no discussion in the argument of the subsidy benefiting those for whom it was not intended.

C. No. The argument never claims that the subsidy was meant to help other people aside from those in rural areas.

D. No. While the argument doesn't address the possibility raised by this choice, it's not a logical flaw in its reasoning.

E. Yes. The argument incorrectly assumes that for the subsidy to achieve its intended purpose, it would have had to help everyone to whom it was applicable, not just some populations.

7. **A** Parallel Flaw

This argument is diagrammable. April rainfall exceeds 5 centimeters → trees blossom in May; → ~trees blossom in May → ~April rainfall exceeds 5 centimeters. April rainfall exceeds 5 centimeters → reservoirs full on May 1; ~reservoirs full on May 1 → ~April rainfall exceeds 5 centimeters. Conclusion: ~reservoirs full on May 1 → ~trees blossom in May. The conclusion claims that the reservoirs not being full on May 1 is sufficient to know that the trees will not blossom in May, while the evidence does not support this claim. The argument doesn't flip the terms in the contrapositive of the first premise.

A. Yes. Garlic in pantry → still fresh; ~still fresh → ~garlic in pantry. Garlic in pantry → potatoes on basement stairs; ~potatoes on stairs → ~garlic in pantry. Conclusion: ~potatoes on stairs → ~garlic still fresh.

B. No. Held over burner for two minutes → optimal temperature; ~optimal temperature → ~held over burner for two minutes. Optimal temperature → contents liquefy immediately; ~liquefy immediately → ~optimal temperature. Conclusion: held over burner for two minutes → liquefied immediately. This argument is not flawed.

C. No. More than 200 years old → classified "special"; ~classified "special" → ~more than 200 years old. Set with wooden type → more than 200 years old; ~more than 200 years old → ~set with wooden type. Conclusion: ~classified "special" → ~printed with wooden type. This argument is not flawed.

D. No. Mower operates → ~engine flooded; engine flooded → ~mower operates. Foot pedal depressed → engine flooded; ~engine flooded → ~foot pedal depressed. Conclusion: ~foot pedal depressed → mower operates. This argument is flawed, but not in the same manner as the original argument.

E. No. Kiln too hot → plates crack; ~plates crack → ~kiln too hot. Plates crack → redo; ~redo → ~plates crack. Conclusion: ~redo → ~kiln too hot. This argument is not flawed.

8. **D** Reasoning

The executive concludes that consumer response to the set of advertisements run in the print version of a travel magazine was probably below par. He bases this conclusion on the fact that consumer response to the same set of ads run on the magazine's website was more limited than is typical for website ads.

A. No. The executive bases his prediction of consumer response to the print ads on the response garnered from the website ads, so this choice, especially the part about the cause of the phenomenon, doesn't match the argument.

B. No. The executive uses information about consumer response to ads run on a website to draw a conclusion about the probable consumer response to ads run in print, an event of a different kind.

C. No. The executive does not make a statistical generalization; he is only referring to a specific set of ads.

D. Yes. He uses the evidence from the website ads to draw a conclusion about the results of the print ads, for which no direct information is available.

E. No. Future events are never referred to in the argument.

9. **B** Inference

You're looking for an answer that directly contradicts information in the paragraph. Four of the answer choices will be consistent with the information provided, even if they contain ideas that are not directly expressed in the argument.

A. No. This is consistent with the last sentence of the paragraph.

B. Yes. This cannot be true. The second sentence suggests that it is possible for two groups living in different environments to face the same daily challenges, so those challenges cannot be unique to those environments.

C. No. This could be true, as it doesn't contradict anything stated in the passage.

D. No. This could be true, as it is in line with the information found in the second and third sentences.

E. No. This could be true, as you know from the argument that they lived in different environments.

10. **E** Resolve/Explain

A pack of ten coyotes, which are known to prey on wild cats and plover, was removed from a small island because the coyotes were supposedly decimating the plover population. However, once they were removed, the plover population decreased significantly, and within two years no plover could be found on the island. Why did the plover population shrink after the coyotes were removed?

A. No. This suggests that the plover population should have recovered after the coyotes were removed.

B. No. This is irrelevant; it doesn't explain why the plover population plummeted.

C. No. By itself, this choice isn't enough to explain why the plover disappeared; you don't know that a disease that commonly infects plover would result in its decimation.

D. No. This is irrelevant and doesn't tell you why the plover population decreased.

E. Yes. If the coyotes were removed, then the number of wild cats would no longer be held in check; a greater number of wild cats preying on plover would result in the elimination of the plover population.

11. **E** Inference

Pick the answer best supported by the passage.

A. No. The passage does not mention the motivations of those who make statutes.

B. No. The passage claims that, in order to have a sound basis for preferring a given set of laws to any others, laws must be viewed as expressions of a transcendental moral code.

C. No. The passage suggests that the moral rules have the preferred status, not the laws. Also, the last sentence suggests that moral behavior and compliance with laws are at least sometimes distinguishable.

D. No. This is too strong. The passage doesn't say that there is no statute that the citizens have a moral obligation to obey.

E. Yes. If the laws are to be seen as expression of a moral code that has precedence over these laws, and that measures the adequacy of these laws, then there shouldn't be an absolute moral prohibition against the violation of statutes. What if, for example, there was a statute that wasn't in accord with the moral code?

12. **E** Principle Match

Diagram the two pieces of information provided in the argument. Intermittent wind and temperature below 84 degrees → pleasant; ~pleasant → ~intermittent wind or temperatures at 84 degrees or higher. High humidity with either no wind or temperatures above 84 degrees → oppressive; ~oppressive → ~high humidity and some wind and temperatures at 84 degrees or lower. Match the principle diagrammed to a correct weather report in the answer choices.

A. No. To be pleasant, there must be intermittent wind; however, this says there was no wind.

B. No. To be oppressive, there must be high humidity; however, this says humidity levels were low.

C. No. To be pleasant, the temperature must be below 84 degrees; however, this says the temperature stayed at 84 degrees.

D. No. To be oppressive, the temperature must rise above 84 degrees; however, this says the temperature did not do so.

E. Yes. High humidity and ~wind → oppressive.

13. **B** Main Point

Mariah concludes that Adam should not judge the essay contest. Her reasons for this, however, are different from those of Joanna, who thinks Adam would be biased because several of his classmates have entered the contest. Mariah believes that Adam should not judge the contest because he has no experience in critiquing essays.

A. No. Mariah discounts Joanna's suspicion of bias, so this choice is not relevant.

B. Yes. Mariah's conclusion that Adam should not be a judge is based on his lack of expertise.

C. No. Mariah is concerned about expertise, and since she seems to believe that Adam would not have a bias, you don't know whether she would consider objectivity more important than expertise.

D. No. Again, Mariah favors expertise, and since she seems to believe that Adam would not have a bias, you don't know whether she would weigh fairness over expertise.

E. No. Since Mariah dismisses the idea that Adam would be biased, this isn't relevant to her conclusion.

CHAPTER 3: READING COMPREHENSION

Answers for Passage (Pages 195–197)

1. **A** PrepTest 124, Section 4, Question 1
2. **C** PrepTest 124, Section 4, Question 2
3. **D** PrepTest 124, Section 4, Question 3
4. **C** PrepTest 124, Section 4, Question 4
5. **D** PrepTest 124, Section 4, Question 5
6. **D** PrepTest 124, Section 4, Question 6

Explanations

Step 1: Prepare

Prepare this passage like any other RC passage: look for key conclusions, transitions, and expressions of the author's opinion; define the central theme or purpose of each paragraph and how those paragraphs relate to each other; and articulate the basic Bottom Line of the passage. If a question asks about some small detail or about a concept you have not yet fully understood, go back to the passage with that specific issue in mind. And remember that POE is your friend. Often you don't need to fully understand the right answer as long you have good reasons to eliminate the other four.

Paragraph 1: In the first paragraph, the author introduces the contrast between most Asian American poetry from Hawaii and the recent work of Wing Tek Lum.

Paragraph 2: In the second paragraph, an example of Lum's poetry is introduced in order to illustrate how, through the presence of immigrants, Lum is able to refer both to the traditional culture of his Chinese homeland and to the flux within Hawaiian society. A laudatory poem to a famous Chinese poet is introduced to illustrate Lum's refusal to offer a stereotypical nostalgia for the past while still participating in a distinguished literary tradition.

Paragraph 3: In the third paragraph, the author discusses the final poem in Lum's volume. This poem illustrates the complex relationship between heritage and local culture in determining one's identity. In this poem, Lum acknowledges the hope that many immigrants have for their lives in the United States while cautioning that immigrants should come to terms with the strong cultural emphasis in the United States on individual drive and success so as to form a healthy new sense of identity.

Bottom Line: The author critiques the recent work of the Asian American poet Wing Tek Lum, claiming that his book, *Expounding the Doubtful Points*, demands to be understood on its own terms. This contrasts with typical Asian American poetry from Hawaii, which can be characterized either as portraying a model multicultural paradise or as exemplifying familiar Asian American themes like generational conflict. The purpose of this passage is to Advocate or Defend Wing Tek Lum's book of poetry.

Note: In this passage, the Bottom Line is laid out in the first paragraph. The rest of the passage supports the author's main defense of Lum's poems. On your first reading, keep your focus on the larger purpose of those second and third paragraphs, and don't get bogged down in the details.

Steps 2–4: Assess, Act, and Answer

Note: In the explanations for these questions and answer choices, we will put special emphasis on self-evaluation: if you picked or lingered over a wrong answer, why? And what could you have done to avoid it or eliminate it faster?

---

1. Which one of the following most accurately expresses the main point of the passage?

(A) The poetry of Lum departs from other Asian American poetry from Hawaii in that it acknowledges its author's heritage but also expresses the poet's search for a new local identity.

(B) Lum's poetry is in part an expression of the conflict between a desire to participate in a community with shared traditions and values and a desire for individual success.

(C) Lum writes poetry that not only rejects features of the older literary tradition in which he participates but also rejects the popular literary traditions of Hawaiian writers.

(D) The poetry of Lum illustrates the extent to which Asian American writers living in Hawaii have a different cultural perspective than those living in the continental U.S.

(E) Lum's poetry is an unsuccessful attempt to manage the psychological burdens of reconciling a sense of tradition with a healthy sense of individual identity.

Here's How to Crack It

Step 2: Assess

This is a Big Picture: Main Point question.

Step 3: Act

Remind yourself of your Bottom Line: "The author critiques the recent work of the Asian American poet Wing Tek Lum, claiming that his book, *Expounding the Doubtful Points*, demands to be understood on its own terms."

Step 4: Answer

Note: Even though this is not a Structure: Organization question, breaking down the answer choices as you would for that question type can help you to (1) understand what each part and the whole of the choice is saying and (2) look for pieces that have gone wrong.

Choice (A) mostly matches the Bottom Line. The passage highlights how Lum's poetry is striking in its departure from other Asian American poetry from Hawaii. Lum does address his own heritage but combines that with a search for a new local identity.

Choice (B) seeks to define Lum's poetry in specific terms, but fails to address the broader points of the passage. While *individual success* mentioned in this choice is addressed in the passage, it is only mentioned at the end of the last paragraph and only in reference to a caution that Lum raises for immigrants. The focus on a such a relatively minor point of the passage is a good reason to eliminate this choice. If you chose it, be careful not to put undue emphasis on topics that appear later in the passage.

Choice (C) does not match the passage and can be eliminated. The passage does not discuss Hawaiian writers in general or their popular literary traditions. Avoid answer choices on Main Point questions that attempt to make the point of the passage broader than it really is.

Choice (D) makes an interesting argument about Lum, but does not match the defense provided in the passage. Since the author claims the poetry of Lum is different from that of other Asian American writers in Hawaii, it can't illustrate something about Asian American writers in Hawaii as a whole.

Choice (E) goes in the wrong direction from the passage. The author's main point is a defense of Lum's poetry as something unique. The author uses positive language to describe Lum's poetry, so the author would not say that Lum's poetry is unsuccessful. It is common for a wrong answer choice on a Main Point question to go in the opposite direction of the passage.

Choice (A) is the credited response because it is the only one that matches the Bottom Line.

2. Given the information in the passage, which one of the following is Lum most likely to believe?

(A) Images in a poem should be explained in that poem so that their meaning will be widely understood.

(B) The experience of living away from one's homeland is necessary for developing a healthy perspective on one's cultural traditions.

(C) It is important to reconcile the values of individual achievement and enterprise with the desire to retain one's cultural traditions.

(D) One's identity is continually in transition and poetry is a way of developing a static identity.

(E) One cannot both seek a new identity and remain connected to one's cultural traditions.

Here's How to Crack It

Step 2: Assess

This is an Extract: Inference question.

Step 3: Act

Refer back to the passage to find support for an answer choice. The author provides examples of Lum's ideas in the second and third paragraphs, so the credited response will probably come from one of those examples.

Step 4: Answer

Choice (A) suggests that Lum believes images in a poem should be explained, but the images mentioned in the examples cited by the author in the second or third paragraph provide no evidence that Lum explains his images in great detail. It could be true that Lum believes images should be explained, but there is no evidence in the passage to prove it, so get rid of this answer choice.

Choice (B) is a tough one. In the poem cited in the beginning of the second paragraph, Lum addresses how connections to the homeland are necessary but that one needs to have a new sense of family. However, this is in reference only to someone who has already immigrated. Lum never advocates immigration per se. This is an answer choice that many people hold on to on a first pass but ultimately get rid of because the support for it is not explicit enough.

Choice (C) is directly supported by the text of the poem cited in the third paragraph. The author states that Lum believes *the strong cultural emphasis in the U.S. on individual drive and success that makes retaining a sense of homeland tradition* should be addressed in a way that allows people to find a new identity.

Choice (D) seems to go against the claims made by the author about Lum. Lum's poetry attempts to discover and retain a local sensibility while keeping ties to the homeland. This choice illustrates a dynamic identity, not a static one. Eliminate it.

Choice (E) contradicts the passage too. In the poem cited at the beginning of the second paragraph, Lum says that it's *comforting and necessary* to keep ties to one's homeland. Eliminate this choice too.

Therefore, (C) is the credited response.

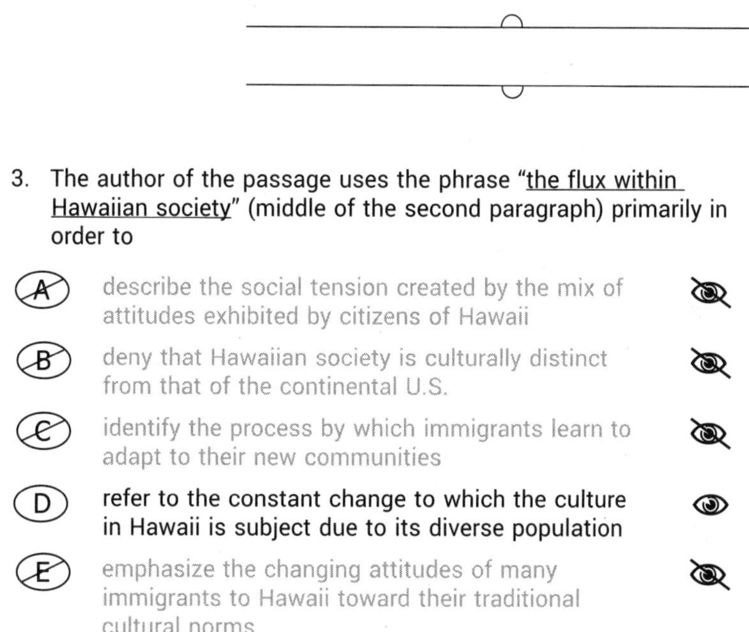

3. The author of the passage uses the phrase "the flux within Hawaiian society" (middle of the second paragraph) primarily in order to

(A) describe the social tension created by the mix of attitudes exhibited by citizens of Hawaii

(B) deny that Hawaiian society is culturally distinct from that of the continental U.S.

(C) identify the process by which immigrants learn to adapt to their new communities

(D) refer to the constant change to which the culture in Hawaii is subject due to its diverse population

(E) emphasize the changing attitudes of many immigrants to Hawaii toward their traditional cultural norms

Here's How to Crack It

Step 2: Assess

This is a Structure question.

Step 3: Act

Refer back to the passage and note that the author uses the phrase "the flux within Hawaiian society" in order to highlight the continuous changes in that society brought about by the influx of immigrants.

Step 4: Answer

While (A) discusses the mix of attitudes mentioned in the second paragraph, it is primarily about the attitudes of *citizens of Hawaii*, whereas the topic of the second paragraph is the continuous changes in that society brought about by the influx of immigrants. Since this choice is only partially connected to the passage, eliminate it.

Choice (B) is about the comparison between Hawaii and the continental United States. The author discusses the United States broadly in the third paragraph, but this question is about the second paragraph. Wrong answer choices are often about different parts of the passage than the question. Cross this one off.

Choice (C) is about immigrants, so it is on the same topic as the second paragraph. However, the paragraph is about how those immigrants deal with the conflict of staying tied to a homeland while having a new sense of family in the Hawaii. There is no discussion of a process of adaptation, so cross this one off too.

Choice (D) matches the prediction well. It suggests there are continuous changes in Hawaiian society brought about by the influx of immigrants.

Choice (E) flips the message of the passage. The passage discusses the role of immigrants bringing changes to the Hawaiian society, not that the Hawaiian society changes the traditions of immigrants. The LSAT often flips the order of ideas in order to make a wrong answer choice seem right. Eliminate this one.

This leaves you with (D) as the credited response.

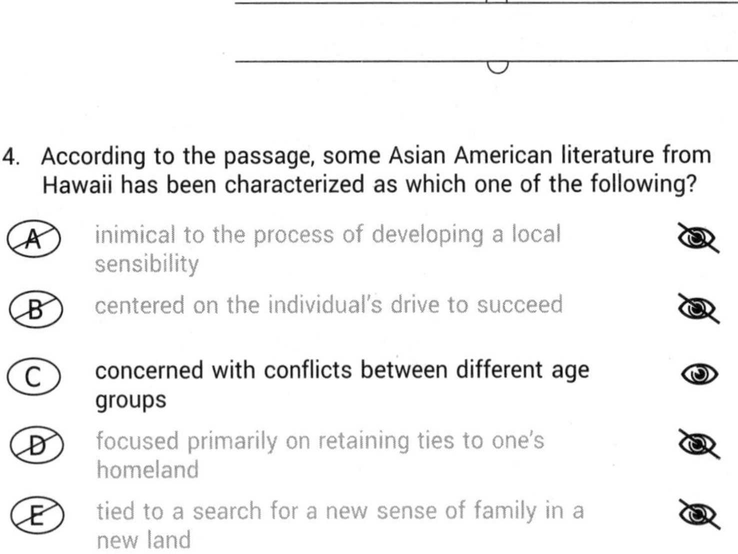

4. According to the passage, some Asian American literature from Hawaii has been characterized as which one of the following?

(A) inimical to the process of developing a local sensibility

(B) centered on the individual's drive to succeed

(C) concerned with conflicts between different age groups

(D) focused primarily on retaining ties to one's homeland

(E) tied to a search for a new sense of family in a new land

Here's How to Crack It

Step 2: Assess

This is an Extract: Fact question.

Step 3: Act

Look for a fact mentioned in the passage.

Step 4: Answer

In (A), the word *inimical* is too strong. The passage does not explicitly state that any Asian American literature from Hawaii is totally opposed or against the process of developing a local sensibility.

Choice (B) suggests that some Asian American literature from Hawaii is centered on individual achievements. The reference to individual success appears in the third paragraph and refers specifically to the United States' strong cultural emphasis. Since this idea is not mentioned as a characteristic of Asian American literature from Hawaii in the passage, eliminate this choice.

Choice (C) suggests that some Asian American literature from Hawaii is centered on age group conflicts. This conflict was cited as a characteristic of one of two types of Asian American literature from Hawaii in the first paragraph. Keep this choice.

Choice (D) suggests that some Asian American literature from Hawaii is focused on retaining ties to one's homeland. This is not discussed in reference to Asian American literature from Hawaii.

Choice (E) is true of Lum's poetry, which is strikingly different from Asian American literature from Hawaii.

Therefore, the credited response is (C).

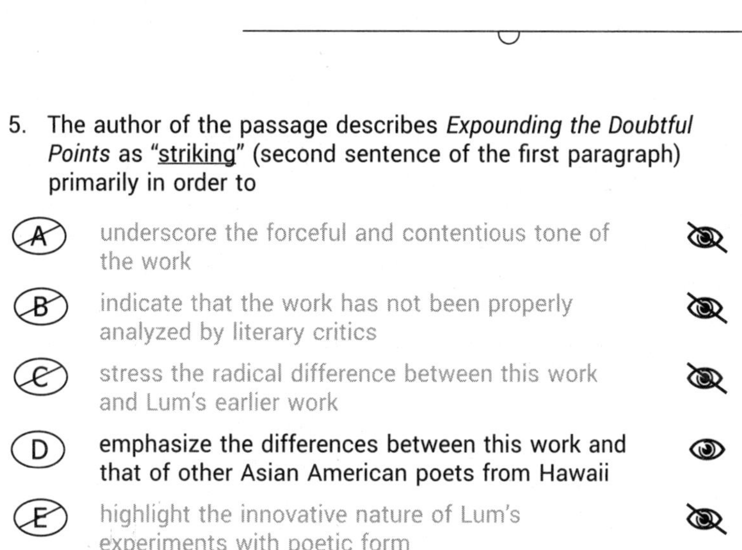

Here's How to Crack It

Step 2: Assess

This is a Structure question.

Step 3: Act

Refer back to the highlighted portion and read the sentence above and below it. The author describes *Expounding the Doubtful Points* as *striking* in order to emphasize how different Lum's recent work is from the usual Asian American poetry from Hawaii.

Step 4: Answer

The author does not describe Lum's work as *contentious*, so eliminate (A). The generational conflict mentioned in the first paragraph is a common topic of Asian American poetry in Hawaii, but the author refers to Lum's work as *striking* because it is not characterized by these themes.

While (B) does address a possible belief of the author who advocates for Lum's work to be considered unique, the word *striking* refers to a feature of Lum's work specifically. Eliminate this answer choice since it is not about a feature of Lum's work.

Choice (C) compares *Expounding the Doubtful Points* to Lum's earlier works, but the passage never mentions Lum's earlier works or compares this book to others by the same author. Cross it off.

Choice (D) matches the prediction that *striking* is used in order to emphasize how different Lum's recent work is from the usual Asian American poetry from Hawaii. Keep this one.

The passage discusses Lum's work as *striking* in its choice of topic, but (E) argues that Lum's work experiments with poetic form. The passage never discusses the poetic form of *Expounding the Doubtful Points*, so cross this one out.

Therefore, the credited response is (D).

---

6. With which one of the following statements regarding Lum's poetry would the author of the passage be most likely to agree?

(A) It cannot be used to support any specific political ideology.

(B) It is an elegant demonstration of the poet's appreciation of the stylistic contributions of his literary forebears.

(C) It is most fruitfully understood as a meditation on the choice between new and old that confronts any human being in any culture.

(D) It conveys thoughtful assessments of both his ancestral homeland tradition and the culture in which he is attempting to build a new identity.

(E) It conveys Lum's antipathy toward tradition by juxtaposing traditional and nontraditional images.

Here's How to Crack It

Step 2: Assess

This is an Extract: Inference question. Treat it much like an inference question on Arguments and look for support in the text of the passage.

Step 3: Act

Remind yourself of your Bottom Line: "The author critiques the recent work of the Asian American poet Wing Tek Lum, claiming that his book, *Expounding the Doubtful Points*, demands to be understood on its own terms."

Step 4: Answer

The author does not discuss the political ideology mentioned in (A) at all, so you don't know whether the author would agree with this claim. Cross this one out.

The author never mentioned whether Lum's poetry exhibits appreciation of stylistic contributions, so you don't know whether the author would agree with the claim in (B). Eliminate it too.

Choice (C) makes a claim that is broader than any discussed in the passage. The author never mentions the universality of the topics Lum addresses in his book. The author and Lum appear to address the culture of Asian Americans in Hawaii exclusively, so you don't know whether the author would agree with this claim about people in all cultures. Cross this one off.

The author cites assessments of homeland traditions and building a new sense of family in the discussion of the example in the first part of the second paragraph. Since (D) is directly supported by an example in the passage, this appears to be a good choice. Keep it.

Choice (E) has a tone that does not match the rest of the passage. The author discusses the fact that Lum recognizes the value of tradition, so the author would not claim that Lum's poetry conveys antipathy toward tradition. Eliminate this choice.

This leaves (D) as the credited response.

CHAPTER 7: ARGUMENTS PRACTICE

Answers for Arguments Practice (Pages 229–240)

1. **D** PrepTest 125, Section 2, Question 1
2. **E** PrepTest 125, Section 2, Question 2
3. **A** PrepTest 125, Section 2, Question 3
4. **E** PrepTest 125, Section 2, Question 4
5. **B** PrepTest 125, Section 2, Question 5
6. **C** PrepTest 125, Section 2, Question 6
7. **C** PrepTest 125, Section 2, Question 7
8. **A** PrepTest 125, Section 2, Question 8
9. **A** PrepTest 125, Section 2, Question 9
10. **B** PrepTest 125, Section 2, Question 10
11. **B** PrepTest 125, Section 2, Question 11
12. **D** PrepTest 125, Section 2, Question 12
13. **B** PrepTest 125, Section 2, Question 13
14. **C** PrepTest 125, Section 2, Question 14
15. **E** PrepTest 125, Section 2, Question 15
16. **D** PrepTest 125, Section 2, Question 16
17. **D** PrepTest 125, Section 2, Question 17
18. **C** PrepTest 125, Section 2, Question 18
19. **D** PrepTest 125, Section 2, Question 19
20. **E** PrepTest 125, Section 2, Question 20
21. **A** PrepTest 125, Section 2, Question 21
22. **E** PrepTest 125, Section 2, Question 22
23. **C** PrepTest 125, Section 2, Question 23
24. **A** PrepTest 125, Section 2, Question 24
25. **D** PrepTest 125, Section 2, Question 25
26. **D** PrepTest 125, Section 2, Question 26

Explanations

1. **D** Flaw

Since a survey of retirees is being used to support the claim that the company has good relations with its employees, the integrity of the survey must be examined.

A. No. The premise is the results of a survey, and accepting the results of a given survey does not require believing the company's general claim.

B. No. There is no reason to think the survey's results cannot be verified; rather, there is reason to think the survey's results are insufficient to prove the company's general claim.

C. No. The word "fairly" is used the same way both times.

D. Yes. Retirees who enjoyed working for the company may be more likely to respond to the survey than disgruntled former employees, and the retirees' experiences may not be representative of current relations between the company and its employees.

E. No. There is no mention of changing managing methods at all.

2. **E** Necessary Assumption

You need to prove that some people who are most opposed to animal cruelty actually contribute to animal cruelty. You know that some people who are most opposed to animal cruelty keep pets and feed those pets meat. You need to get from feeding those pets meat to contributing to animal cruelty.

A. No. You are trying to prove a claim about someone's cruelty; love is out of scope.

B. No. You are trying to prove a claim concerning some people who keep pets; people opposed to keeping pets are out of scope.

C. No. You are trying to prove a claim regarding people opposed to animal cruelty who feed their pets meat. People who work in labs, slaughterhouses, and farms are irrelevant unless you know they feed their pets meat.

D. No. A claim about popular pets is out of scope.

E. Yes. Negated, this would say "feeding meat to pets doesn't contribute to animal cruelty," which ruins the only shred of evidence provided in the argument.

3. A Weaken

Over the last five years, national publicity campaigns have tried to encourage people to read more fiction, but bookstores are making less money selling fiction. Therefore, the author concludes that those campaigns have been unsuccessful. You must accept that bookstores are selling less fiction, but look for an answer that allows you to believe the campaigns have still been a success.

A. Yes. Here's a potential sign of the campaigns' success.

B. No. This doesn't help defend the fiction campaigns.

C. No. The argument is about fiction, so biographies are out of scope.

D. No. The argument is about fiction, so books on careers and business are out of scope.

E. No. The argument refers only to national campaigns; overseas customers are out of scope.

4. **E** Resolve/Explain

On one hand, honey is high in sugar and sugar leads to tooth decay; on the other hand, people who eat honey have fewer cavities. There must be something about eating honey that discourages cavities even more than the sugar content promotes tooth decay.

A. No. Even if all their sugar is from honey, they eat a lot of honey and that still suggests they would have tooth decay problems.

B. No. Does dissolving sugar neutralize its effect on tooth decay? Since you aren't told what effect dissolving the sugar has, this can't be the credited response.

C. No. This doesn't tell you anything about people who consume honey.

D. No. You don't know whether honey is an unrefined sugar, so this choice doesn't resolve the paradox.

E. Yes. Here's a positive dental health feature of eating honey.

5. **B** Flaw

Two of the club's bylaws are explained; violating either would get you suspended. Thibodeaux got suspended. The conclusion assumes that since he didn't do one of those two things, he must have done the other. Why do we have to pick from just these two things? There are probably plenty of things that could get you suspended. Breaking either bylaw is sufficient (→) to get you suspended, but that doesn't mean we can assume getting suspended guarantees (→) you had to break one of those two bylaws.

A. No. Missing a monthly general meeting gets you suspended, not being late. This is irrelevant.

B. Yes. This identifies the assumption that there could not have been other ways to get suspended besides the two bylaws initially mentioned.

C. No. This answer is tempting—the argument took for granted that breaking one of two bylaws was necessary for someone to get suspended when in fact it was only sufficient for someone to get suspended. This choice, however, says the argument took for granted that something was sufficient just because it was necessary.

D. No. It is true that the argument doesn't define late, but that is not a logical problem with the reasoning.

E. No. No part of the argument discusses how long one has been an officer, making this choice irrelevant.

6. **C** Necessary Assumption

The argument concludes that in a future world dominated by recycled paper, more filler will have to be used than is used now. What do you know about recycled paper? The first three sentences combine in a chain of reasoning to tell you that recycled paper requires more filler than other paper if you want to make it white. What remains to be established, though, is that in a future world, people will still want their paper to be white.

A. No. Since the argument is based on recycled paper replacing other types of paper, this answer choice is going against the conclusion.

B. No. Harm to the environment is out of scope when you're only trying to prove that more filler will be used.

C. Yes. Negated, this says that the natural gray hue of recycled paper will be a universally acceptable alternative to white. That means far less filler will be used than is used now.

D. No. This idea of a "whiteness threshold" is irrelevant, and the idea goes against the direction of the conclusion by presenting a reason to potentially stop adding filler.

E. No. This does not need to be true. Manufacturing the current amount of worldwide paper with only recycled paper would still prove the conclusion true.

7. **C** Inference

There is a chain of conditional ideas that ultimately results in the idea that if a nation has to singlehandedly bear the burden of curbing industrial emissions, it won't, and therefore the world's carbon dioxide problem will run amok. The conclusion is essentially naming the contrapositive. If the world is to avoid these carbon dioxide problems, then nations cannot be made to singlehandedly bear the burden of curbing industrial emissions.

A. No. This goes in the opposite direction of the argument, which suggests that nations need to be more concerned with pollution than with economics for emissions control to occur.

B. No. The argument was concerned with the behavior of nations, not corporations.

C. Yes. This sounds like nations not singlehandedly bearing the burden of emissions control.

D. No. There was no mention of distrust and the idea that it could be eliminated is way too extreme.

E. No. This is close, in the sense that it also sounds like nations would not be singlehandedly bearing the burden, but the idea of needing to form a world government in order to fairly distribute the burden of emissions control amongst many nations is extreme.

8. **A** Principle Match

A positive aspect of digital technology (being a pattern of electronic signals minimizes waste) is identified, and then a downside of that same aspect is identified (being a pattern of electronic signals makes losing a document easier).

A. Yes. This matches the information perfectly.

B. No. The idea that more problems are created than are benefits is not supported by the passage. The benefit of and problem with digital technology are stated objectively without any evaluation of which is better or worse.

C. No. Nothing is compared and so there is no support for the idea that one thing is more important than another.

D. No. The innovation of digital technology increases the risk of destroying documents. There is no mention of document storage technology.

E. No. This is all positive and lacks any mention of the downside.

9. **A** Necessary Assumption

The argument concludes the museum will have to raise fees or reduce services. Why? Because the government mandate will increase the minimum wage rate, which in turn will increase the museum's operating expenses. Does the museum employ anyone at minimum wage? You don't know. If it doesn't, the mandate won't force the museum to change its payroll in any way, and therefore the operating expenses won't be changing.

A. Yes. Negating this means the museum has higher paid people on its payroll, so not only might it not be compelled by the mandate to raise any salaries, but any minimum wage salaries it may have to raise could be offset by lowering the higher salaries to retain the same level of operating expenses.

B. No. Since you can't change the premise (fact) that the revenue does not exceed the operating expenses, it doesn't matter whether the revenue fluctuates or not.

C. No. This is the opposite of what you want to assume. Negating this would tell you that everyone at the museum makes minimum wage, which would greatly strengthen the argument. The negation should never strengthen the argument.

D. No. Crowd size doesn't matter when you can't change the fact that expenses outweigh revenue.

E. No. This also relates to revenue intake. Since you can't change the fact that expenses outweigh revenue, this is irrelevant.

10. **B** Reasoning

Helen argues that time spent reading a book is an investment in the eventual benefits yielded by reading it. Randi does not disagree with that general idea but says that it applies only to vocational books. Randi argues that the act of reading fiction is as time-wasting as watching a sitcom.

A. No. Helen's "evidence" was nothing more than her own thoughts, so Randi does not question how she gathered them.

B. Yes. Randi thinks Helen's analogy applies only to vocational books and uses an analogy to sitcoms to show there's a difference when it comes to reading fiction.

C. No. Randi agrees with Helen's conclusion as it applies to vocational books, so it is not an absurd conclusion.

D. No. Helen presents an analogy, not an example, and Randi's analogy contrasts with Helen's.

E. No. Helen presents an analogy, not an example, and Randi accepts Helen's analogy when applied to vocational books, so its relevance is never denied.

11. **B** Main Point

The argument concludes no hardware store will be opening in the shopping plaza. Why? If someone were going to open a store, there would be publicity. The contrapositive of that states the following: If there's no publicity, no one's opening a store. There is no publicity; therefore, no one's opening a store.

A. No. The argument doesn't attempt to prove anything about some people believing a store will open.

B. Yes. It's an almost verbatim paraphrase of the argument's conclusion.

C. No. This reiterates a premise.

D. No. The idea that it would be "unwise" to open a store is unsupported by the argument, which only tries to prove that a store will not open.

E. No. This reiterates a premise.

12. **D** Inference

The important details marked off here are that science's value system does not require scientists to consider harmful consequences when deciding on research and that ordinary morality requires people to take foreseeable consequences into account when making decisions.

A. No. There is no discussion of responsibility for actions, and so there is no evidence for this answer.

B. No. This is close, but the facts actually say ordinary morality would say a scientist is acting immorally by failing to consider the harmful consequences in the first place, whether or not the research ever yields those consequences. Furthermore, if the harmful applications weren't foreseeable, then ordinary morality as described in the argument wouldn't really apply to this particular case.

C. No. The first sentence contradicts the idea that science is morally neutral.

D. Yes. Scientists deciding on research with potentially harmful consequences would be simultaneously following one part of their value system while violating a part of ordinary morality.

E. No. The idea that the effects of scientific knowledge can never be foreseen is extreme and can't be supported.

13. **B** Sufficient Assumption

The argument concludes that companies offering neither best price nor highest quality will go bankrupt. How can you prove a company will go bankrupt? Not attracting consumers → bankruptcy. In order to prove the conclusion, you need to know that offering neither best price nor highest quality → not attracting consumers. Scan answer choices for those two concepts.

A. No. This contains nothing about attracting consumers, which is your only logical path to proving a business will go bankrupt.

B. Yes. This is the conditional idea you needed.

C. No. You're trying to prove a claim about companies that don't offer the highest quality or lowest price. This is out of scope.

D. No. This has weak language ("some consumers"), which is generally useless on Sufficient Assumption questions. This implies that there may still be some other consumers who might patronize a company out of brand loyalty, which actually goes against the direction of what you're trying to prove because it makes a company with mediocre products less likely to go bankrupt if it has consumers with brand loyalty.

E. No. It's irrelevant to this argument to know whether there are other reasons a company may fail; in order to prove your conclusion, you still need to establish that companies with mediocre products fail to attract consumers.

14. **C** Weaken

The argument concludes that a reduction of the speed limit in 1986 led to a decrease in serious accidents. Why? The number of serious accidents in the five years after 1986 is less than the number of serious accidents in the five years before 1986. You need to accept that the number of serious accidents has gone down, but find an answer choice that lets us believe this is not due to the change in speed limit.

A. No. If more speeding tickets were issued in greater numbers before or after 1986, you could consider whether that means that more people are dangerously speeding (causing more accidents) or whether cops are enforcing the speed limits more, leading people to drive more carefully (causing fewer accidents). Since the number of tickets is constant, however, this gives you nothing.

B. No. More police presence might let you think that "fear of a ticket" was causing the decrease in accidents more so than the reduced speed limits themselves. Less police presence tells you nothing.

C. Yes. This lets you believe fewer cars on the road, not a lower speed limit, led to the reduction in accidents.

D. No. This only changes the relative proportion of hospitalization accidents to fatal accidents, but since they are both lumped together as one under the category of "serious accidents," the proportion of one to the other tells you nothing.

E. No. This would lead you to think that if they had used the same classification for "serious accident" during the whole 1981 to 1990 time period, there would be an even greater discrepancy between the accident-prone early years and the less accident-prone later years.

15. **E** Flaw

The argument concludes that humans are not rational. Why? They engage in irrational behavior such as pollution and bad farming. The concept of being rational is defined as having a capacity for well-reasoned behavior. Because humans sometimes behave irrationally, does that mean they have no capacity for rationality?

A. No. There is no inherent contradiction in the definition of rationality as "a capacity for well-considered thinking and behavior."

B. No. The argument does not need to assume humans are aware of irrational behavior. The argument thinks the mere fact that humans do behave irrationally is proof of their lack of rationality.

C. No. It doesn't need to show this since the argument is designed to lump humans in with other animals as being not superior to them.

D. No. The argument is trying to prove humans are no better than other animals; proving humans are not worse is irrelevant.

E. Yes. This addresses the fact that examples of irrational behavior don't necessarily rule out a capacity for rationality.

16. **D** Inference

"Must be true" answers normally come from a combination of quantity statements or conditional rules. All good hunters have a high muscle-to-fat ratio. Most wild cats are good hunters (therefore, most wild cats have a high muscle-to-fat ratio). Some domestic cats are good hunters (therefore, some domestic cats have a high muscle-to-fat ratio).

A. No. While possible, this is not provable; you have no evidence about cats that are not good hunters to even consider.

B. No. You can't prove a comparative quantity type claim when nothing in the evidence compared quantities.

C. No. You know good hunter → high ratio, but you can't then assume bad hunter → low ratio. You can never go from knowing A → B to assuming ~A → ~B.

D. Yes. That's one of the two inferences you were able to make.

E. No. It's possible that there are bad hunters with a high muscle-to-fat ratio, and so it's possible that they can't kill heavy prey.

17. **D** Reasoning

First, identify the conclusion—legal responsibility is different than moral responsibility—and the premises—drunk driving penalties vary according to the consequences of an action while moral responsibility depends only on the intentions of the action. The claim you are asked about is one of the premises.

A. No. The language that legal responsibility is based solely upon unintended features of an action is not supported by the argument.

B. No. This is close, but it's not clear that the criteria for legal responsibility always include those for moral responsibility. In the drunk driving example, it is possible that the driver's intentions are not a criterion at all when considering legal penalties.

C. No. The conclusion is just that moral and legal responsibility do not always overlap; this answer choice portrays a different, more specific claim as the conclusion.

D. Yes. This choice paraphrases the conclusion but still effectively identifies both ingredients.

E. No. This choice incorrectly represents the conclusion as being only about moral responsibility.

18. **C** Principle Match

The argument concludes it is best not to take a strong position until one has considered all important evidence. Why? Taking a strong position hinders your ability to consider conflicting evidence, which compromises your ability to understand an issue fully. So the underlying principle seems to be as follows: Don't take a strong position until you've understood an issue fully.

A. No. The argument made a claim about when you should not take a strong position, so the principle shouldn't address when you should.

B. No. We must accept the premises as true, and this tries to contradict the first sentence by wanting to undo that strong positions are sufficient to make one misinterpret or ignore conflicting evidence.

C. Yes. This paraphrases your prediction well.

D. No. This is incorrectly trying to move backward through the conditional statements of the premises, which say that as soon as you take a strong position, you are bound to be biased against conflicting evidence, which in turn precludes you from considering that evidence fully.

E. No. The argument made a claim about when you should not take a strong position, so the principle shouldn't address when it is reasonable to take a strong position.

19. **D** Flaw

The argument concludes that if Jennifer plays in the game, the Eagles will win. Why? So far, the team has lost only when Jennifer was not playing. Not only does that correlation fail to prove that Jennifer's absence caused the team to lose each time, it also fails to prove that Jennifer's presence causes the team to win.

A. No. This is close, but incorrect on two counts. First, Jennifer's not playing a game is not a factor that is sufficient to bring about the result of the Eagles losing. However, even if it were, the argument would be inferring that the absence of that factor (Jennifer playing the game) would be sufficient, not necessary, to bring about the opposite result (Eagles winning).

B. No. The logical flaw of this argument relates to correlations being treated as causal factors. The computer-related content was incidental.

C. No. As the argument states, no computer was necessary to uncover the evidence the argument uses to support its conclusion, so flaws relating to computer analysis are irrelevant.

D. Yes. The argument assumes that because the team has never lost while Jennifer was playing, they will never lose when Jennifer plays.

E. No. The conclusion is not about the value of computer analysis; it is that if Jennifer plays, the Eagles will win.

20. **E** Inference

Styrofoam egg cartons are identified as among the easiest to make because they don't need to be thoroughly cleaned, as the egg shells will provide an insulating barrier between the food and the Styrofoam.

A. No. Egg cartons are among the easiest to make, so there could be other food containers that have the same characteristics.

B. No. You have no evidence about anything that cannot be packaged in recycled Styrofoam.

C. No. You have no evidence to justify calling anything a main reason, and presumably the Styrofoam is cleaned for the sake of food that will come into contact with it.

D. No. You have no evidence to support a claim about most egg cartons, only some.

E. Yes. Translate "Not all A are B" statements into "Some A are NOT B." This is saying that some recycled Styrofoam food containers allow food to come into contact with the container. Egg cartons fit this description because the eggs are allowed to touch the Styrofoam.

21. **A** Parallel Flaw

Correlation = Causality flaw. Because most people who have condition A (migraines) had condition B (depression) as children, the argument erroneously concludes that having condition B as a child makes it likely to have condition A as an adult.

A. Yes. Most dogs with A (good tempers) had B (rabies vaccine) as puppies; therefore, it assumes that having B as a puppy makes you likely to have A as an adult.

B. No. This says most dogs with A (vicious tempers) had B (ill treatment) when they were young, but it concludes that if a pet owner's dog has A, then it is likely to have had B when young.

C. No. This says most dogs with A (good behavior) had B (obedience training), but it concludes that if you did not have B you will not have A.

D. No. This does not take a single correlation between two factors and manipulate those two factors.

E. No. This is not a correlation between two different factors; it assigns one factor (being taken from a mother) to a certain time (eight weeks) and concludes that anything after that time will have that factor.

22. **E** Flaw

The argument concludes that if Professor Vallejo is correct, glassblowing did not originate in Egypt. Why? If Professor Vallejo is correct, there is currently insufficient evidence to prove glassblowing originated in Egypt. Do you have any evidence it originated anywhere else? Not that you know of, so you can't prove that glassblowing did or did not originate in Egypt.

A. No. Contradicting majority opinion is not a logical flaw.

B. No. It does not presuppose Vallejo's claim is true because the conclusion is phrased "If Professor Vallejo is correct..."

C. No. It is true that the argument failed to provide this criteria, but this choice doesn't address any logical flaw.

D. No. The phrase that relates the traditional view to the majority view is neither a premise nor the conclusion and therefore has nothing to do with the reasoning process.

E. Yes. The argument assumes that an inability to prove glassblowing did originate in Egypt proves that it did not originate in Egypt.

23. **C** Parallel

This is a valid argument that establishes the only mattresses in Southgate Mall are at Mattress Madness. All the mattresses at that store are 20 percent off. Therefore, all the mattresses at Southgate Mall are 20 percent off.

A. No. There could be food in Diane's refrigerator that she didn't purchase in the past week.

B. No. There could be food elsewhere in Diane's apartment that was not purchased in the past week.

C. Yes. The only food in her apartment is in the refrigerator and all the food in her refrigerator was purchased this past week. Therefore, all food in her apartment was purchased this past week.

D. No. Diane could have purchased food in the past week and left some of it in her car or at her office.

E. No. Diane could have month-old food sitting in her pantry or somewhere else in her apartment other than the refrigerator.

24. **A** Strengthen

This argument attempts to solve a problem with methane production by concluding that cows should be given better-quality diets. What is the methane problem? Worldwide, there are over a billion cows (and counting) to meet our meat and milk demands. These cows produce methane gas, which isn't desirable (global warming). Cows produce less methane gas when given higher-quality diets. Does this solve the original problem? It seems as though it might. Does it create any problems of its own? It's not certain. You need to assume that all other relevant factors about cows (environmental impact and meat/milk production) would not be worsened.

A. Yes. This choice rules out the possible concern that a higher-quality diet may lead to less meat/milk production, which would force farmers to keep more cows in order to meet world demand (thus undermining any methane reduction obtained).

B. No. This doesn't make any difference, particularly since it applies uniformly to low- and high-quality diets.

C. No. The willingness of farmers to make this switch is out of scope; the argument is only trying to prove that if you made the switch, you would reduce methane production.

D. No. The relative proportion of which cows are guiltier of methane emissions is irrelevant, since they all have to be fed anyway.

E. No. The extent to which methane contributes to global warming is irrelevant when the argument is only trying to prove that changing cow feed would reduce methane.

25. **D** Inference

Our first sentence says face danger solely to obtain pleasure → ~courage. Our second sentence says courage → persevere in the face of fear. These two ideas don't chain together, so we should be ready for either contrapositive. The first contrapositive: courage → ~solely for pleasure. The second contrapositive: ~overcame fear → ~courage.

A. No. Avoiding future pain is not a concept ever mentioned, so you will not be able to prove anything about it.

B. No. The necessary condition to call something courageous is that someone perseveres in the face of fear of one or more dangers involved. This answer choice nearly contradicts that.

C. No. This is too broad a statement to prove. You're labeling actions as courageous or not courageous, not people. Just because a person derives pleasure from some dangerous activities doesn't mean that they couldn't be involved in a situation in which no pleasure is derived from danger, which still leaves open the possibility for acting courageously.

D. Yes. This just reiterates the conditional of the second sentence, courageous (only if) → persevere in the face of fear.

E. No. This choice states that everyone else would fear something → this person doesn't. However, that leaves open the possibility that there could be a situation in which this person does fear something that everyone else would not fear. That leaves open the possibility for this person to act courageously by persevering in the face of fear.

26. **D** Sufficient Assumption

The argument concludes that if the newspaper is right, the public will be safer in future severe weather. What does the newspaper predict? New sirens installed → public safety in severe weather improved. Do you have a way to prove that new sirens will be installed? Replacement parts for old sirens are difficult to obtain → government will install new sirens. Do you have a way to prove that replacement parts for old sirens are difficult to obtain? The local company the government has previously used to buy those parts has since gone out of business. We just need to know that government can't get parts from its normal company → replacement parts are difficult to obtain.

A. No. Sufficient assumption answers need to tell you that IF a premise obtains, THEN the conclusion follows. Any answer that begins by saying IF the conclusion obtains is useless.

B. No. You don't need to establish the newspaper was correct. The conclusion is only trying to prove something that follows if the newspaper is correct.

C. No. This is close to the relationship you wanted, but it needs to be more explicit. It's possible that it is simple for the government to obtain replacement parts from a nonlocal company, in which case the old sirens will be retained and the conclusion will not follow.

D. Yes. This is the link you need.

E. No. This is also close, but it needs to be more explicit. It's still possible that the government takes a reckless attitude toward solving the problem of finding replacement parts and does not care that the parts are of inferior quality. If it was easy for the government to obtain those parts, there is no reason to believe the government will be forced to buy and install new sirens.

CHAPTER 8: READING COMPREHENSION PRACTICE

Answers for Reading Comprehension Practice (Pages 241–251)

1. **A** PrepTest 125, Section 1, Question 1
2. **C** PrepTest 125, Section 1, Question 2
3. **D** PrepTest 125, Section 1, Question 3
4. **D** PrepTest 125, Section 1, Question 4
5. **E** PrepTest 125, Section 1, Question 5
6. **B** PrepTest 125, Section 1, Question 6
7. **E** PrepTest 125, Section 1, Question 7
8. **E** PrepTest 125, Section 1, Question 8
9. **B** PrepTest 125, Section 1, Question 9
10. **B** PrepTest 125, Section 1, Question 10
11. **C** PrepTest 125, Section 1, Question 11
12. **A** PrepTest 125, Section 1, Question 12
13. **C** PrepTest 125, Section 1, Question 13
14. **D** PrepTest 125, Section 1, Question 14
15. **C** PrepTest 125, Section 1, Question 15
16. **E** PrepTest 125, Section 1, Question 16
17. **E** PrepTest 125, Section 1, Question 17
18. **A** PrepTest 125, Section 1, Question 18
19. **A** PrepTest 125, Section 1, Question 19
20. **A** PrepTest 125, Section 1, Question 20
21. **C** PrepTest 125, Section 1, Question 21
22. **C** PrepTest 125, Section 1, Question 22
23. **B** PrepTest 125, Section 1, Question 23
24. **E** PrepTest 125, Section 1, Question 24
25. **E** PrepTest 125, Section 1, Question 25
26. **A** PrepTest 125, Section 1, Question 26
27. **B** PrepTest 125, Section 1, Question 27

Explanations

Questions 1–5

This passage addresses problems created for "traditional legislation and law enforcement" by the international flow of information on the Internet. The first paragraph defines the Internet and states the thesis. The second paragraph explains that a government can enforce control only over something contained within its national borders and it would be forced to enact a restrictive, unpopular policy of denying its citizens access to the Internet if it wanted to prevent or monitor all transmissions. The third paragraph examines the specific difficulties of trying to enforce trademark laws on the Internet. The fourth paragraph discusses the need for regulation regarding Internet transmissions that travel through several jurisdictions.

1. **A** Big Picture

   A. Yes. It identifies that certain aspects of the Internet make it problematic for existing legal enforcement and regulation.

   B. No. The passage does not make reference to weakening a government's power over any sort of financial transactions.

   C. No. This addresses only one sentence at the end of the second paragraph.

   D. No. The passage never refers to global crime.

   E. No. The passage never addresses the stability of many nations.

2. **C** Structure

   This paragraph is examining the need for regulation to determine what rights nations have concerning Internet transmissions passing through their borders.

   A. No. This does not address the purpose of the paragraph.

   B. No. This does not address the purpose of the paragraph.

   C. Yes. This is a hypothetical example given so the reader may consider an unresolved regulatory question involving international Internet transmissions.

   D. No. This paragraph has nothing to do with trademarks.

   E. No. The origins of the Internet are never discussed.

3. **D** Extract Fact

   The first sentence of the second paragraph states the defining attribute of sovereignty.

   A. No. Control over business enterprises is not stated.

   B. No. Authority over communicative exchanges is not stated.

   C. No. Power to regulate trademarks is not stated.

D. Yes. This is almost the passage's wording verbatim.

E. No. Authority over all commercial transactions is not stated.

4. **D** Extract Infer

A. No. The context in which this word is used suggests no attitude.

B. No. This relates to the attitude of the "affected citizens."

C. No. This relates to the attitude of the "affected citizens."

D. Yes. By using "draconian," the author suggests such a measure would be unthinkably restrictive.

E. No. The context in which this word is used suggests no attitude.

5. **E** Structure

A. No. This paragraph does not question the discussion of sovereignty.

B. No. Although there is one hypothetical consideration, this paragraph provides no practical illustrations.

C. No. This paragraph does not summarize but rather moves into a new aspect of the overall topic.

D. No. This paragraph does not extend the discussion of trademarks.

E. Yes. By introducing the topic of the need for new regulations to handle issues unique to the Internet, the fourth paragraph extends the thesis from the first paragraph.

Questions 6–12

Passage A

The author provides a general summary of the function, composition, and practical considerations of drilling fluids and drilling muds. The first paragraph explains the function of drilling fluids. The second paragraph identifies common compositions of drilling muds. The third paragraph discusses reasons the composition of some muds may be hard to ascertain.

Passage B

The author discusses drilling muds in the context of their potential environmental hazards. The first paragraph describes the general function and use of drilling mud. The second paragraph describes a relatively harmless mud, water-based mud (WBM). The third paragraph describes a more environmentally damaging mud, oil-based mud (OBM).

6. **B** Big Picture

A. No. Passage A does not mention any type of environmental pollution.

B. Yes. Both passages explain the makeup of drilling muds.

C. No. Passage A does not deal with environmental impact.

D. No. Passage B does not explain why drilling muds are necessary.

E. No. Passage B does not discuss difficulties inherent in drilling regulations.

7. **E** Extract Fact

A. No. This is not mentioned in passage A.

B. No. This is not mentioned in passage A.

C. No. This is not mentioned in passage A.

D. No. This is not mentioned in passage B.

E. Yes. Both passages acknowledge that barite is a heavy mineral.

8. **E** RC Except

A. No. Both passages indicate the presence of clay in drilling muds.

B. No. Passage B indicates WBM is allowed to be dumped into the sea.

C. No. Passage B mentions the environmental effects of OBM, which implies that some study of its effects has been conducted.

D. No. Passage B indicates OBM is 30 percent oil and it is regulated.

E. Yes. Neither passage supports the idea that drilling mud is "continuously" discharged into the sea.

9. **B** Extract Infer

A. No. The "most environmentally damaging" drilling mud is not supported by either passage.

B. Yes. Passage B indicates the potentially dangerous effects of dumping barite into the sea, while passage A indicates that barite is included in some foods and in a normal medical procedure during which humans ingest it.

C. No. No comparison between offshore and land-based drilling is made.

D. No. Neither author argues for tightened regulations of drilling muds.

E. No. Passage A does not refer to offshore drilling at all.

10. **B** RC Except

A. No. This is stated in the final sentence of the first paragraph of passage B.

B. Yes. Neither passage supports the idea that governments require disclosure of "all" ingredients. Passage A's reference to secret recipes seems to contradict this as a possibility.

C. No. This is stated in the final sentence of the second paragraph of passage A.

D. No. This is implied by the discussion of drilling through rock in the first paragraph of passage A.

E. No. This is stated in the first two sentences of the last paragraph of passage B.

11. **C** RC Reasoning

The difference stated in passage B between OBMs and WBMs is that OBMs are needed for drilling at greater depths.

A. No. It's possible that the cost of OBMs may also increase, depending on which ingredients are affected.

B. No. This by itself does not suggest any need for change in the future.

C. Yes. If in the future companies must drill deeper to access oil reserves, they will likely make greater use of OBMs when drilling.

D. No. This would seem to reduce the likelihood of using OBMs.

E. No. This by itself does not suggest any need for change in the future.

12. **A** Extract Fact

A. Yes. This is stated in the middle of the last paragraph ("they do not disperse as readily").

B. No. This is not stated.

C. No. This is not mentioned specifically as an environmental hazard.

D. No. This is not mentioned specifically as an environmental hazard.

E. No. This is not stated.

Questions 13–19

The passage discusses the African American choreographer, performer, and dance teacher Aida Overton Walker and examines the proliferating appeal of a dance form she helped popularize. This dance form, "the cakewalk," was embraced by many different social and ethnic groups, including upper-class members the dance was originally designed to parody.

The first paragraph introduces Walker and details the African roots of the cakewalk. The second paragraph discusses the European elements that were added to the cakewalk and describes how they originally served to parody those who would later find the dance form appealing. The third paragraph explains the social and cultural conditions that allowed for the cakewalk's increased popularity. The fourth paragraph examines how Walker was able to win over audiences from different social backgrounds and racial groups.

13. **C** Big Picture

A. No. This focuses only on Walker, whereas the focus of the passage was on Walker's popularization of the cakewalk.

B. No. This choice relates to only one particular audience, described in the second-to-last sentence of the passage, with whom Walker achieved success.

C. Yes. This choice discusses Walker's success in terms of the unique social breadth of the cakewalk's appeal.

D. No. This introduces a false distinction between initial versions of the cakewalk and a supposedly definitive version Walker popularized.

E. No. Different social niches adapted the dance to their own demands, while this answer choice says the dance was preserved in its original form.

14. **D** Structure

The passage says the socioeconomic flux of the time created a diverse cultural atmosphere that demanded art forms with versatile appeal, which explains why the layering of parody present in the cakewalk facilitated a broad audience.

A. No. "Only" makes this too strong of a claim.

B. No. There is no discussion of performers in this paragraph.

C. No. The "socioeconomic flux" was not a target of parody.

D. Yes. This identifies that the social backdrop influenced the way the popularity of the cakewalk spread.

E. No. This too narrowly focuses on European American versions of the dance, while the paragraph makes no mention of European Americans at all.

15. **C** RC Reasoning

The cakewalk was originally intended to mock European Americans by using elements familiar to them, but this aspect contributed to them embracing the dance.

A. No. The passage never ranks any version of the cakewalk as being more popular than another.

B. No. This doesn't demonstrate that the people being parodied became fans of the music themselves.

C. Yes. Popular music was parodied by a particular style of music, but the elements that were included expressly for that purpose contributed to that style's appeal to pop music audiences.

D. No. This has no sense of parody and instead refers to regaining popularity by cashing in on a current trend.

E. No. This choice discusses only appropriation of elements, not parody.

16. **E** Extract Fact

A. No. There is no mention of how well known the cakewalk was before Walker.

B. No. There is no evidence that Walker and only a few others performed it professionally.

C. No. The passage discusses only the layering of parody that was instrumental to the popularizing of the dance, not whether Walker diminished the frequency of the parodies with her interpretation of the cakewalk.

D. No. There is no support for any statements concerning what was "commonly known" of the cakewalk's West African roots.

E. Yes. Support for this statement can be found in the second sentence of the second paragraph.

17. **E** Extract Infer

A. No. A claim about satiric art forms in general cannot be supported by the passage.

B. No. "Mimetic vertigo" was not discussed in relation to common interactions between African Americans and European Americans.

C. No. There is no discussion of European Americans admiring other African American dances.

D. No. There is no discussion of the post-cakewalk influence of African dance forms.

E. Yes. The last sentence of the passage explains that industrialists and financiers saw the cakewalk as a means through which to express their social rank.

18. **A** Extract Infer

A. Yes. The first sentence of the last paragraph and the last paragraph in general explain that Walker accentuated different aspects of the cakewalk in order to appeal to the "varied and often conflicting demands" of different audiences.

B. No. Nothing is known about the size of the audiences to whom previous versions of the dance appealed. Also, Walker accentuated different elements of the dance, satire being only one of those that ingratiated the dance with different audiences.

C. No. This is close, but the claim that she choreographed different versions of the dance is not supported by the evidence that she "addressed within her interpretation" varying aspects that would appeal to different audiences.

D. No. The idea that Walker inserted imitations of others' performances of the dance into her own work is unsupported, and the only discussion of "mimetic vertigo" did not ascribe anything to Walker.

E. No. Neither the idea that the dance needed to be revitalized nor the idea that its mixture of cultural elements needed to be disentangled is supported.

19. **A** Extract Fact

A. Yes. The last sentence of the first paragraph explains that gliding steps and improvisation were traditional African elements retained in the cakewalk.

B. No. The first performer of the cakewalk is never mentioned.

C. No. Other North American dances were not mentioned.

D. No. The specifics of what certain parodies circulating at the end of the nineteenth century added to the cakewalk are never mentioned.

E. No. The duration of the cakewalk's popularity is never stated.

Questions 20–27

The passage discusses group cohesion, saying that in principle a greater degree of group cohesion leads to better decision making because group members are less apprehensive about dissenting, but in practice a very cohesive group can succumb to a phenomenon termed groupthink, which results in poorer decision making due to less critical discussion of problems and alternatives. The first paragraph sums up the conventional wisdom that holds that the less cohesive a group is, the more its members will be dissuaded from disagreeing with the majority opinion. The second paragraph segues into problems associated with too much group cohesion and introduces groupthink. The third paragraph explains and discusses the factors that lead to and facilitate groupthink.

20. **A** Big Picture

A. Yes. This acknowledges the potential value of group cohesion and the potential detriment of its contribution to groupthink.

B. No. This is too narrowly focused on how individuals can prevent groupthink.

C. No. This is better but still too narrowly focused on groupthink, with no reference to the lengthy discussion of group cohesion.

D. No. The passage generally did endorse a preference for higher cohesion.

E. No. This focuses unduly on the prospects of future research helping to prevent groupthink, while the passage was an explanatory discussion of group cohesion.

21. **C** Extract Infer

A. No. Chronic indecision is not a concept supported by the passage.

B. No. This is not groupthink because there was legitimate argument over competing options.

C. Yes. Because the scenario involved disagreement over competing options, this does not fit the definition of groupthink, which is specifically characterized by a lack of disagreement over alternatives.

D. No. "Illusion of unanimity" is one of the telltale signs of groupthink, so this example simply does not qualify as groupthink.

E. No. The inefficiencies mentioned as a result of groupthink relate to pressure to conform and unwillingness to disagree, not a failure to study information thoroughly.

22. **C** RC Reasoning

The author lists "cohesiveness of the decision-making group" as a necessary precursor to group-think.

A. No. This addresses no relevant influence on groupthink and presumes that most groups will fall victim to it.

B. No. This addresses only group cohesion and does not relate it to groupthink in any way.

C. Yes. General distrust of other group members indicates low cohesion, which should preclude groupthink from occurring.

D. No. Stubborn resistance to a consensus is the opposite of groupthink.

E. No. Willingly submitting to the majority opinion is a central factor identified as a contributor to groupthink, so this would weaken the author's explanation of groupthink.

23. **B** Extract Fact

A. No. This suggests low group cohesion, which precludes groupthink.

B. Yes. The first sentence of the final paragraph supports this.

C. No. Unusually high stress is not mentioned in the passage.

D. No. This is mentioned in the first paragraph as a characteristic of intimidated members of groups with low cohesion.

E. No. This is the opposite of groupthink.

24. **E** Extract Infer

A. No. It's not possible to support the idea that groupthink occurs in all cohesive groups.

B. No. Just because the passage states that some contributing factors are still unknown, it isn't possible to support the notion that the factors are unique to each case.

C. No. There is no support for the pessimism of "probably fruitless."

D. No. The strength of "cannot influence" is not supported by the information given in the passage.

E. Yes. In the first sentence of the second paragraph the author foreshadows groupthink as a "pitfall" of group cohesiveness, and the researchers in the final paragraph characterize groupthink primarily in negative terms.

25. **E** Extract Fact

A. No. The idea of enforced conformity is not mentioned in the passage.

B. No. The expectations of military decision-making groups are not mentioned.

C. No. The idea of inappropriate conformity is difficult to support and definitely never mentioned in relation to inadequate information.

D. No. No comparison is made between voluntary and enforced conformity.

E. Yes. The second sentence of the first paragraph supports this.

26. **A** Structure

The discussion in the first paragraph of low cohesion revolves around the idea that in principle low cohesion is less desirable than high cohesion in group decision making.

A. Yes. The first paragraph portrays the expectation that higher group cohesion will better promote an environment of healthy dissension.

B. No. Groupthink is not mentioned until later and is exclusively associated with high cohesion.

C. No. There is no discussion in this paragraph of ways to improve groups' openness regardless of their cohesion.

D. No. This is specifically contradicted by the last sentence of the passage.

E. No. The subsequent discussion in the passage centers entirely on the pitfalls of highly cohesive groups.

27. **B** Extract Infer

A. No. Highly cohesive groups are more likely to have a healthy level of internal disagreement, but the language of "confrontational negotiating styles with adversaries" is too strong to support.

B. Yes. The last sentence of the first paragraph affirms that cohesion is positively correlated with hearing the honest opinions of all group members. The second sentence of the first paragraph suggests that in groups with low cohesion, members will be pressured to conform.

C. No. The passage continually affirms that consideration of varied perspectives is a healthy component of decision making.

D. No. The passage never cites any particular factors as "the key factors in the formation of groupthink."

E. No. This is contradicted by the last sentence of the passage, which states that high cohesion is a necessary condition of groupthink.

NOTES

NOTES

NOTES